EMOTIONAL LEADERSHIP

Using emotionally intelligent behaviour to enjoy a life of EASE

Enjoy your life of EASE!

Chris Gosling

19/11/05

Karen Gosling

ON **EMOTIONAL LEADERSHIP**

"A thought-provoking, sometimes personal, vision of how emotional intelligence might be applied to everyday living, from an author with considerable experience in the counselling and behavioural coaching field."

- Dr John (Jack) Mayer
Creator and Co-Author of the ability measure of emotional intelligence
The MSCEIT™ - Mayer-Salovey-Caruso Emotional Intelligence Test
University of new Hampshire, Department of Psychology
www.unh.edu/psychology/faculty/fac_mayer.htm

"Mike Gosling is a committed, caring and highly competent educator, counsellor and behavioural coach in the field of emotional well-being. If you want to boost your own emotional health, and the well-being of those around you, to enhance your customer service, this is a valuable book to study."

- Ron Kaufman, bestselling author, *UP Your Service!*
www.RonKaufman.com

Published by Goslings International Pte Ltd

199A Thomson Road, Goldhill Centre, Singapore 307636

www.goslings.net

EASEQuadrant®
Change for The Better   and **EASEQUADRANT®** are registered trade marks of Goslings International Pte Ltd.

Cataloguing-in-Publication Data:

Gosling, Mike
Emotional Leadership.

ISBN 981-05-1600-2   376 pages, includes index.

1. Leadership   2. Emotions   3. Emotional Intelligence
4. Self-development   4. Behavioural change   6. Title

Cover design by Denis Wong and Ivo Widjaja
Typography, page layout, and design by Pagesetters Services Pte Ltd.
Edited by Michelle Jones-White.
Logos and web site design by Ivo Widjaja.
Set in MinioMM . Printed in Singapore.

Publisher's Note

This book accompanies The EASEQuadrant® Workshop – a two-day program on integrated emotional leadership, offered by Goslings International Pte Ltd, Singapore. Website: www.easequadrant.com Discounts on bulk quantities of this book are available to corporations, professional associations and other organisations. For details contact Goslings International Pte Ltd. Tel: (65) 6256 7710, Fax: (65) 6255 0497, Email: EmotionalLeadership@goslings.net

EMOTIONAL LEADERSHIP

Using emotionally intelligent behaviour to enjoy a life of EASE

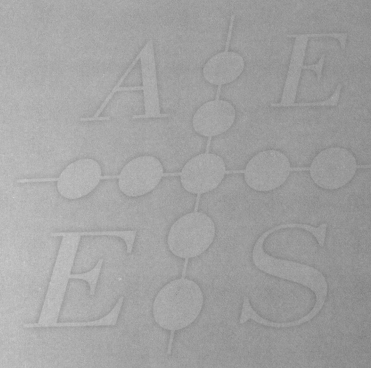

Mike Gosling & Karen Gosling

CONTENTS

LEVEL 1: EXPERIENTIAL EMOTIONAL LEADERSHIP

CHAPTER 1: EMOTIONAL LANDSCAPE

LEVEL 2: STRATEGIC EMOTIONAL LEADERSHIP

CHAPTER 5: CREATING TRANSITION

AUTHOR MIKE GOSLING

Born and raised in the Fijian Islands, Mike Gosling is a third-generation Anglo-Fijian – now an Australian citizen and permanent resident of Singapore. Mike immigrated to Australia in 1973 at the age of 24. He spent the next ten years working in Adelaide, in the professional accounting, manufacturing, and commercial sectors of industry. He moved to Singapore to live and work in March 1997, after travelling to 38 countries and completing further undergraduate and master of business administration degrees in South Australia. From 1993 to 1999 Mike worked as a university academic in Australia and Singapore teaching financial management and entrepreneurship.

MIKE THE BUSINESSMAN

Whilst living and working in Adelaide, Mike acted as a registered tax agent and operated a 30 hectare "weekend" sheep farm with 120 border leicester ewes. From 1984 to 1988 he owned and operated a convenience food outlet on the Gold Coast, Queensland, Australia, with his wife – Karen Gosling.

In January 1998 Mike co-founded a cognitive-behavioural counselling practice in Singapore with Karen, and in July 1999 he joined the business full-time as Managing Director. His organisation – Goslings International Pte Ltd – provides executive behavioural coaching, professional counselling,

The EASEQuadrant® Workshop, emotional intelligence assessments and reporting, corporate employee assistance, and emotional leadership training.

MIKE THE AUTHOR

From March 2002 to March 2004 Mike wrote *Emotional Leadership* in collaboration with Karen Gosling – Co-founder of Goslings International Pte Ltd and his business partner. Much of the work on emotional intelligence in the book derives from Mike's PhD program on the "Emotional Intelligence of Managers in Singapore", due for completion in 2004.

A COMMITMENT TO EMOTIONAL LEADERSHIP EDUCATION

Mike created *The EASEQuadrant® Workshop* – an eight-stage emotional leadership programme – to teach individuals the emotionally intelligent strategies that have served him so well over the years, allowing him to become emotionally wise. The children's edition of this book, *Emotional Leadership For Kids,* will help children learn emotional leadership skills, and is to be published by Asiapac Books, and released in June 2005 at the annual World Book Fair.

Work is currently underway on the online modules of *The EASEQuadrant® Workshop*. These online modules offer worldwide interactive participation in Mike's journey to emotional wisdom; promoting Goslings mission to raise the emotional well-being of people around the world.

AUTHOR KAREN GOSLING

Born and educated in Adelaide, South Australia, Karen spent one year as an exchange student in Germany, before graduating in social work studies at the University of South Australia in 1976. She worked as a community welfare worker for six years – with the Department for Community Welfare in South Australia – before spending two years with the Royal Society for the Blind, as a supervisor and senior social worker. Karen married Mike Gosling in 1977 and for six years they lived on a small rural property whilst working full-time in the city. Mike's daughters – Kristie and Talei – would spend their holidays with Karen and Mike, on the farm.

In 1984 Karen travelled widely with Mike through Asia, India, Africa, UK, and Europe. In 1985 they settled in Queensland – on Australia's Gold Coast – where Karen worked as a senior social worker at the Gold Coast Hospital. Four years later she returned with Mike to Adelaide. He to study, and she to commence six years of fulfilling work in the spinal injuries rehabilitation centre of the Royal Adelaide Hospital – the largest teaching hospital in South Australia. During this time their two sons, Daniel and William, were born. With Mike mostly at home, the flexibility of the working hours at the rehabilitation unit, and a wonderful childcare centre, the stress of caring for their sons in their infant years was reduced significantly. From March 1995 until May 1997 Karen was senior medical social worker at the Royal Adelaide Hospital. She was instrumental in establishing a 24-hour counselling service to victims of trauma, as part of the hospital's regional trauma service.

Karen joined Mike in Singapore in June 1997. In January 1998 she co-founded Goslings International Pte Ltd with Mike where she is Counselling Director. Karen was a part-time lecturer in medical social work at the National University of Singapore (NUS) from 1998 to 2000.

Karen finds the counselling work at Goslings the most rewarding professional work of her 28-year career. She says, "Assisting people to gain greater awareness of their issues and emotions is fulfilling in itself. But observing the outcome after providing the tools, thereby enabling people to change their behaviour and their lives – that's exhilarating!"

The EASEQuadrant® Workshop and this book were born out of Karen and Mike's desire to share with others an understanding of how and why we feel things during times of stress or change. And to provide the tools for individuals to manage these feelings so that they can remain in control of their behaviour – to enjoy a life of EASE!

ACKNOWLEDGEMENTS

To Karen
- Don't ever stop giving of yourself to others. I love you.

To Mike
- I love you in so many ways … the best gift my life ever received was you.

To Daniel, William, Talei and Kristie
- We love you. Think about the kind of person you want to be.

To Ms Cecilia Abordaje
- Thank you, Cecilia, for making our home so welcoming and for looking after our children and boarders.

To Dr Mark Vawser
- You are the one displaying the symptoms.

To Ms Annette Berwald
- Know your inner voice and use the cognitive framework.

To Mr Jon Flaherty
- You're talking to the wrong kind of people.

To the 'men of the church'
- We forgive you. Your decision was made in limited awareness.

To Mr Ivo Widjaja

- Thank you for your friendship and unselfish voluntary contributions.

To Dr John (Jack) Mayer

- I began my research into emotional intelligence (EI) in July 1999. I was initially drawn to Dr John (Jack) Mayer's work – with Dr Peter Salovey and Dr David Caruso – on the MSCEIT model of EI. I could see immediately that I could apply their model in our clinical practice to assist people having difficulty understanding their emotions. I first met Jack Mayer at the inaugural conference on Applying Emotional Intelligence to Business Solutions and Success held in Toronto, Canada, in August 2001 organised by Multi-Health Services, Inc., where he was a speaker. And I was affirmed in my earlier decision to work with his model. Jack's command and profound insight of his subject was evident. He has encouraged my work enormously, providing positive feedback and generously sharing his knowledge and recent research on emotional intelligence. Jack's articles and "ability model of emotional intelligence" were my inspiration and the key theoretical resource for this book and *The EASEQuadrant®*. Thank you, Jack.

To Mrs Pauline Ong

- Pauline is our mentor and friend. She understands our vision. Together with her husband, Dr Ong Beng Hock, she has generously provided us with personal friendship and support in Singapore. Welcoming our family into her home, taking an interest in our children, and introducing us to her valuable friends.

To Mr Koh Hock Seng & Ms Rhonda Willson
- Thank you for providing us your insight and expertise on publishing scenarios.

To Ms Karen Quek Soo Inn
- Soo Inn is our Business Development Manager in Singapore. She has assisted us immensely with the launch and distribution of this book. Thank you for your commitment and loyalty.

To Mrs Pee-Koh See Hua
- Thank you for bringing me to Singapore in 1997 to teach at Ngee Ann Polytechnic. Without which, none of this might have happened.

To Ms Michelle Jones-White
- Michelle's ability as an editor to encapsulate ideas succinctly is a gift. Her lead and suggestions for changes to the book title, text, text flow, headings, and layout were brilliant, challenging, and very much appreciated.

To Mr Ron Kaufman
- Thank you Ron for being our guide to the world of writing and workshops. For your generosity in providing advice, inspiration, and the slogan for our programme: *EASEQuadrant®* – Change for The Better.

To Mr Don Mathews
- Don attended *The EASEQuadrant® Workshop* in August 2003 and provides an empowering endorsement of our program. He is one of a growing number of leaders of organisations in Singapore who

recognise the strategic importance of implementing effective "EQ" knowledge and skills training in children and the workplace. Don introduced us to the publisher of the children's edition of this book, Asiapac Books. *Emotional Leadership For Kids* is to be released in June, 2005 at the annual World Book Fair. Thank you, Don, for your unwavering support.

To Clients of Goslings International Pte Ltd
■ Thank you for trusting us with your personal issues. It has been a privilege to serve and help more than 1,650 clients from 73 ethnic groups since January 1998. Without realising, all of you have helped us to achieve our goal of writing this book. Through *Emotional Leadership* we hope that others will use the tools and techniques developed in our clinical practice to raise their emotional well-being.

To *The EASEQuadrant® Workshop* participants
■ Thank you for joining our programme. For the moments we shared together and for your feedback – which assists us to improve our workshops, for the benefit of those who follow you.

To our friends, family members, business associates, referring health practitioners and professional associates.
■ Please accept our gratitude and appreciation for your ongoing support and encouragement.

INTRODUCTION

You are what you think. You create your mood and emotional style. You are responsible for your behaviour. Only *you* can make yourself angry or anxious. You *can* change the way you think and your behaviour. You can choose to own your feelings and take responsibility for them. You can choose to use emotionally intelligent behaviour to enjoy a life of EASE. Or you can choose to be a victim.

Emotional Leadership is a pathway to better health. Good health derives from a balanced combination of the physical, mental, social and spiritual. Clean air, clean water, good nutrition, the effective elimination of waste toxins made by the body, correct breathing, exercise, meditation, relaxation, social relationships, a balanced emotion state and individual spirituality are all crucial to better health. This book explains how to treat the cause – not the symptoms – of emotional dis-*ease*; the emotional constipation that is the cause of stress felt in the body, with attendant physiological effects. This book provides a road to better health.

Our belief is that our brain controls our emotional health. When we have a balance between positive and negative emotions derived from our cognitions – the way we think – we experience emotional freedom, and a state of emotional well-being. A precursor to better health.

This book is your journey to emotional freedom. Your path to emotional wisdom; knowing how to behave, when you don't know what to do. This book will help you to become emotionally wise. Able to better understand your mood, emotional style and impact on others – and respond effectively to internal and external events in your life. When you are emotionally wise you will experience emotional freedom. You will use the behaviour of the person you *want* to be. People who behave with emotional wisdom experience better health and enjoy a life of EASE.

Emotional wisdom is acquired in the drama of life, exercising emotional leadership. Every minute, in every hour, of every day, there is opportunity to exercise emotional leadership. Whether it is in your business, professional or social relationships. Leadership in relationships is about building a long-term feeling of trust. Emotional leadership is choosing to behave with emotional intelligence. Learning and applying behaviours that gain long-term trust and promote emotional wisdom in you and in those with whom you have relationships.

JOURNEY TO EMOTIONAL WISDOM

Emotional wisdom comes by practising the eight stages of emotional leadership (see page xxv). Your journey to emotional wisdom is depicted in Figure 1, which illustrates the interrelationship between the three phases to becoming an emotionally intelligent (wise and trusted) leader; awareness (strategy), skill (tactic), and choice (value).

Figure 1. Journey to emotional wisdom
The Three Phases of Emotional Leadership (EL)

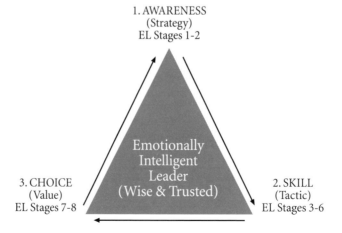

1. AWARENESS
(Strategy)
EL Stages 1-2

Emotionally
Intelligent
Leader
(Wise & Trusted)

3. CHOICE
(Value)
EL Stages 7-8

2. SKILL
(Tactic)
EL Stages 3-6

1. Awareness (strategy) – Knowing your emotional landscape.
   – Awareness of who you choose to be and behave, is your strategy – leading long-term emotionally intelligent behaviour to live a life of EASE.
2. Skill (tactic) – Listening to your body.
   – Skill in listening to your body, dealing with difficult emotions ("energy surges") that impact physiologically on your body, is your tactic – practising emotionally intelligent behaviour to live a life of EASE.
3. Choice (value) – Sowing emotional leadership.
   – Choosing to sow emotional leadership, your journey to emotional wisdom (knowing how to behave when you don't know what to do), is your value – managing emotionally intelligent behaviour to live a life of EASE.

THE EIGHT STAGES OF EMOTIONAL LEADERSHIP

This book presents a programme of integrated emotional leadership, bringing together our combined 35 years of experience in the fields of cognitive-affect-behaviour and emotional intelligence (EI). The programme – which we call *The Eight Stages of Emotional Leadership* (Figure 2) – integrates theoretical aspects of the ability model of emotional intelligence[1] and cognitive-affect-behaviour with our 'hands on' experience in the field. The book accompanies *The EASEQuadrant® Workshop,* our two-day course in behavioural change.

Emotional intelligence refers to an ability to recognise the meanings of emotions and their relationships, and to reason and problem-solve effectively. It further involves employing emotions to enhance cognitive abilities. Emotional intelligence is the emotional knowledge and skills you are able to develop and nurture to make your relationships work.

Cognitive-behavioural counselling and behavourial coaching are disciplines that can help you to understand your behaviour. They provide you with an opportunity to change your behaviours through actively participating in reframing cognitions that drive behavioural responses, reactions, feelings, or emotions.

Through our clinical practice, workshops, and seminars, we realised that people who are strong in emotional intelligence lead happier lives. Karen and I created *The EASEQuadrant® Workshop* with the goal to help others reach their potential through information, education and empowerment. Specifically, this book will help you:

- Explore the nature and potential of emotional health.
- Assess your emotional abilities and competencies (emotional intelligence) and identify areas for development.
- Understand your mood and emotional style, in order to build long-term trust in business, professional, and personal relationships.
- Build emotional self-awareness, create opportunities for individual transition, and promote successful self and social management.

Figure 2. The Eight Stages of Emotional Leadership

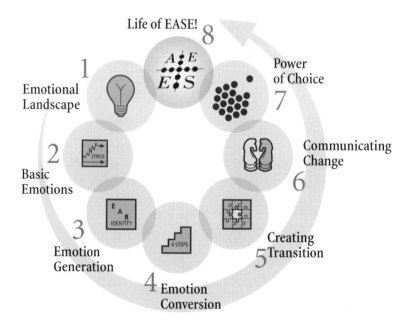

You will be motivated to apply the concepts and tools in this book to raise your level of emotional happiness and well-being, and encouraged to assist others in developing effective habits in the home, workplace and community.

English novelist and critic, Aldous , said, "Experience is not what happens to you; it is what you *do* with what happens to you." What you learn from this book and what you do about it is your choice.

What happens in your life is also unfolding in other peoples' lives every day – you are not alone.

- Employees dealing with customers constantly seek to provide prompt, effective, quality service.
- Managers and supervisors skilled in active listening and giving quality feedback are assisting employees to manage change and emotional distress in the workplace.
- Professional coaches and counsellors are helping angry, anxious, or depressed people cope with the struggle of everyday life and make life-changing decisions.
- An empathic parent or partner is helping to ease the pain of unresolved hurts in relationships, or bringing joy to a family member suffering social or psychological problems.

An outcome of the book is that when you choose to understand your mood and emotional style, and change your behaviour accordingly, you will be a person acting with emotional leadership. Able to help raise the emotional well-being of people around you. Equipped with a better understanding of how you perceive, use, understand, and manage your emotions (emotional intelligence) and increased emotional knowledge and skills from participating in every stage of this journey, you will be a more confident and content individual. And an effective communicator in whatever situation you find yourself – particularly in your personal relationships.

This book will teach you how to apply your emotional intelligence to create the behaviour you want in your relationships – every day of your life.

By applying what you learn in this book, you will be contributing to increasing human wellness and will have moved a step closer to fully realising your life goals.

THE LEARNING PROCESS

Throughout *The Eight Stages of Emotional Leadership* you develop and practise emotional leadership on **two levels** of *The EASEQuadrant®* – experiential and strategic, and in **four quadrants** – evaluating, affirming, sealing, and enjoying a life of ease – that together lead you to a life of EASE (Figure 3).

Figure 3. *The EASEQuadrant®*

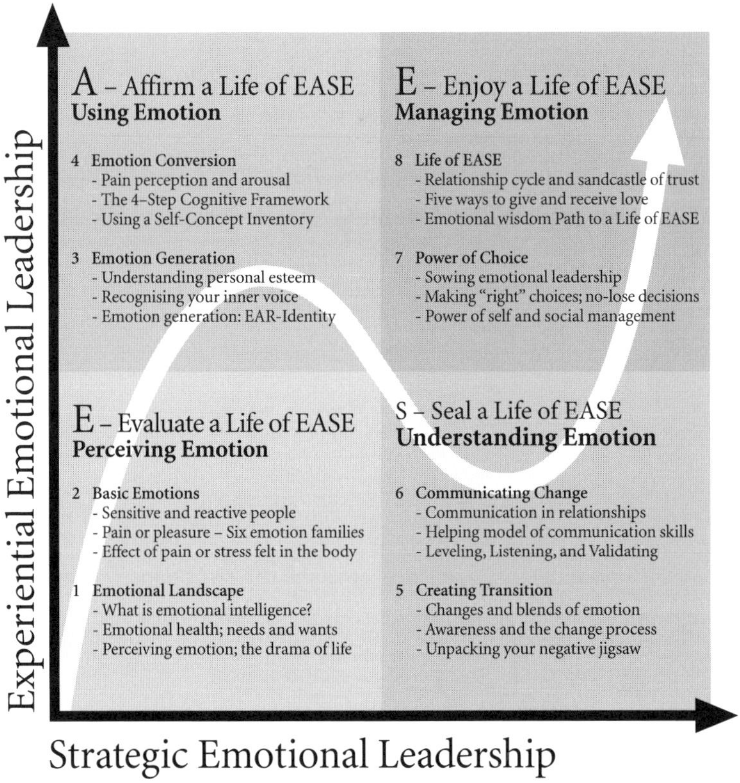

A – Affirm a Life of EASE
Using Emotion

4 Emotion Conversion
- Pain perception and arousal
- The 4–Step Cognitive Framework
- Using a Self-Concept Inventory

3 Emotion Generation
- Understanding personal esteem
- Recognising your inner voice
- Emotion generation: EAR-Identity

E – Enjoy a Life of EASE
Managing Emotion

8 Life of EASE
- Relationship cycle and sandcastle of trust
- Five ways to give and receive love
- Emotional wisdom Path to a Life of EASE

7 Power of Choice
- Sowing emotional leadership
- Making "right" choices; no-lose decisions
- Power of self and social management

E – Evaluate a Life of EASE
Perceiving Emotion

2 Basic Emotions
- Sensitive and reactive people
- Pain or pleasure – Six emotion families
- Effect of pain or stress felt in the body

1 Emotional Landscape
- What is emotional intelligence?
- Emotional health; needs and wants
- Perceiving emotion; the drama of life

S – Seal a Life of EASE
Understanding Emotion

6 Communicating Change
- Communication in relationships
- Helping model of communication skills
- Leveling, Listening, and Validating

5 Creating Transition
- Changes and blends of emotion
- Awareness and the change process
- Unpacking your negative jigsaw

Experiential Emotional Leadership

Strategic Emotional Leadership

THE *EASEQuadrant*®

Four quadrants form *The EASEQuadrant*® (Figure 3) – a matrix for emotional leadership set on the two axes of experiential emotional leadership and strategic emotional leadership. Each of the four quadrants is right of passage along your journey to emotional wisdom and a life of EASE.

You begin your journey with an **evaluation** of your emotional landscape– your emotional intelligence and level of emotional awareness. Next you explore your EAR–Identity (the behaviour you want to be) and learn a key cognitive technique to **affirm** (reframe) your memory, thoughts, values, beliefs and expectations. Quadrant three teaches you how to increase your understanding of emotion chains and blends, and practise effective communication skills to help you **seal** your new identity. Finally, making right choices about how you want to behave, and learning the secret of building long-term trust through improved self and social management, will guarantee that you **enjoy** a life of EASE.

Learning about emotions involves emotional practice; applying your emotional intelligence – how you perceive, use, understand and manage emotion. Throughout this book we integrate and explain how applying your emotional intelligence can create a life of EASE.

The EASEQuadrant® *Workshop* participants complete two online emotional intelligence tests – the MSCEIT™[2] and BarOn EQ-i®[3] – reporting on emotional abilities and competencies respectively, and receive feedback on areas for emotional development. Participants plot their emotional intelligence scores for experiential and strategic emotional leadership onto the *The EASEQuadrant*® grid (Figure 4), showing them where they sit in their journey toward emotional intelligence – and a life of EASE. The goal is to achieve an emotional intelligence score in the top right hand corner of *The EASEQuadrant*® grid. It is within this section, that you realise strong abilities in both experiential and strategic emotional leadership. And it is at this point on the grid where you will begin to exhibit the behaviour necessary to truly enjoy a life of EASE.

Figure 4. *The EASEQuadrant® Grid*

Plot your MSCEIT™ Branch EIQ scores on *The EASEQuadrant®*

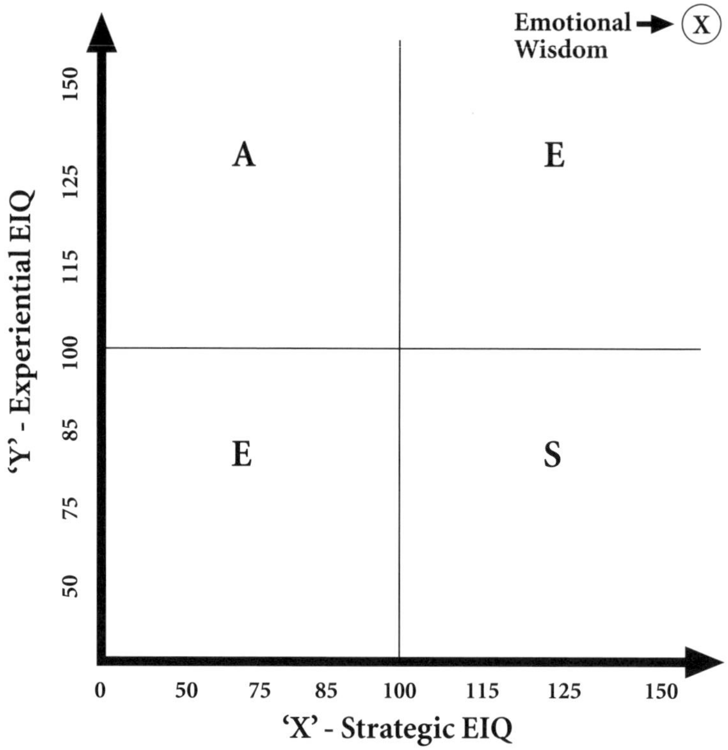

If you want to complete the two emotional intelligence tests online, contact me by email at MikeGosling@goslings.net. I am accredited by Multi-Health Systems Inc., Toronto, Canada to administer the MSCEIT and EQ-i. Alternatively, enquire at www.mhs.com.

For those interested in attending *The EASEQuadrant® Workshop,* we use film and media, real-life case studies on emotional issues, role-play, slide presentations, reflective individual exercises, and small group discussions to facilitate the learning process. Throughout this book you will find many workshop examples that illustrate real world applications of emotional leadership. For example, understanding what comprises the compound emotion of disgust serves as a lead-in to discussing other compound emotions.

In this book, as in the workshop, the exercises and case studies are styled as Emotional Leadership Practice (ELP) and are marked with this icon ✎.

Throughout *Emotional Leadership* you will also come across text boxed as "Emotional Wisdom". These are key learning points and emotional tips collected as a result of research, academic teaching, and hands-on experience with many individuals who have participated in our clinical practice and *The EASEQuadrant® Workshop*. The names of clients and participants and any identifying details, have been altered to protect their confidentiality and anonymity. These accounts are used to reinforce the behaviour you want to achieve; a result of applying emotional intelligence, cognitive-behavioural techniques and other strategies, detailed in the eight stages of emotional leadership.

How to use this book

This book is organised logically. The theoretical explanation of emotional intelligence and emotional health is at the beginning, forming the first of eight stages of your journey to emotional wisdom and a life of EASE.

LEVEL ONE: EXPERIENTIAL EMOTIONAL LEADERSHIP

We begin with a look at your emotional landscape. How well are you in tune with your own emotions? You learn about emotional health; the needs, values and motives that drive you to appreciate the dramas of life. You identify the functions of emotions, and explore the primordial drive to survive, and the evolved desire to thrive. Our programme develops the need for personal self-awareness. An understanding of emotional constipation, and how emotions impact on your body. And a study of cognitive-affect-behavioural issues, that underpin your emotional well-being.

CHAPTER ONE: EMOTIONAL LANDSCAPE

Emotions impact on individual health. In chapter one you will learn to better understand your needs and wants, and evaluate how you **perceive** emotion. How you receive and interpret information from both external (world) and internal (body) environments. Emotional intelligence involves the ability to understand emotions in yourself and others. How you relate to peers and family members, and adapt emotionally to your changing environment. The way you perceive things from here on depends upon what you do about your experiences – what you do about what happens to you.

- The true test of intelligence lies in the drama of life.
- Understanding your emotional intelligence scores.
- Emotional health – needs and wants.
- Perceiving emotion – the brain.
- Knowing yourself and understanding change.

CHAPTER TWO: BASIC EMOTIONS

Delving further we compare the differences between men and women, and explore the variations between sensitive and reactive people. There are two basic emotions – pain and pleasure – and six emotion "families" that help you to deal with life's tasks. Learn to recognise your emotional signals. Learn to *experience* your feelings. Learn not to block them by recognising the physical, cognitive and emotional symptoms that arise from negative thoughts. You will begin to identify the true intensity of your feelings with the help of the pain timeline. And you'll understand that stress is a buildup of negative emotion felt in the body.

- Differences between men and women.
- Sensitive people versus reactive people.
- Identify emotion families and understand the pain timeline.

CHAPTER THREE: EMOTION GENERATION

Events in your life such as actions, thoughts, beliefs, values and expectations, are appraised or interpreted to generate emotional and physical responses. Learn to recognise lowered self-esteem. Identify the emotions that arise from you judging and rejecting yourself. Identify your inner voice. Understand and evaluate the components of your EAR-Identity.

- Understanding personal esteem – your inner-view of self.
- Recognise your inner voice and challenge its message.
- EAR–Identity – using emotion to facilitate thought.

CHAPTER FOUR: EMOTION CONVERSION

Learn to live in "present-moment awareness"[4]. Experience growing self-confidence as you tell your inner voice to check out! You are ready and equipped to construct your new identity. The 4-step cognitive framework is the key to dealing with unpleasant sensory and emotional experiences.

- Pain perception and arousal.
- From anger to assertion, from fear to appreciation.
- 4-Step cognitive framework and self-concept inventory.

LEVEL TWO: STRATEGIC EMOTIONAL LEADERSHIP

The second level of strategic emotional leadership, is developing long-term techniques to take account of your self-inventory – your propensity for self-judgement – and recognising and embracing change *before* emotional arousal. You will develop a checklist of what to do – and what not to do – to communicate effectively.

You learn to sow emotional leadership. To develop your emotional intelligence to empower no-lose decision making that will serve you, your partner, family, workmates and community. Finally, the programme integrates the management of emotions in self and in others, to heal emotional wounds and give and receive love to build extraordinary relationships.

CHAPTER FIVE: CREATING TRANSITION

Individual transition begins with awareness – acknowledging your need to change. Change is a process. Unfortunately, change is often sought too late. It usually follows a crisis – the "Oh shit!" experience – that has caused a person to become more aware of unacceptable behaviour, its cost and the barriers he or she has erected against change. It is far better for *you* to recognise your need for change, and embrace it *before* emotional arousal.

- Understanding changes and blends in emotion.
- Awareness and the change process.
- Unpacking your negative jigsaw.

CHAPTER SIX: COMMUNICATING CHANGE

Clearly expressing your thoughts and feelings, is vital for building intimacy and trust. Adopt language appropriate to the situation. Understand the communication model. Use communication skills to reflect content and feelings. Focus on the person. Practise levelling, active listening and validating. Use leading responses and open-ended questions. Place acceptance before judgement. Use "I" statements and not "You" statements to disarm your critics, affirm yourself and influence others.

- Communication in relationships.
- Helping model of communication skills.
- Levelling, listening, and validating.

CHAPTER SEVEN: POWER OF CHOICE

Develop your emotional abilities and competencies so that you make no-lose decisions that will serve you, your partner, family, workmates and community. Motivating yourself to deal with difficult emotions is the point of transformation. In sowing emotional leadership you are choosing to give to others in a way that honours their right to be heard, validated and respected.

- Sowing emotional leadership – the onward path.
- Making "right" choices – no-lose decisions.
- Power of self-management and social management.

CHAPTER EIGHT: LIFE OF EASE!

Be challenged to recognise that you are today what you have chosen to be. Learn the secrets of what makes an intimate relationship special. Are you communicating effectively? Are you giving love according to how your partner receives love? Have you built your sandcastle of trust? Set your intentions, desires and goals into the spiritual realm. Remain detached from the outcome and let wisdom work its work.

- Relationship cycle and sandcastle of trust.
- Five ways to give and receive love.
- Emotional wisdom – pathway to a Life of EASE!

BEHAVING WITH EMOTIONAL INTELLIGENCE

Behaving with emotional intelligence is a life-long adventure of learning and growing. American journalist and writer, David Grayson, said, "Adventure is not outside a man (or woman), it is within."

Your journey to emotional wisdom – a life of EASE – never ends. Life is a series of events, and every event is an opportunity for change. This book is about experiencing change from inside out. It is from the most painful events felt within that you journey the most.

Take time to;
- Commit yourself to developing your emotional intelligence and emotional self-awareness.
- Find someone to join you in discussing the points raised in this book. This will help to clarify your thoughts, provide valuable input for others and enrich the learning experience.
- Use the Emotional Leadership Practice (ELP) activities in this book to apply what you are learning.
- Implement effective communication skills in your relationships.
- Write to us and ask others about the views expressed in this book, to broaden your knowledge and exposure to the topic and receive combined wisdom.
- Give us appropriate feedback to help improve the learning process set out in this book, and for those attending *The EASEQuadrant® Workshop*.

■ Read and re-read this book. The best learning will take place as you apply the principles and techniques in the drama of life – living day-to-day. Individual transformation will only come through practise and commitment to the proven techniques and strategies set out in this book.

Your adventure will continue long after you finish reading this book. Emotionally intelligent people take on the responsibility for teaching others what they have learned, and behaving toward them in an emotionally intelligent way.

Notes

1 Mayer, JD & Salovey, P 1997, *What Is Emotional Intelligence?* in Salovey, P and Sluyter, D eds, *Emotional Development and Emotional Intelligence: Educational Implications*, Basic Books, New York.
2 MSCEIT™ Copyright ©1999, 2002. Multi-Health Systems Inc. All rights reserved.
3 BarOn EQ-i Copyright ©1997, 1999. Multi-Health Systems Inc. All rights reserved.
4 Chopra, D 1996, *The seven spiritual laws of success*, Bantan Press, London, p. 73.

CHAPTER 1

EMOTIONAL
LANDSCAPE

THE WAY YOU PERCEIVE THINGS FROM HERE ON DEPENDS
UPON WHAT YOU DO ABOUT YOUR EXPERIENCES – WHAT
YOU DO ABOUT WHAT HAPPENS TO YOU.

INTRODUCTION

Your emotional landscape is typified by deep valleys of anger and resentment, rapid-filled rivers of fear and anxiety, black volcanic plugs of disgust, dark bottomless chasms of sadness, shimmering lagoons of surprise, and occasionally, harbour-fringing mountains of joy and appreciation.

Events in your life trigger behaviours – a response, reaction, feeling or emotion. The intensity of your behavioural response to *an event* will vary from person-to-person. No two people respond to an event with exactly the same emotion, or intensity of emotion. For example, I may feel **irritated** when my wife comes home at two o'clock in the morning after a girl's night out, whereas you may feel **outraged** when your partner does the same. Your behaviour as a response to an event in your life is predetermined by your emotional landscape. Meaning that, the choices you have made so far determine the person you want to be.

You create your emotional landscape. Equally, you have the power to change it.

DRAMA OF LIFE

1. PRIMORDIAL DRIVE TO SURVIVE VERSUS EVOLVED DESIRE TO THRIVE

In the primordial drive to survive, physiological arousal or feedback – a heart that is beating hard – helps you to interpret or appraise a situation. For example, if you've been out for a walk you know your heart is pounding and you know why – so you are not frightened by it. But if the situation is perceived as threatening – for example, someone is following you up a dark street –

anger or fear is experienced, and "fight or flight" is the primordial drive shown.

We cannot be humanly alone. Emotion plays a vital function in the primordial drive to connect and bond you with others. For example, if a situation appears to be safe, a person may feel relaxed and show contemplative and attachment behaviours.

This evolved desire to thrive promotes altruism and self-actualisation. When a person is in control of his or her situation the person feels self-confident, secure, successful – even ecstatic. They will display high levels of energy, inspiring them to self-actualise and fulfil their potential. In this situation a person will feel energetic and creative.

In the drama of life emotions signal a higher level of need. Anger and fear based reactivity – negative emotion – can lead to an increased risk of illness and chronic pain. Understood as stress felt *in* the body, negative emotion affects health adversely. Conversely, positive emotion can help you to change the thoughts that are keeping you ill. The continual internal feedback about your body's state of physiological arousal, helps you interpret the situation or event that has given rise to the complex emotional response that is generated.

2. FUNCTIONS OF EMOTIONS

Emotions – felt as physiological arousal in the body – signal increased risk of illness, emotional distress, and/or psychosocial problems that are played out in the drama of life. Emotional constipation is the binding of internal negative emotions unable to be released or *let go*. This stagnation will lead to serious physiological impairments in the body if not addressed.

Your emotions:
1. Give you feedback and help you survive.
2. Connect and bond you with other people in relationships.
3. Cause you to act with altruism and to self-actualise – to fulfil your potential.

Emotional Leadership Practice
ELP 1.1   Identifying emotions in films

Think of a film you have recently seen. Take note of a particular scene, and write down what you feel, and what you think the main actor in the film is feeling. Ask a friend to do the same and discuss your lists of feeling words. Notice how your view about what the actor was feeling may be quite different to what your friend thought the actor was feeling.

YOUR OWN FEELINGS	FEELINGS OF ACTOR

THE GODFATHER

One of my favourite films – for what it teaches us about emotions – is *The Godfather*. The film is notable for the totally different responses that two of the main characters, Sonny and Michael Corleone, portray.

There is a scene in the film where the Godfather has been shot and is lying in hospital. Michael arrives to visit and finds his father completely alone. The guards are nowhere to be seen. Not at the entrance to the hospital, reception, or outside his father's room. In fact, it seems that the guards have made a hasty exit – notable by the unfinished sandwich sitting on the reception desk. Michael hurries *to* his father's side, brushing the protestations of a nurse who appears from nowhere aside. He picks up the phone and calls Sonny.

Sonny's response to the news that his father is unattended is reactive anger. "Don't panic", he cautions Michael, "I'll get someone over there right away." Sonny has no self-awareness of his own and panics. He attributes his state of panic to someone else – Michael. Sonny processes his emotion and ineffectively uses anger to control the situation. He rids himself of a feeling he doesn't like, through anger.

Sonny is prone to panic. This is reinforced in another scene where Sonny is enraged to learn that his brother-in-law has physically abused his sister – again. He flies out of the house in an uncontrollable rage and drives off, to deal with the situation in his own way, by himself. For those who don't know the film, Sonny has been set-up and is gunned down at a tollbooth on the freeway. A very ineffective use of emotion, wouldn't you say?

Back to the original scene… despite Michael's obvious concern for his father's safety, and his feelings of anxiety and fear when he arrives and reaffirms that there are no guards standing watch over his father, Michael's response is positive assertion. He quickly assesses what he is feeling, why he is feeling it, and the impact on others. Michael's stress tolerance – his ability to manage his own anxiety – assists him in achieving his goal of protecting his father from the enemies coming to kill him. He sums up the situation, and assertively enlists the nurse's help to move his father out of the hospital room by warning her, "Do you know my father? Men are coming here to kill him." While Michael and the nurse are moving the Godfather out of the room, Enzo arrives to pay his regards to the Godfather – and is oblivious to what is going on. Enzo then supports Michael by posing as guard outside the hospital entrance.

In this scene from *The Godfather*, Michael processes his emotion by generating sufficient anger to overcome his fear and anxiety, and acts assertively to deal with the situation. Often when you are busy your reflective space becomes diminished. For example, the nurse pushed Michael. If that had happened to many of us we would have become upset. Michael used "reality testing" effectively. He observed the situation and made clear decisions about what was happening. He used positive assertion – the capacity to put into words your feelings and directions, while being sensitive to others. Unlike Sonny, Michael exercised impulse control. His relationship with the nurse started badly. She was adversarial in her tone, instructing him to leave. Michael could have reacted angrily – as would Sonny – but instead, he chose to act collaboratively. He responded, "People are coming here to kill my father. We have to get him out. Will you help?" *Emotional Leadership* will help you to see that empathy and self-awareness are necessary to develop trusting relationships. They are a necessary prerequisite for love – but they do not guarantee it.

Perceiving emotion is an ability we all have. Recent research into emotional intelligence has determined the ability to perceive emotion, as one of four branches of emotional intelligence. People vary in their ability to perceive emotion. This is discussed at length later in this chapter.

 Emotional Leadership Practice

ELP 1.2   Identifying emotions in faces

Look at each face below. Write down what "feeling" you think is expressed by each face.

Emotional Leadership Practice

ELP 1.3   Identifying the functions of emotions.

Discuss the following questions with a friend or partner. Use the space provided to write down your observations.

1. How do emotions give you feedback and help you survive?

2. How do emotions connect and bond you with other people in relationships?

3. How have your emotions served you in a recent work or social experience, in your relationships with others?

4. Who are the people that benefit most from your service? How will your emotions signal to you that they are in need of attention?

5. In what ways will your emotions cause you to act with altruism and to self-actualise?

WHAT IS EMOTIONAL INTELLIGENCE?

1. TEN RAMPANT EI MYTHS IN CORPORATE CULTURE

Emotional intelligence is a relatively new field of research. The words "emotional intelligence" were first used by John Mayer and Peter Salovey in 1990[1]. As with anything new, it is taking time for people to learn about emotional intelligence and accept it as a purposeful addition and enhancement to a body of existing knowledge on intellectual and social intelligence, personality, and cognitive-affect-behaviour. For example, emotional intelligence (EI) – often referred to as "EQ" – is seen by some as a passing fad and unnecessary. As is personality testing.

In August 2001, I attended the inaugural conference on Applying Emotional Intelligence to Business Solutions and Success held in Toronto, Canada. In his closing talk, "On the road to emotional intelligence", Scott Halford[2] described ten rampant myths about emotional intelligence in corporate culture.

1. EI is too difficult to see in action.
2. EI is not scientifically based.
3. EI is a corporate flavour-of-the-month trend.
4. EI is like Meyers-Briggs and DiSC Classic.
5. If my EI is high, I can afford to be stupid.
6. I'm too old for EI.
7. I can read one bestselling book or attend one conference on EI and know everything there is to know about it.
8. EI is just another way of saying "kum-ba-yah".
9. EI doesn't have substance or application.
10. I don't need EI. I got to where I am without it.

Taken together, these myths would give ample reason not to even begin writing this book. But they can be dispelled quite simply.

1. EI is too difficult to see in action.

Emotional intelligence is being witnessed all around you every day. People behaving toward you with compassion, and showing empathy toward you and your situation, are everywhere. For example, the Child Protection Officer who – thanks to her compassionate nature – never loses her temper with a client in trying circumstances. The taxi driver, who returns your passports inadvertently left in his taxi and will not accept a reward. I'm sure you can recall a host of examples of emotionally intelligent behaviour that you've observed.

2. EI is not scientifically based.

Emotional intelligence is quite new. It was first written about – as a topic in it's own right – in 1990. We will see that the body of scientific literature on emotional intelligence is extensive, and that there is a growing field of research studies. Eminent writers have written popular books on the topic, relying on a significant volume of scientific research. *Emotional Leadership* uses the ability model of emotional intelligence as its theoretical base.

3. EI is a corporate flavour-of-the-month trend.

Research in North America shows that emotional intelligence is vital for the future development of team building, leadership and management, in corporations, government and other organisations. Emotional intelligence is widely used by management consultancy organisations – such as the Hay Group – that typically serve Fortune 500 companies.

On the launching of the second volume of his memoirs, the Senior Minister of Singapore – Mr Lee Kuan Yew – said, "What we (Singapore) need now is to increase the competence of our people at all levels, so we can have stronger teams for the enterprises to produce goods and services that can compete in world markets. They must be able to keep learning and retraining throughout their working lives." (*The Straits Times*, 17 September 2000, p. 1). Fielding questions from Harvard Professors in the *Lessons in Leadership* series at Harvard University on 17 October 2000, Senior Minister Lee said, "No one can succeed or last long as a leader if he does not have a high EQ." (*The Straits Times*, 20 October 2000, p. 12).

4. EI is like Meyers-Briggs and DiSC Classic.

In recent correspondence, Dr Jack Mayer says, "I sought to create an ability measure of emotional intelligence because I believe that to be the very best kind of measure for the area. Self-report measures of EI basically ask people how well they believe they can perform at emotional problem-solving, and then feeds that same information back to the individuals who provided it in a nicely organised package. In contrast, the MSCEIT™ actually measures EI directly, and tells the person something that they may not already know.

The true EI ability measured by the MSCEIT™ has been shown to measure something never-before-measured by a commercial scale. That is, in a number of now-published studies, the MSCEIT™ has been shown to be independent of self-reported EI, independent of other personality measures, and independent of other intelligence measures.

At the same time, the MSCEIT™ predicts important outcomes. People high in EI form better, more cooperative, and more meaningful relationships with others; those low in EI experience more difficulties, including aggressive encounters, alcohol and drug abuse, and similar problem behaviours."

5. If my EI is high, I can afford to be stupid.

Perhaps this is just a facetious comment regarding emotional intelligence. Stupidity rests with those who refuse to develop emotional awareness and emotional intelligence. Someone high in EI will be completely aware. They will have taken on the responsibility of passing on emotional intelligence in their behaviour toward others – a desired outcome of this book.

6. I'm too old for EI.

I am reminded of my interview for enrolment into the cadet officer training school, for the Adelaide University Regiment in the late 1970's. A reviewing officer asked me, "Aren't you a bit old to be doing this, Gosling?" – I was 26 years of age at the time. I replied, "Well Sir, if I don't start now I *will* be a lot older when I finally do." I passed the application stage. No one is too old for EI. Today, at 55 years of age, I'm only just beginning to scratch the surface!

7. **I can read one bestselling book or attend one conference on EI and know everything there is to know about it.**

Learning emotionally intelligent behaviour is a lifetime experience – as you will discover from reading this book. We are not born with a sufficient amount of emotional intelligence to see us through life. We need to nurture and value what we have been given by our creator. An emotionally intelligent person is always open to change. They recognise their responsibility to seek out new knowledge, and they learn to respond to events using consistent emotionally intelligent behaviour – a difficult task even for the most skilled practitioner, human nature being what it is.

Anyone who thinks that they can read one book, and attend one conference, and know everything there is to know about emotional intelligence, simply needs to walk through a library and research laboratory to be minimised by the extent of literature already available on this topic.

8. **EI is just another way of saying "kum-ba-yah".**

Measurement of emotional intelligence is now conducted by many organisations around the world. I include both the MSCEIT™ and EQ-i® tests in *The EASEQuadrant® Workshop* to provide an emotional abilities test and emotional competency (self-report) test. As already mentioned in point four, the MSCEIT™ predicts important outcomes. Additionally, research[3] shows that the MSCEIT™ is mostly separable from personality and well-being tests. Whereas the EQ-i® is highly related to personality.

The MSCEIT™ is the measure of choice as a mental model of EI that "… predicts important life criteria." The MSCEIT™ measures a distinct mental ability – the capacity to reason, in regard to emotions, and the capacity to use emotion to assist cognition. The MSCEIT™ taps into individual differences not contained in a self-report on aspects of personality traits, such as optimism, neuroticism, motivation, extraversion, openness to experience, agreeableness, and conscientiousness. The EQ-i® is not so readily distinguishable from these personality measures.

By measuring a workshop participant's emotional intelligence it gives both of us a starting point from where we can work together, to build their new identity, using behaviour they want to be.

If this is "kum-ba-yah" to some folks, I would simply say, "Is that so?"

9. EI doesn't have substance or application.

In our clinical practice in Singapore we use emotional intelligence testing to work with clients experiencing ongoing psychological and personal problems. We find time and time again, that clients are able to use the results from their EI tests to zero in on problem areas in their behaviour. Once made aware, they are enthusiastic about making the suggested changes to their lives.

For example, Client A reported back that she has been helped greatly by the discovery of an emotional intelligence she didn't know she had. Her increased understanding of her emotional abilities is now helping her in her business and social relationships. She now understands why she has been successful in her work as a manager, and can see the areas she can improve on.

Client B has finally understood why people have told her that they don't want to continue a friendship with her. The MSCEIT™ indicated that she scored very low score on sensations – what we describe as an ability to be empathetic. She then realised that her inability to empathise with others, and therefore being quite blunt and self-focused in her talk with friends, has caused her to lose relationships. By addressing and discussing what the MSCEIT™ is saying about her emotional abilities and the potential for change, we helped her address this issue – for which she was very grateful.

10. I don't need EI. I got to where I am without it.

Everyone needs to develop their emotional intelligence if we are serious about raising the emotional well-being of the people we have an impact on within our families, work places, and communities.

The question is not, "How did I get to where I am?", but rather "Can I remain where I am without an understanding of my own and others' emotional intelligence?"

I argue that you cannot and *Emotional Leadership* explains why.

Emotional Leadership Practice

ELP 1.4   What is emotional intelligence?

Each of the following acronyms describes a view of emotional intelligence. Write down a brief description for each acronym and the author of the instrument.

IQ

EQ

EQ-i®

MSCEIT™

ECI

BOEI

2. TRUE TEST OF INTELLIGENCE

It was once thought that having a high IQ was all one needed to be successful and fulfil one's potential. A high IQ is a human characteristic valued by almost everyone. Achieving a high grade in a test, or having the ability to do well academically, is important.

Cognitive intelligence – measured as IQ (Intelligence Quotient) – is to do with your cognitive capacity to;

■ Be analytical and logical in thinking, problem solve (thought).

■ Remember and recall information (memory).

■ Compute accurately (mathematics).

■ Have a general fund of information (day-to-day link).

However, today the reliability and validity of IQ tests are not beyond question. There is a tendency to test the critical components of skills in questions – such as competency levels. These at best are indicators of something

deeper and more important. We now know that things like perseverance, self-discipline, achievement, and emotional abilities, are more important than having a high IQ.

Ultimately, emotional health is dependent upon having a firm grip on how you behave when you don't know what to do. How you use your emotional abilities – emotional intelligence – in various situations.

The term emotional intelligence consists of two parts;

1. **Emotions** – Signals that convey meanings about relationships. Some basic emotions are regarded as universal.
2. **Intelligence** – Refers to your ability to reason with, or about, something.

You are what you think. Emotional intelligence is your potential, or set of abilities, to reason with emotions and emotional signals, and use emotion to enhance thought. An emotionally intelligent person has a firm grip on how to behave, when he or she doesn't *know* what to do.

3. TRADITIONAL VIEW OF EMOTION IN RELATION TO COGNITION

Researchers (Salovey, Bedell, Detweiler, & Mayer 2000) have provided a sequence of how emotional intelligence has risen from a large body of literature, to be a field of research on its own. Here are some traditional views of emotion in relation to cognition, and within the following section, a critique of the narrow definition of intelligence, gleaned from these researchers.

Traditional views of emotions include;

- Passion and reason are opposites.
- Emotions are chaotic and immature.
- Emotions "get in-the-way" of rational decision-making.
- "Rule your feelings, lest your feelings rule you." – *Publilius Syrus (First century BC)*
- "[Emotions cause] a complete loss of cerebral control [and contain] no trace of conscious purpose." – *PT Young (1936)*

From 1940 a paradigm shift occurred. Emotions are now seen to be functional and adaptive, not chaotic;

- "[Emotions] arouse, sustain, and direct activity." – *RW Leeper (1948)*
- Intelligence is "the aggregate or global capacity of the individual to act purposely, to think rationally, and to deal effectively with his environment." – *D Wechsler (1958)*

Emotions arouse our thinking and motivate us;

- "Emotions are adaptive, functional, and organising of cognitive activities and subsequent behaviour." – P*eter Salovey PhD Yale*
- "The emotions are of quite extraordinary importance in the total economy of living organisms and do not deserve being put into opposition with 'intelligence'. The emotions are, it seems, themselves a high order of intelligence." – *OH Mowrer (1960)*

4. INTELLIGENCE IS TOO NARROWLY DEFINED

In the past, intelligence has been too narrowly defined. Analytical (thinking) abilities are but one kind of intelligence. Sternberg (1985)[5] argues that we must also consider;

- Creative intelligence. For example, being street smart – one's degree of common sense.
- Practical intelligence that is context specific. That is, knowledge is contextualised for survival in the wild – the drama of life.

"Intrapersonal" intelligence may be one kind of intelligence.

> Access to one's own feeling life – one's range of affects or emotions:
> the capacity instantly to effect discriminations among these
> feelings…label them…enmesh them in symbolic codes…and draw
> upon them (use them) as a means of understanding and guiding one's
> behaviour. - Gardner (1983), *Frames of Mind*.

Emotional intelligence is often thought to be new. In fact, emotional
intelligence has been around since Charles Darwin wrote about the functional
purpose of emotions in The expression of the emotions in man and animals
(1872/1965)[6].

Darwin's functional view of emotions was;
- Emotions are intelligent.
- Emotions ensure survival.
  - Energising required behaviour.
  - Signalling valued information.

Darwin's functional view of emotion

EMOTION	EXPRESSION	SIGNALS INTENTION TO OTHERS
Anger	Bare teeth	I'm going to bite you
Fear	Raise eyebrow; open mouth	I'm going to run away
Sadness	Frown	Take care of me
Joy	Smile	It's safe to approach me

5. THE ARRIVAL OF EMOTIONAL INTELLIGENCE

Emotional intelligence thus rose out of the fields of personality, social psychology and neuropsychology. Personality is a set of behaviours acquired through learning – past experience. Social psychology focuses on what people *do* rather than what people are *like*. And neuropsychology is the study of the relationship between brain function and behaviour.

The term "emotional intelligence" is described in many different forms due to the history of the field.

John Mayer and Peter Salovey (1997), the first researchers to use the term "Emotional Intelligence" in 1990, define emotional intelligence as;

> "The capacity to reason with emotion in four areas: to perceive emotion, to integrate it in thought, to understand it, and to manage it.

> The ability to perceive, appraise, and express emotion accurately and adaptively; the ability to understand emotion and emotional knowledge; the ability to access and /or generate feelings when they facilitate thought; and the ability to regulate emotions in ways that assist thought.

> Emotional intelligence involves the ability to understand emotions in oneself and others, relate to peers and family members, and adapt emotionally to changing environmental concerns and demands."[7]

Daniel Goleman's book *Emotional Intelligence* (1995) popularised the concept of emotional intelligence and equated it with good social behaviour. This stretched the meaning of emotional intelligence.[8] Goleman describes emotional intelligence as;

> "The abilities called here *emotional intelligence*, which include self-control, zeal, and persistence, and the ability to motivate one-self." [9]

In his later book, *Working with Emotional Intelligence* (1998), Goleman describes emotional intelligence as;

"The capacity for recognising your own feelings and those of others, for motivating ourselves, and for managing emotions well in ourselves and in our relationships."[10]

Other researchers define emotional intelligence as good character or social skills, and test emotional intelligence as a set of emotional competencies, observed in overt emotionally intelligent behaviour.

Reuven Bar-On (2001) says that emotional intelligence is…

"…an array of noncognitive capabilities, competencies, and skills that influence one's ability to succeed in coping with environmental demands and pressures."[11]

Goleman and Bar-On refer to outcomes of emotional intelligence. If you measure these competencies and call them EI, then you have the best test. It may be better to ask, "Do these skills affect your competence in the workplace?" If yes, then you have a responsibility to improve them.

In summary, emotional intelligence is to do with two areas:
1. Emotional abilities (skills and knowledge) – For example, do you or do you not have the ability to be empathetic? Emotional abilities can be measured using the MSCEIT™ .

    Empathy is the ability to see the world through another person's perspective regardless of what you think, of the other person's perspective. Empathy is taking an adversarial relationship and turning it into a collaborative alliance.

    You will lack the ability to be empathetic if you have not had help in nurturing these skills growing up. If you were brought up to believe that, "If you can't say anything nice, don't say anything at all", you will have trouble criticising people. If dad knows best and mum knows nothing, then you will have problems with authority figures. People who lack empathy can be assisted to develop the ability by linking emotions. Having a high ability to perceive and understand emotions, will assist you in developing an ability to empathise with others.

2. Emotional competencies – your view of your "EQ". For example, how good are you at being empathetic? Emotional competencies can be measured using the EQ-i®.

   Emotional competencies – such as high flexibility and optimism – are linked to empathy. Understanding your emotional competencies and the links between them, will assist you to develop the areas in which you are weak, and moderate the areas in which you score high. For example, a high flexibility score may indicate that you are unable to be very assertive.

6. MEASURING EMOTIONAL INTELLIGENCE

Emotional intelligence tests have been developed by Bar-On, Mayer et. al, and Goleman to help answer this basic question;

> "Why do some people with a high IQ fail in life, while others with a moderate IQ succeed?"

Brief overview of the MSCEIT™

John Mayer, Peter Salovey, and David Caruso began constructing their model of emotional intelligence – the MSCEIT™ (pronounced "Mes-keet") – with the idea that emotions contain information about relationships. They argue that, "EI refers to an ability to recognise the meanings of emotions and their relationships, and to reason and problem-solve on the basis of them. It further involves employing emotions to enhance cognitive abilities."[12]

The Mayer-Salovey-Caruso Emotional Intelligence Test (MSCEIT™), which participants of *The EASEQuadrant® Workshop* complete, is designed to assess emotional intelligence. It is an ability-based scale. That is, it measures whether you do or do not have an ability to *perform tasks* and *solve emotional problems*. Rather than simply asking you for a subjective assessment of your emotional skills – that is, a self-report test.

The MSCEIT™ model – you will find a brief outline in Appendix B – is the first measure of emotional intelligence that reports valid scores in each of the four central areas of emotional intelligence, which are developed in *Emotional Leadership* in the following chapters.

The ability to;

1. Accurately perceive emotions – Chapters 1 and 2,
2. Use emotions to facilitate thinking, problem solving, and creativity – Chapters 3 and 4,
3. Understand emotions – Chapters 5 and 6,
4. Manage emotions for personal growth – Chapters 7 and 8.

The MSCEIT™ Mayer-Salovey-Caruso Emotional Intelligence Test[13], measures your potential – or set of abilities – to reason with emotions and emotional signals, and to use emotion to enhance thought. Hence the term "emotional intelligence".

Specifically, the MSCEIT™ tests your potential or ability in four areas;

1. Your ability to perceive and identify emotion in yourself and others. To recognise how those around you are feeling, as well as perceiving emotions in objects, art, stories, music and other stimuli.

    How a person feels based on facial expressions and the extent to which images/landscapes express emotion.
2. Your ability to generate, use and feel emotion as necessary, to communicate feelings or employ them in the cognitive processes.

    How mood interacts and supports thinking and reasoning, and your ability to generate emotion and compare its sensations with other sensory modalities – for example, empathy.
3. Your ability to understand emotional information and how emotions combine and progress through relationship transitions.

Understanding emotional chains – how emotions transition from one to another. For example, anger to rage, sadness to despair. And understanding emotional blends – how simple emotions assimilate together into complex feelings. For example, how acceptance, joy, and warmth equal contentment.

4. Your ability to be open to feelings, and to manage emotion in yourself and others to promote personal understanding and growth.

Your ability to incorporate your own feelings into decision making for self-management. For example, using anger assertively. And incorporating emotions into decisions that affect other people for relationship management. Such as, using or acknowledging another person's anxiety to help formulate a decision.

We will return to review MSCEIT™ scores in item 9 below – Understanding your emotional intelligence scores.

"EQ" and the Bar-On EQ-i®

The term "EQ" is commonly used to refer to emotional intelligence. "EQ" stands for "emotional quotient". It derives from Bar-On's emotional intelligence test – the Bar-On EQ-i® (Emotional Quotient Inventory)[14] – that provides a subjective assessment (self-report), as to how well you meet a specific standard. That is, how competent you are at using your emotions.

The Bar-On EQ-i® looks at environmental and social factors. The test provides 133 social 'standards', 'statements', or 'competencies' and measures how you perform these 'competencies' in your environment. In ELP 1.5 (following) we have listed the 15 conceptual components of emotional intelligence, that are measured by the Bar-On EQ-i® subscales.

Your total EQ-i® scale score encapsulates how successful you are in coping with environmental demands, and presents a snapshot of your present emotional well-being measured over a five point scale – 1 being *very seldom true of me*, and 5 being *very often true of me*.

Scoring is grouped into five EQ composite scale scores and 15 EQ subscale scores. The five EQ composite scale scores are,

1. Intrapersonal EQ Scale (RAeq)
2. Interpersonal EQ Scale (EReq)
3. Adaptability EQ Scale (ADeq)
4. Stress Management EQ Scale (SMeq)
5. General Mood EQ Scale (GMeq)

The 15 EQ Subscales are listed in ELP1.5.

 Emotional Leadership Practice

ELP 1.5   What are emotional competencies?

Emotional intelligence develops over time, changes throughout life, and can be improved through training and remedial programs as well as therapeutic techniques.

Study the following factorial components of Reuven Bar-On's concept of emotional intelligence, measured by the EQ-i®. Which of these emotional competencies do you recognise in yourself?

1. **Emotional Self-Awareness**: The ability to recognise one's feelings.
2. **Assertiveness**: The ability to express feelings, beliefs and thoughts and defend one's rights in a nondestructive manner.
3. **Self-Regard**: The ability to respect and accept oneself as basically good.
4. **Self-Actualisation**: The ability to realise one's potential capacities.
5. **Independence**: The ability to be self-directed and self-controlled in one's thinking and actions, and to be free of emotional dependency.
6. **Empathy**: The ability to be aware of, to understand, and to appreciate the feelings of others.
7. **Interpersonal Relationship**: The ability to establish and maintain mutually satisfying relationships that are characterised by intimacy, and by the giving and receiving of affection.

8. **Social Responsibility**: The ability to demonstrate oneself as a cooperative, contributing, and constructive member of one's social group.

9. **Problem Solving**: The ability to identify and define problems, as well as to generate and implement potentially effective solutions.

10. **Reality Testing**: The ability to assess the correspondence between what is experienced and what objectively exists.

11. **Flexibility**: The ability to adjust one's emotions, thoughts, and behaviour to changing situations and conditions.

12. **Stress Tolerance**: The ability to withstand adverse events and situations without "falling apart", by actively and positively coping with stress.

13. **Impulse Control**: The ability to resist or delay an impulse, drive or temptation to act.

14. **Happiness**: The ability to feel satisfied with one's life. To enjoy oneself and others and to have fun.

15. **Optimism**: The ability to look at the brighter side of life and to maintain a positive attitude – even in the face of adversity.

(BarOn EQ-i®: Copyright© 1997, 2002, Multi-Healths System Inc. All rights reserved. Reproduced with permission.)

7. DO IQ AND EI EQUATE WITH HAPPINESS?

Emotional intelligence is as important as IQ – if not more so – in dealing with how well people meet new situations, absorb new knowledge, perform tasks and solve problems. Emotional abilities are innate. But you *can* learn to nurture and develop how you perceive, use, understand and manage, your emotions.

Intellect and emotion are two sides of the same coin. Emotional distress is an illness of how you think. How you feel depends on how you think. This is good, because thoughts that are keeping you ill can be reframed or restructured.[15] Happiness and personal fulfilment, and a life of ease will not come from either IQ or EI alone. But from interplay of all your personality traits, competencies, thinking and emotional abilities, communication skills, right choices focused on opportunity, and recognising the way you and your partner give and receive love.

8. VALUE OF EMOTIONAL INTELLIGENCE AT WORK

Research has shown that emotional intelligence is vital for the future development of team building, leadership and management in corporations, government and other organisations. Emotional intelligence has become a recognised factor in leadership and management for a number of reasons. Emotional abilities are essential to self management and social management. Emotional competencies identify star performers and retaining emotionally intelligent people is the key to an organisation adding economic value.

Mayer (1999) says, "… emotional intelligence – if substantiated – broadens our understanding of what it means to be smart."

In his article, *"What makes a leader?" (Harvard Business Review, 1998)*, Daniel Goleman says, "…my research along with other recent studies, clearly shows that emotional intelligence is the sine qua non of leadership".

Research points to emotional intelligence being important for success in work and in life. Non-cognitive (emotional) abilities that play part of successes at work include:

1. **Learned optimism** – The causal attributes people make when confronted with failure or setbacks.

   Optimists make specific, temporary external attributions. For example, "It's the economy, stupid."

   Pessimists make global, permanent, internal attributions. For example, "I'll never succeed" or "It's my fate to be a follower".
2. **Ability to manage negative feelings** – That is, stress.
3. **Ability to generate empathy** – People who are best at identifying other's emotions, are more successful in their work and social lives. We resist displaying empathy as we may not have had help nurturing these skills growing up.

Emotional Leadership Practice

ELP 1.6   Value of emotional intelligence at work

Think about experiences you have had with emotional intelligence at work. Discuss these with your colleagues.

9. UNDERSTANDING YOUR EMOTIONAL INTELLIGENCE SCORES

Interpretive guidelines for MSCEIT™ scores[16] are assessed as follows

Your MSCEIT™ Total and Branch Scores can be plotted on a normal distribution curve. The curve (see item 10, page 26) allows you to compare your scores to the frequency distribution of the normative sample of 5,000 respondents, who form the test base of the MSCEIT™.

The highest frequency falls in the centre, at the mean – 100 in the case of the MSCEIT™. This means that half the values fall below the average and half above it. The further away any particular value is from the mean, the less frequent that value will be. The area under the curve will contain the total of all values in the sample population of 5,000. Mathematical calculations record 68 percent of all scores fall within one standard deviation from the mean – in areas A and B – and about 27 percent of all scores will fall into areas C and D. About 5 percent of scores fall outside of areas A, B, C and D.

For the MSCEIT™, one standard deviation has been calculated at 15. If you have a score between 85 and 115, your score falls in areas A or B. A score of around 100 means you are in the average range of emotional intelligence. A person obtaining a score of 115 has high emotional intelligence, compared to others in the normative sample.

Interpretive guidelines for EQ-i®[17] scores are assessed as follows;

EQ-i standard scores have a mean – or average – score of 100, and a standard deviation of 15. The majority of respondents – approximately 68 percent – will receive scores within 15 points of the mean. That is, between 85 and 115. An even larger number – about 95 percent – will have scores between 70 and 130. These respondents are markedly atypical and need to be examined more closely.

High 'total EQ' scores indicate individuals who are in touch with their feelings, feel good about themselves, and are fairly successful in realising their potential. These individuals understand the way others feel and are generally successful in relating to people. They are good at managing stress and rarely lose control. People with high 'total EQ' scores are realistic, assertive, and fairly successful in solving problems. Individuals who score high on 'total EQ' are generally happy and have a positive outlook on life.

10. THE NORMAL DISTRIBUTION CURVE

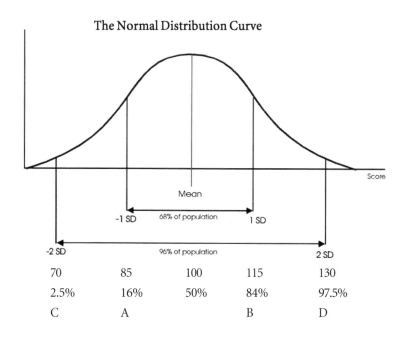

Emotional Leadership Practice

ELP 1.7   Plot your MSCEIT™ scores on a normal distribution curve

The EASEQuadrant® Workshop participants and readers interested in completing the two online MSCEIT™ and EQ-i emotional intelligence tests may use the normal distribution curves below to plot their emotional intelligence scores.

The Normal Distribution Curve

70	85	100	115	130
2.5%	16%	50%	84%	97.5%

Experiental Emotional Intelligence   Strategic Emotional Intelligence

Branch 1: Perceiving Emotion

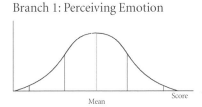

Branch 2: Facilitating Thoughts

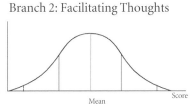

Branch 3: Understanding Emotion

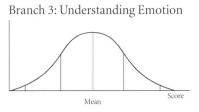

Branch 4: Managing Emotion

Emotional Leadership Practice

ELP 1.8   Plot your EQ-i® scores on a normal distribution curve

Use the normal distribution curves below to plot your emotional intelligence scores.

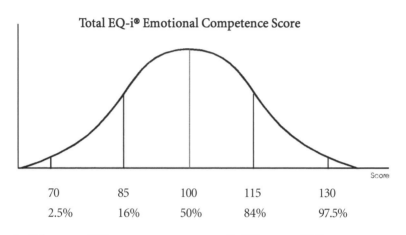

Total EQ-i® Emotional Competence Score

70	85	100	115	130
2.5%	16%	50%	84%	97.5%

IntRApersonal EQ

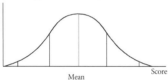

IntERpersonal EQ

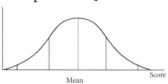

Adaptability EQ

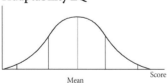

Stress ManagementEQ

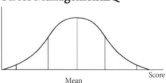

General MoodEQ

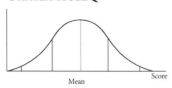

Other EQ Subscale

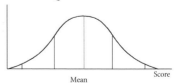

EMOTIONAL HEALTH

1. NATURE AND POTENTIAL OF HEALTH

The best measure of emotional health is; how do you manage the problems and opportunities that you experience in your life each day?

Aldous Huxley said, "Experience is not what happens to you; it is what you *do* with what happens to you." If you experience nervous suffering – but you've found a way to survive a difficult life – you are probably healthier than those who have avoided such experiences, only because they have had easier lives. Emotionally healthy people have learned to live their lives managing their pain. They are self-motivated to raise their own well-being and the well-being of others. They have chosen not to be victims.

 Emotional Leadership Practice

ELP 1.9   How well do you handle the problems of life?

Based on your experience, how well do you handle the problems and opportunities you face in your daily life? How often have you blamed others for what has happened to you, and avoided taking responsibility for the difficulties in your life?

NOTES

Emotional Leadership Practice

ELP 1.10   Consider the signs of emotional health

Can you answer "Yes" to these questions;

☐ Are you usually energetic?

☐ Do you only occasionally make comparisons between yourself and others (less than once a day)?

☐ Do you laugh genuinely and often (many times most days)?

☐ Are you a self-starter?

☐ Are you appropriate with your anger and quick to recover?

☐ Are you only occasionally slowed down by feelings of depression?

☐ Do you only occasionally feel guilty?

☐ Do you have a good, long-lasting relationship with your partner?

☐ Do you have good, long-lasting friendships (at least two or three)?

☐ Do you only occasionally spend time with people who mistreat you or put you down?

☐ Do you make most decisions quickly?

☐ Do you seldom regret your decisions?

☐ Do you recognise sadness, anger, fear, joy, surprise and disgust easily in yourself?

☐ Are you seldom told that you are controlling or manipulative?

☐ Do you know you could survive and thrive – after a grieving period – even if you lost all of the important people in your life?

☐ Do you engage easily with people?

☐ Are you often aware of your mood and its impact on others?

Evaluating and deciding

Each Yes is a remarkable achievement accomplished by a small percentage of people! Compliment yourself sincerely and proudly for every Yes on this page! Each No is a way of saying that you are about average. Read each No again and say; "I could improve this if I wanted to!" Decide whether to change – by weighing the amount of emotional pain your problems cause for you, and for those you love. Decide whether to get professional help – by weighing this pain against the various costs of therapy such as financial, time, privacy and inconvenience.

2. DEFINITIONS OF HEALTH

Most of us have thought of health in a linear way. We are used to a functional definition of health – the absence of disease. Put another way, Winefield and Peay (1980) say, "… illness was simply a matter of bodily disorder."[18]

Two definitions of health are;

1. "Health is a state of complete physical, mental and social well-being and not merely the absence of disease or infirmity".
   – *World Health Organisation*[19]
2. "Health is the optimal condition of being that allows for the ultimate engagement in life". – *Jesse Williams, Physician*[20]

How does one engage life ultimately? We engage life physically, cognitively, emotionally and spiritually. A person who is experiencing the pain and confusion of personal distress and/or social and psychological problems is not healthy. Nervous disorders that affect neocortical functioning (see The Physical Brain, page 39) result in significant behavioural and cognitive impairment. To be emotionally healthy, means potentially to be free of the physical, emotional and cognitive signs and symptoms that unfold in the drama of life – to be free to build intimacy and trust.

The definition of emotional health we will use in *Emotional Leadership* is;

Emotional health is a state of being calm. Of being steady or in a positive state – free of stress. Managing your emotions in present moment awareness.

To be emotionally healthy is to be able to manage the impact of another's behaviour toward you, by recognising the emotion displayed in the other person, and not allowing that emotion to affect you negatively. By applying behaviour you want to be.

Emotional health is facilitated by;

- Developing emotional self-awareness,
- Applying simple cognitive-behavioural techniques,
- Exercising your power-of-choice,
- Implementing effective communication skills,
- Learning to give and receive love, and
- Improving your emotional abilities – emotional intelligence – to enhance self-management and social management.

3. SIGNS OF EMOTIONAL HEALTH

Three important signs of emotional health are; spontaneity, intimacy and awareness.[21]

Spontaneity refers to the immediacy with which we express ourselves. If you are able to appraise events rapidly and not be slowed by caution, then you are spontaneous. *Being spontaneous shows that we trust who we are.*

> **Question 1.1** – Ask yourself; "How often do I respond to things quickly and with enthusiasm?" If you answer "almost always", you are spontaneous and potentially emotionally healthy.

Intimacy refers to feeling safe when we are close to others. If you usually look away when people look your way, or if you often feel lonely – chances are you are not very intimate. *Being intimate shows we trust ourselves socially.*

Question 1.2 – Ask yourself; "How often do I feel completely safe when I look into other people's eyes?" If you answer "almost always", you are intimate and potentially healthy emotionally.

Awareness refers to our ability to see and hear clearly and to believe what we see and hear. If you often doubt your perceptions of people and situations, you are not very aware. Or you are very aware and don't know it – a common problem. *Being aware shows we are alert, rather than mentally preoccupied.*

Question 1.3 – Ask yourself; "How often am I wrong about my perceptions? How often do I ask other people to confirm my perceptions and thinking?" If you answer "almost never" you are aware and potentially healthy emotionally.

 Emotional Leadership Practice
ELP 1.11   Self-awareness – 'The Johari Window'

[Originally developed by Joseph Luft and Harry Ingham. Luft, J 1969, *Of Human Interaction*, Palo Alto, CA, National Press Books; Luft, J 1970, *Group Processes: An Introduction to Group Dynamics*, Palo Alto, CA, National Press Books.]

The name 'Johari Window' was derived from the first names of the two people who developed the model – Joseph Luft and Harry Ingham – 'Johari'.

The Johari Window has four basic areas, or quadrants. Each quadrant contains a somewhat different self. The model is particularly helpful in enabling you to increase your self-awareness. No one knows you better than you which quadrant dominates your view of yourself.

The Johari Window is helpful in enabling you to raise your emotional self-awareness. It is a tool for changing behaviour. Self-awareness helps you identify your strengths and weaknesses, so you can work on your strengths. Your communication becomes more effective when you know the effect it has on others. Self-awareness assists you in exercising control over your behaviours. For example, if you're aware that talking about yourself and not enquiring about others upsets others, you can decide to change your behaviour.

Figure 4. The Johari Window

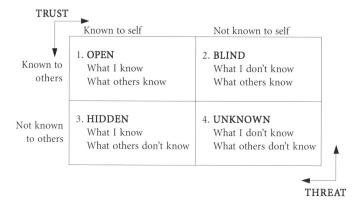

Trust and threat are the factors that alter the Johari Window. To be open, a person must be open to feedback and to disclosing themself. If a person cannot be open to another, then communication shuts down. It is threatening to be open and honest with others. But you are less effective if you have to shut down and not be open. Effective relationships occur if there is a fair balance between self-disclosure and feedback. Threat tends to decrease awareness, mutual trust tends to increase awareness.

Why don't people have trust?
- Because people expect the worst in others.
- We guard information closely.
- Leadership is built around control.
- We measure conformance.
- We communicate on a "need to know" basis.
- We shoot the messenger. A person brings us news and we jump on him – so he stops giving the message.

- Decision-making is centralised.
- Personnel systems often deny the motivated worker.
- Policing communicates distrust.
- Promises go unfulfilled.
- We don't even trust ourselves.

1. **Open: The Open Person** – Reasonably confident. Good communicator. Trusting – has open arena for disclosure with others. Is open to feedback.

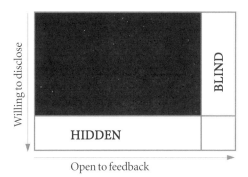

2. **Blind: The Bull In A China Shop** – The boring person is very willing to disclose – a talker. Not receptive to feedback. Wall of words is a defence against lack of confidence. Fill all the spaces with words so that you don't have to give anything. Blind to behaviour that is involved in interactions.

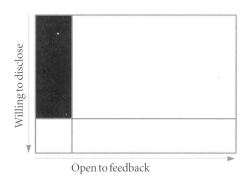

3. **Hidden: The Interviewer** – Asks questions. Is open to feedback, but won't disclose much about how he feels about the feedback. Hides a lot by questioning, "Tell me about you. Now I've told you a little about me, tell me all about you." Lacking in confidence.

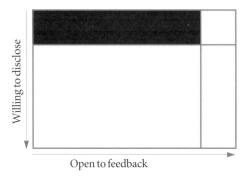

4. **Unknown: The Turtle** – A poor communicator – the introvert. Not a risk taker. Huge potential. Large blind spots. Not much disclosure. Barriers to feedback. Not aware of who they are and how they are seen by others.

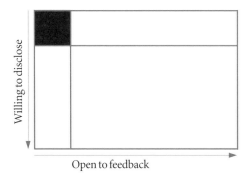

NEEDS AND WANTS

1. HIERARCHY OF NEEDS

Perception is influenced by needs and expectations. In 1943, Psychologist Abraham Maslow (1908-1970) published his taxonomy of five basic needs; physiological, safety, belonging, esteem and self-actualisation.[22]

The most basic need is your **physiological need**. To have enough food, oxygen, water, minerals and vitamins to survive. You would die if you didn't take care of your needs. An adult needs the same things that an infant needs. You need food, air, water, space, exercise and to avoid being too hot or too cold. You need to get rid of wastes efficiently – otherwise you die.

When the physiological needs are largely taken care of, you become interested in finding a place to be **safe and secure** from physical and psychological harm – danger, threat, and anxiety.

In turn you begin to feel a need for friends, and have a desire to be loved and to love – a need for **affection and belonging**. We all need attention and "strokes" from each other. A sense of belonging, a feeling of acceptance, and the ability to give and receive love.

Now you look for a little **esteem** from others and from yourself. You have a need for the respect of others – reputation, prestige, recognition and appreciation. And a need for self-respect – self-confidence, competence, achievement, independence, freedom, knowledge and strength.

Maslow held that as one level of your needs is satisfied, a higher level of need is activated. The process continues until you reach **self-actualisation** – the finding of self-fulfilment and realising one's potential. At this point there is continual self-development, creativity and realising one's potential.

Adapting Maslow's model to emotional leadership, this book argues that self-actualisation includes improving your emotional intelligence – through applying emotional leadership – to realise fully your life goals.

2. ENERGY SURGES SIGNAL NEEDS

The human body gets its primary energy from burning sugar. You get your energy from taking care of your body well – not perfectly. In fact, you only need to eat, sleep, and exercise "well enough" for your body to give you all the information you will ever need through your feelings. Feelings are energy surges that tell you what you need or want. When you notice these feelings, you usually have enough energy to handle the need or want, they are telling you about. For example, when you feel hunger you have the energy to get up and make something to eat. But sometimes the need for sleep overrides the feeling of hunger.

3. DEVELOPING EMOTIONAL AWARENESS

Emotions signal a level of need. A need for food and water, safety, love and esteem. Emotions are feelings linked to a thought. The emotional states of anger, fear, sadness, surprise, enjoyment and disgust originate in your mind. Your appraisal of your thoughts produces physical manifestations that you have learned to call feelings. Feeling plus thought is experienced in the body as emotion. Emotions can create chemical imbalances and actual toxins, that cause deterioration of your body or lead to illness. The way to cure the illness that you have created for yourself, is to develop emotional awareness.

Awareness is – the degree of clarity you have at the time you perceive, and understand, the need at hand. You will always choose an action that seems most likely to meet your need at the time. The potential benefits of the action you choose might seem – at least at the time – to outweigh the foreseeable disadvantages. For example, you may choose anger as a payback for a hurt you feel. This meets your need, but is possibly an inappropriate response because of the impact of your anger on the other person.

As you recognise and understand your needs and wants – and despair that they are not being met – you become open to thoughts and feelings that are mostly painful. You may have an "Oh Shit!" experience. You may begin to ask yourself, "Why is everything going wrong? Why am I feeling forsaken? Why am I feeling rejected? Why am I always angry? Why am I treated so badly? Why did he or she leave me? What's wrong with my behaviour? Why am I so depressed?" Sooner or later your stored hurts will start to overwhelm you.

> **Emotional Wisdom**
>
> Retaining your creative potential is the mark of wisdom. Passing it by – in favour of old habits, rituals, rigid beliefs and outworn behaviour – is the mark of a fool. The way to end a painful emotion, is to perceive it to end. To develop emotional awareness.

When you begin to ask yourself these questions, you are developing emotional awareness. You are recognising and examining major physiological problems in your body. People who don't ask themselves these questions simply blame others for the discomfort they feel. Their emotional constipation – negative emotions – remain. In blaming others and not owning your feelings, you give someone else the *responsibility* for your feelings. *You* are responsible for your actions in that you will inevitably pay the price – willing or not, consciously or unconsciously – for your lack of awareness.

Becoming emotionally aware means becoming a responsible person. Knowing the price you pay for your actions. It's worth the effort. Low emotional awareness means that you are later surprised – even dismayed – at the cost of some of your decisions.

PERCEIVING EMOTION

1. THE PHYSICAL BRAIN

To perceive emotion is to receive and interpret information from both external (world) and internal (body) environments. Your senses – sight, smell, touch, taste and hearing – connect you to the world around you, through your physical brain.

Perception is the whole process by which information (events) about the outside world impinges on the sensory organs and is then decoded and interpreted by the brain – resulting in a conscious experience. It is one aspect of cognition – all the mental activities which enable us to know and make decisions (appraisals) about the world (our environment). (Winefield and Peay, 1980 p. 53).

Four major brain regions are; the brain stem, cerebellum, neocortex (cerebrum) and limbic system.

Emotional Leadership Practice
ELP 1.12   Two views of the brain

Refer to figures 1.1. and 1.2. Identify four major regions of the brain. Discuss with a friend or partner how the brain has evolved through its primitive and intermediate stages to the present large human rational brain, a highly complex net of neural cells. Identify the major components of the limbic system – the centre of emotions. What is the amygdala?

Figure 1.1. Side view of brain

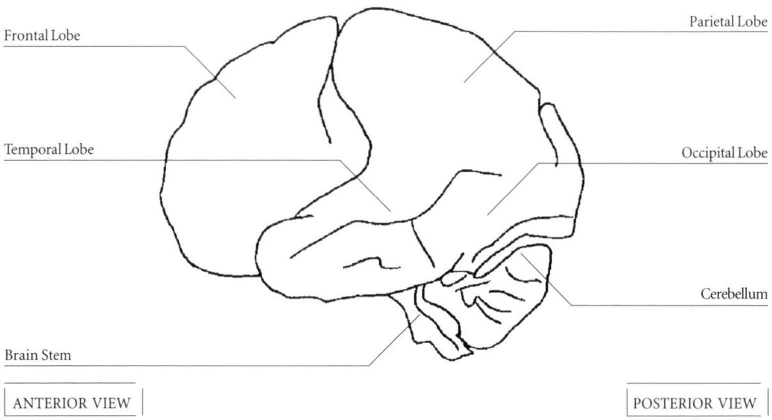

Frontal Lobe

Parietal Lobe

Temporal Lobe

Occipital Lobe

Cerebellum

Brain Stem

| ANTERIOR VIEW |

| POSTERIOR VIEW |

1. The **brain stem** is an extension of the spinal cord. Its major component is the medulla that controls functions necessary for survival such as breathing, digestion, heart rate and blood pressure.
2. The **cerebellum** is located at the rear of the brain. It controls movement, balance, muscle coordination and arousal – being awake and alert.
3. The **neocortex** contains the cerebrum – the largest part of the brain. Its outer surface is the cerebral cortex composed of gray matter, responsible for all perceptions and complex thought. The cerebrum is divided into two hemispheres. The left hemisphere is for sequential analysis, language, abstraction and reasoning. The right hemisphere deals with visual and spatial abilities, and specialises in artistic and musical tasks.

    The neocortex is divided into four arbitrary functional areas or lobes;

    a. Frontal lobe for higher cognitive functions including; concentration and elaboration of thought, personality, behaviour and emotions, through intense connections with the thalamus, amygdala, and other subcortical structures.
    b. Parietal lobe at the top of the brain for motor functions and monitoring skin senses.
    c. Occipital lobe at the back of the brain for vision.
    d. Temporal lobe with auditory, speech reception, memory retrieval and expressed behaviour functions.

4. The **limbic system** – comprising the thalamus, hypothalamus, hippocampus, amygdala, and connecting pathways – mediates and expresses emotional, motivational, sexual and social behaviours, and memory.

Figure 1.2. The Limbic System

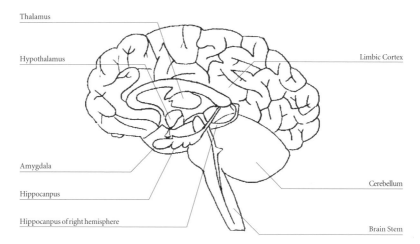

Thalamus

Hypothalamus

Limbic Cortex

Amygdala

Cerebellum

Hippocanpus

Hippocanpus of right hemisphere

Brain Stem

The brain controls all involuntary functions at the same time. These include breathing and heartbeat, as well as higher mental processes such as thought, and physical activities of breathing, movement, and coordination, plus non-physical functions such as emotions. It regulates bodily functions and is the seat of your personality. The brain absorbs information from the outside world, interprets it, and makes the body act accordingly. It does this through a fascinating process of communication between specialised brain or neural cells – called neurons – that fire electrical impulses, or thoughts.

The brain is made up of gray and white matter. The white matter of the brain supports cells by bringing food and nutrition – it contains the wires that "hold" the brain together. The gray matter of the brain is the most important. It contains neurons that transmit and communicate information by means of electrochemical pulses.

Each pattern of light, sound, heat, pain, scowl or snap of a finger – each thought, translates into a sequence of electric pulses. Neurons connect themselves to each other in chains and nervous impulses pass from the point of stimulus, through the spinal cord, and along the membranes of neurons to the limbic system – located in the brain's medial temporal lobe.

The mass of electrochemical pulses – or neuron connections – swirling around the brain, is the brain's most significant quality; "mind" or "consciousness" – with all its great powers and uniqueness. Consciousness is your total thinking, personality, emotion and warmth. Consciousness emerges from all the activities of the cerebral network as an independent entity, influenced by subjective human values. By impacting on consciousness, human values become an underlying key to change.[23]

2. THE AMYGDALA VERSUS NEOCORTICAL FUNCTIONING

The largest web of neocortical functioning in the brain is between the prefrontal area and the limbic structures. This perhaps explains the great variety of feelings and emotions that humans experience.

The limbic system includes;

- Thalamus – the processing centre of the cerebral cortex which contributes to affectual expression. This relays and translates information from senses – except smell – to higher levels of the brain, and is a gateway to the amygdala – where emotional significance is attached to sensory signals.
- Hypothalamus – the primitive integration centre of the autonomic nervous system (ANS), that regulates hunger, thirst, body temperature and endocrine function. Activates physical expression of emotion – for example the fight or take flight stress response, and controls parasympathetic activity – reduces heart rate, quiets the body and conserves energy. The hypothalamus is the central core from which all emotions derive their motive force.[24] The Hypothalamus controls the "Four F's" – fighting, feeding, fleeing and fornicating.
- Olfactory pathways – translate information from smell.
- Hippocampus – particularly involved with the formation of long-term memory, enables you to compare present threats with past experiences – thus choosing the best option.
- Amygdala – centre of emotional energy in the brain. Pre-eminent

role in the development of emotional memory, mediation and control of major affective activities such as friendship, love and affection. Being the centre for identification of danger, the amygdala is critical for self-preservation. When triggered it gives rise to fear, getting the person ready for "fight or flight" by exciting and driving the hypothalamus and motor centres.

The amygdala is the nucleus responsible for the lurch you feel in your stomach when you feel fear for the first time. Electrical stimulation of the amygdala results in sex related reactions such as ovulation, uterine contractions and penile erections.

The amygdala plays a large role in emotion processing. In his book *A Celebration of Neurons*, Robert Sylwester says,

The amygdala complex is composed of two almond-shaped, finger-nail-sized structures that are richly and reciprocally connected to most brain areas – especially advanced sensory-processing areas. Its principal task is to filter and interpret sophisticated incoming sensory information in the context of our survival and emotional needs, and then to help initiate appropriate responses.[25]

It seems that the limbic system is not only involved in all aspects of emotion – including sexual behaviour and the production of emotional speech – but may be responsible for gender differences in thought, feeling, and even language.

3. ALL EMOTIONS HAVE A PHYSICAL COMPONENT

Throughout this book you will explore ways to experience a state of assertion and appreciation (positive emotions) where control of the signals sent to your brain from your senses, human values and environment, is wrestled away from the amygdala by the neocortex – the cognitive brain – to give rise to selfless acts of love and a life of EASE.

> **Emotional Wisdom**
>
> Your journey of emotional leadership is the personal discovery that all your emotions have a physical component, a normal biological response that requires management. You should not feel guilty about any feelings that you may have. Emotional health is what you *do* about your (biological) feelings.

4. KNOWING YOURSELF AND UNDERSTANDING CHANGE

You create your own emotional health. Your mind and body are inseparable, bound together in a field of energy and information called awareness – your feelings, thoughts, beliefs, assumptions, expectations and perceptions. Information in the form of electrical signals from sensory cells (neurons) streams along pathways from many access points en route to the brain for appraisal. It is only after the brain has completed processing complex categories of information, that it signals the way you perceive your environment. You can use your awareness to build the mind (thoughts) and body (behaviour) you want. Self-actualisation is achievable if you are self-aware and self-accepting, and are living in present-moment awareness.

In the **old paradigm** of unawareness, reality is experienced in your body through your senses. This reinforces the message that things *are* what they seem. It seems as though external events or other people are causing you pain. Outside circumstances are to blame and you are the victim.

- Pain or pleasure is experienced from external events and your unyielding expectations – you are merely the victim.
- A basic value you hold, you assume to be true about reality. Your identity is constructed in current reality from memory and fantasy.
- You want to force other people and external events to be what you want. Your point of view is all knowing. Black is black.

In the **new paradigm** of self-awareness and self-acceptance embracing change, reality is dictated by how you have now *learned* to perceive it. When you change your perceptions by developing self-awareness, you change the experience of your body.

- Pain or pleasure is experienced from how you have learned to perceive and appraise events – you are the victor.
- A basic value you hold is something you know to be true for your reality. Your identity is constructed in current reality – present moment awareness.
- You rise from your point of view to your viewing point. You embrace openness, self-disclosure, and a tolerance for ambiguity.

The way you perceive things from here-on-in depends upon what you do about your experiences – what you do about what happens to you. Something already stored in your brain as memory may cause you to store new information incorrectly. The key is to recognise that it is your perception (appraisal) of events that causes emotional distress and behavioural problems. Not the events themselves. Appraisal is the topic of chapter three.

Emotional Leadership Practice
ELP 1.13   Perceptions: Illusions of women

What do you see the first time you look at the following picture?

Two different women can be seen. One young, one old. But it depends upon your point of view – your perception. With some practice you can "reverse" the puzzle-pictures that contain optical illusions. The picture illustrates that your brain creates its own words, based upon your perception (appraisal) – not the picture itself.

 Emotional Leadership Practice
ELP 1.14   Perceptions: The Lollipop

Go out and buy yourself a lollipop. Hold the lollipop out in front of you with one hand. Start to turn it in an anti-clockwise direction if you're right handed – clockwise if you're left handed – while slowly raising it above your head. Keep your eyes on the lollipop as you continue turning it, watching it as it rises above your head. What direction is the lollipop turning once you have raised it above your head?

This exercise is about perception. We each have a perception about events that happen in our lives. The way you see things is not always the way others see things. Often your business, professional, or social partner has no idea that you have a different perception to them. This is because most of the time we are fixed in our point of view. We may have no awareness that somebody else sees things from a different perspective to our own.

Summary

Emotional health has to do with how well you manage problems and opportunities that you experience in everyday life. Emotional abilities are innate. But you can develop how to perceive emotions well.

The functions of emotions are to signal your needs and increased risk of illness, emotional distress, and/or psycho-social problems that are played out in the drama of life. The continual internal feedback about your body's state of physiological arousal, helps you interpret the situation or event that has given rise to the complex emotional response generated.

Perception is a dynamic and selective process. An interplay between the functional areas of our brain and our environment. Perception involves reception and appraisal of information. Both from internal (mind) and external (body) environments.

You can raise your emotional health through developing your ability to accurately perceive emotion displayed in others, and changing your perception (appraisal) of events in your environment. Use your ability to perceive emotion to **evaluate** a life of EASE.

Emotional Leadership Practice
ELP 1.15 Key Relationship Response

Think about a key relationship in your life – with a work colleague or loved one. Think about an incident where you felt supported and trusted or where you felt humiliated and disrespected. Recall how you responded to the person in that situation.

Consider the following questions;

1. Describe how the other person acted toward you. What emotions was he or she displaying? What did you think of him or her?

2. Describe how you acted toward the other person. What were you feeling? What did you think of your response?

3. Given your knowledge of your emotional intelligence, or scores from the MSCEIT™ and EQ-i®, online emotional intelligence tests, could you have responded to him or her differently? How? What aspects of your emotional intelligence could you have used to better effect?

4. How may the other person have responded with emotional intelligence?

Emotional Leadership Practice

ELP 1.16 – Applying Emotional Intelligence; ability to perceive emotion.

Max – a successful supervisor and team leader – sought behavioural coaching because he couldn't understand the feelings he was experiencing, gnawing away at his ability to be completely happy. He had a good job that paid well and was fulfilling. He was a good communicator. But he sometimes seemed to rub people up the wrong way. This worried Max and he agreed to complete the MSCEIT™ to see where his strengths and weaknesses lay, with regard to his emotional abilities. Perhaps the results could assist him in understanding where he was going wrong.

Max scored very highly in the areas of his ability to use emotion to facilitate thought and manage emotions. His ability to understand emotions was average, but he needed to work on understanding compound – or blended – emotions. His test results also showed that his "ability for self-management" score was a little low at 90. His result on perceiving emotion was 84, and therefore an area that Max needed to consider improving.

Max's scores are shown below;

Branch	Score
Perceiving emotion	Consider improvement
Facilitating thought	Competent
Understanding emotion	Low average score
Managing emotion	High average score

What do Max's emotionalability scores tell us about his emotional landscape? Make some notes below before reading the answer at the end of this chapter.

NOTES

EMOTIONAL LEADERSHIP CHECKLIST

Use this emotional leadership checklist to evaluate your emotional landscape – the key to achieving your potential.

- Do I know what my emotional landscape is?
- Have I created the conditions to evaluate my life of EASE?
  Can I apply my emotional intelligence to perceive emotion?

EMOTIONAL LEADERSHIP POINT 1
Do I know what my emotional landscape is?

If you complete the online the MSCEIT™ test, record your total, experiential, strategic, and four branch emotional intelligence (EI) scores here.
A score of around 100 means that you are in the average range of emotional intelligence. 85 is low, 115 is high.

Total EI Score

Experiential EI Score

Strategic EI Score

Branch 1 Score – Perceiving emotion

Branch 2 Score – Using emotion

Branch 3 Score – Understanding emotion

Branch 4 Score – Managing emotion

If you complete the online EQ-i® est, record your total and five composite, scale emotional quotient (EQ) scores here.
A score of around 100 means that you are within the average range of emotional intelligence. 85 is low, 115 is high.

Total EQ Score

IntRApersonal EQ Score

IntERpersonal EQ Score

Stress Management EQ Score
Adaptability EQ Score
General Mood EQ Score

Emotional leadership is choosing to behave with emotional intelligence.
Learning and applying emotionally intelligent behaviour builds long-term trust in your business, professional and social relationships. Trust is the key ingredient of any relationship. Building trust requires your commitment to exercising emotional leadership.

EMOTIONAL LEADERSHIP POINT 2
Have I created the conditions to evaluate my ife of EASE?

Using and nurturing emotional intelligence will make your relationships work.

Perceiving, using, understanding and managing your emotions – emotional intelligence – is by far the most effective way to improve individual performance, to reach your personal potential, and achieve life goals.

Function of emotions.

Physiological arousal or feedback – for example, a heart that is beating hard – helps you to interpret a situation. We cannot be humanly alone. Emotions play a vital function in the primordial drive to survive – to connect and bond you with others.
Your emotions;
- Give you feedback and help you survive.
- Connect and bond you with other people in relationships.
- Cause you to act with altruism and to self-actualise. To fulfil your potential.

☐ **Am I emotionally healthy?**

Spontaneity, intimacy and awareness are signs of emotional health. Trust and threat are factors that alter your view of yourself. When a person is not open to another it closes down communication. Individual behaviour is more effective when we have a fair balance between self-disclosure and feedback.

☐ **Have I had opportunities to increase my emotional intelligence in the workplace?**
Employees skilled and knowledgeable in emotional intelligence will enhance relationships in the workplace and create economic value for the business.

EMOTIONAL LEADERSHIP POINT 3
Can I apply my emotional intelligence to perceive emotion?

☐ **Your physical brain.**

The traditional view that passion and reason are opposites, does not recognise that emotions are adaptive, functional, and can organise our cognitions and subsequent behaviour.

> "Emotions are adaptive, functional, and organising of cognitive activities and subsequent behaviour." – Peter Salovey PhD Yale

In the old paradigm of unawareness, reality is experienced in your body through your senses. In the new paradigm of self-awareness, reality is dictated by how you have learned to perceive it. When you change your perceptions through developing self-awareness, you change the experience of your body.

☐ **Use your brain to perceive emotion.**

Wrestle control over your emotions away from the amygdala to the neocortex – your cognitive brain – to give rise to accurate perceptions, and forever change your emotional landscape.

 Emotional Leadership Practice
ELP 1.15 – Applying Emotional Intelligence
Ability to perceive emotion (suggested answer)

Through coaching, Max was able to see he was an empathic leader, able to generate emotion to motivate his team members to do well, so that they all enjoyed fulfilling work. But whilst he did well in socially managing his team, his weakness was his inability to correctly perceive the emotion that people were experiencing, by looking at their faces. Most of the time Max's perception of what people were experiencing was incorrect. This tied in with his low average score on self-management.

The coach pointed out to Max that we can sometimes misread what people are feeling because we project our own feelings of insecurity onto others. For example, if Max was having doubts about his ability to lead the team and was feeling anxious, he could project this feeling onto someone else by saying, "You seem to be angry today. Are you okay?" A team member who feels absolutely fine would then take offence at Max's assumption. This would then cause him or her to have a negative feeling toward Max, as his incorrect perception would rub them up the wrong way – causing them to distance themselves from him.

Max felt uplifted that he finally had an understanding, and an answer to his feelings of unhappiness. He began working hard at changing his perceptions of people by asking hmself, "What is my team member really feeling? If I had that expression on my face what would I be feeling?" before making assumptions of how others felt.

Notes

1   Mayer, JD, Salovey, P & DiPaolo M 1990 'Perceiving affective content in ambiguous visual stimuli: A component of emotional intelligence', *Journal of Personality Assessment*, vol. 54 (3&4), pp. 772-781.

2   From Scott Halford, Complete Intelligence Inc., www.scotthalford.com, scott@scotthalford.com

3   Brackett, MA & Mayer, JD 2003, 'Convergent, discriminant, and incremental validity of competing measures of emotional intelligence', in *Personality and Social Psychology Bulletin*, vol. 29, pp. 1147-1158.

4   Holt, J 1964, 1982, *How children fail*, Pitman Publishing Company, New York. Taken from www.moteaco.com/holt

5   Sternberg, RJ 1985, *Beyond IQ: A Triarchic Theory of Human Intelligence*, Cambridge University Press, New York.

6   Salovey, P Bedell, B Detweiler, JB & Mayer, JD 2000, 'Current directions in emotional intelligence research', in Lewis, M & Haviland-Jones (eds) 2000, Handbook of Emotions, 2nd edn, Guilford Press, New York, p. 505.

7   Mayer, JD, Salovey, P & Caruso, DR 2002, *Mayer-Salovey-Caruso Emotional Intelligence Test (MSCEIT) User's Manual,* Copyright ©1999, 2002. Multi-Health Systems Inc. All Rights Reserved. p. xiv.

8   Mayer, JD 1999, September, 'Emotional Intelligence: Popular or scientific psychology?' in *APA Monitor*, 30, 50. [*Shared Perspectives* column] American Psychological Association, Washington, DC.

9   Goleman, D 1995, *Emotional Intelligence*, Bantam Books, New York, p. xii.

10   Goleman, D 1998, *Working with Emotional Intelligence*, Bantam Books, New York, p. 375.

11   Bar-On, R 1997, The Emotional Quotient Inventory, Technical manual, Multi-Health Systems, Toronto, p. 16.

12   Mayer, JD, Salovey, P & Caruso, D. R. (2002) Mayer-Salovey-Caruso Emotional Intelligence Test (MSCEIT), User's Manual, Copyright © 2002, Multi-Health Systems Inc. All Rights Reserved. P.1.

13   Mayer, JD & Salovey, P 1997, 'What Is Emotional Intelligence?'. in Salovey, P and Sluyter, D eds, *Emotional Development and Emotional Intelligence: Educational Implications*, Basic Books, New York.

14   Excerpted from Reuven Bar-On (1997, 1999) EQ-i™ BarOn Emotional Quotient Inventory, Technical manual, MHS: Toronto, Pages 17-21. Copyright Ó 1997, 1999 Multi-Health Systems, Inc. All Rights Reserved.

15   Adapted from Weekes, C 1972, Peace from nervous suffering. A practical guide to understanding, confidence and recovery, London, Angus & Robertson, p. 10.

16   Excerpted from Mayer, JD, Salovey, P & Caruso, DR 2002, Mayer-Salovey-Caruso Emotional Intelligence Test (MSCEIT) User's Manual, MHS, Toronto, Copyright Ó 2002 Multi-Health Systems, Inc. All Rights Reserved, p. 20-22.

17   Excerpted from Reuven Bar-On 1997, 1999, EQ-i™ BarOn Emotional Quotient Inventory, Technical manual, MHS, Toronto, Copyright Ó 1997, 1999 Multi-Health Systems, Inc. All Rights Reserved, p. 43-48.

18   Winefield, HR & Peay, MY 1980, *Behavioural science in medicine*, The University of Adelaide, Adelaide, South Australia, p. 1.

19   <http://www.who.int/aboutwho/en/definition>

20   <http://www.mindspring.com/~donpow/LifesAnswers/education_health>

21   Adapted from Tony Schirtzinger <http://www.helpyourselftherapy.com/main/write.html>

22   Maslow, A 1943, 'A theory of human motivation', in *Psychological Review*, 50, pp. 370-396.

23   See 'Biographical Memoirs of Roger W. Sperry 1913 – 1994' <http://www.nap.edu/html/biomems/rsperry>

24   <http://www.brain-mind.com/LimbicPrimer>

25   Quoted from *The ASCD* Web <http://www.ascd.org/pdi/brain/amygdala>

CHAPTER 2

BASIC
EMOTIONS

BASIC EMOTIONS FULFILL VITAL LIFE FUNCTIONS. STRESS
IS A BUILD-UP OF NEGATIVE EMOTION FELT IN THE BODY.

INTRODUCTION

We consider something is basic, primary or essential if it performs or fulfills a primary function. For example, you may have a basic or primary way of giving and receiving love. Basic emotions fulfill vital life fuctions.

James Averill (1994) states that, "An emotion may be vital to survival of the species (biological criteria), the society (social criteria), or the self (psychological criteria)."[1] Averill (1994, p.13) holds that social and biological principles must ultimately be manifested in the behaviour of individuals; their psychological principles or "… the personal rules, plans and knowledge structures that determine a person's sense of self." But he disagrees, "with the very notion of basic emotions." On the other hand, Paul Ekman[2] argues that, "… the term basic is to emphasise the role that emotions display, as well as their current function." Ekman believes that, "Emotions evolved for their adaptive value in dealing with fundamental life tasks."[3]

We will use Ekman's six groups of basic emotions, to explore the different intensity levels of emotions we feel, and to explain how a sensitive individual and a reactive individual experience emotion. You will be introduced to the "pain time-line", which describes how we feel negative emotion in the present moment – from present, past and future events.

As the body experiences more and more negative emotion, a person will experience stress. Stress is a build-up of negative emotion felt in the body, experienced as emotional constipation. Too much stress felt in the body produces adrenalin above optimal levels. This excess amount of adrenalin in the body has physiological, cognitive and emotional effects, which can cause a person to become depressed – with a resulting loss of self-esteem. The mission of negative emotion – or stress – is to lower self-esteem. Stress can be alleviated from the body through correct breathing, physical exercise, meditation, relaxation techniques, and colon hydrotherapy.

In this chapter we discuss differences between men and women, sensitive and reactive people, emotion families, negative emotions and their impact on the body, and how to balance your emotions.

Sensitive and reactive people

We can distinguish between two groups of people who experience sensitisation at different levels of intensity. We use the terms *sensitive* and *reactive* to describe either ends of the sensitivity spectrum. We do not intend that reactive people are not sensitive, or that sensitive people are not reactive. Both sensitive and reactive people need to be understanding and aware, and acknowledge the effect of arousal.

> **Emotional Wisdom**
>
> We refer readers to Elaine N. Aron's book, *The Highly Sensitive Person*[4], for a discussion as to how highly sensitive people can learn to live with their trait. Reactive people are referred to; *When Anger Hurts: Quieting The Storm Within*, by Matthew McKay, Peter Rogers and Judith McKay[5] to understand anger, and its impact on your health, and how to combat it.

Often men are regarded as reactive and women as sensitive. Whilst we acknowledge that men and women have traits peculiar to their gender, we use the terms reactive and sensitive – within *Emotional Leadership* – as a means of describing how different people process emotion, based on our many years of clinical experience. We have found that *both* men and women are reactive, and both men and women are sensitive. It is interesting to also note that emotional intelligence tests completed by clients show strong links to what we describe as sensitive and reactive people. We are then able to use the results of emotional intelligence tests to assist individuals in changing their behaviour.

1. SENSITIVE OR REACTIVE – NOT ME!

1. **The sensitive person**

    A **sensitive** person interprets his or her whole world almost totally through feelings. And indeed, often takes things personally – and then holds onto these hurt feelings. When negative emotion is experienced by the sensitive person it is *internalised*. They may feel startled or taken aback – often remaining silent. They may shut down. But anger builds *within* a sensitive person. They often feel unheard, experience guilt, and can be confused as to how to cope with loss – for example, a loss of a relationship or a loss of control. Avoidance of others, addiction and depression may set-in, as a means of dealing with pain. In this way, a sensitive person deals ineffectively with anger. Stored hurts often become overwhelming, causing a person to withdraw while holding onto deep emotional wounds – which project sadness in every part of the body.

2. **The reactive person**

    A **reactive** person interprets his or her world through events and activities. They will often deal with hurt feelings almost immediately by using brief and extreme displays of behaviour; facial expressions, raised voices – sometimes yelling, and physical actions – such as making a fist. Sometimes the gap between the external or internal stimulus, and the display of angry behaviour can be very short in-deed. When a reactive person expresses anger in this way it can be ineffective. It may mask a complicated emotional state, and a trail of damaged feelings and broken relationships, that fill a person with despair – when the enormity of their deeds catches up with them.

Sensitive and reactive people – all of us – need to recognise that it is our appraisal of events that causes a response. We need to learn to avoid the easy emotions – anxiety and anger. And deal with unresolved hurts that are more difficult to confront; feeling unloved, unworthy, rejected, disappointed – or holding on to unmet expectations. We need to experience these feelings – and that can be painful – or we will become immobilised by despair.

Sensitive people need to learn that they don't have the monopoly on negative feelings. They need to recognise that they have a responsibility to deal with their own arousal and not expect the other person, often a reactive person, to be the one to change all the time.

 Emotional Leadership Practice

ELP 2.1   Are you a sensitive person?

Read the statements on the next page and answer true or false. If you answer true to 12 or more statements, chances are – you're a sensitive person.

Are you a sensitive person?

1. Other people drive me crazy when they are not considerate of other peoples' feelings or mine.   true   false
2. I seem to notice more of what's going on around me than others do.   true   false
3. I remember dates of special occasions – the day I first met my spouse, first kiss, etc.   true   false
4. I explode when someone irritates me. Or when they say something that seems stupid and unnecessary.   true   false
5. I get a "racy" feeling to caffeine or pseudoephedrine in decongestants.   true   false
6. I become overwhelmed in a crowded and slow moving lift.   true   false
7. I get worked up when running late for an appointment.   true   false
8. I go crazy when my kids fight all the time – I'll constantly tell them to settle down.   true   false
9. I will get up and leave a violent sex or torture scene in a film or on television.   true   false

10. When someone offends me, or when I feel injured by someone, I deal with the hurt almost immediately.	true	false
11. I like to see all the credits at the end of a movie.	true	false
12. I get irritated when my partner flicks the remote control across television channels.	true	false
13. I avoid shopping centres on weekends.	true	false
14. I am a light sleeper.	true	false
15. When I have a lot to do, I never know where to start.	true	false
16. I resort to lists to prevent me forgetting to do something.	true	false
17. I usually say "yes", when people ask me to take on more tasks or responsibilities.	true	false
18. I need to talk about my feelings, but often feel cautious about getting started.	true	false
19. I shut down if anyone raises his or her voice at me – I can't speak.	true	false
20. I keep the peace at all costs, as I function best when there is harmony in my environment.	true	false

Total true statements about you

2. WHAT MEN AND WOMEN NEED TO KNOW[6]

Relationships fail for three main reasons; unresolved hurts, ineffective communication, and a lack of awareness about how we each give and receive love. Many relationship problems start with the *hurts*. Soon there is a *communication problem*. Next the Housemate Syndrome (see page 205) sets in. Many problems in relationships are not resolved simply because men and women don't understand each other. Men, in particular, don't understand what women need to be happy. And women don't know how to communicate their needs in language that men understand. Men need to be understood – just as women do. It's just that to understand men a woman must think like a man, and vice versa. Men and women must learn from each other if they are to maintain fulfilling relationships in the workplace and the home.

3. WHAT MEN NEED TO UNDERSTAND ABOUT WOMEN

- Communication is a woman's chief coping mechanism.
- Women use conversations to understand their relationships.
- Women communicate to fully explore feelings within themselves.
- Women cope with stress through sharing in nurturing relationships.
- When a woman seeks a partner she looks for someone to protect her emotional security – allowing her the freedom to express her true self.
- When a woman is upset she needs to talk, to sort out how she feels. She is not demanding agreement.
- Women have a primary need to be heard.
- Women ask questions and make statements, as a plea for men to hear them out and have their concerns explored.
- Women feel better and more nurtured when men share in their understanding of a situation – without necessarily agreeing with the woman's assessment.

> **Emotional Wisdom**
> Women typically enter into a relationship through communication and emotional stability, wanting a caring, loyal and understanding partner. They will only seek sexual fulfilment once emotional intimacy and trust is established.

- When a woman feels the right to be upset, the less upset she will be.
- When a woman has a chance to share her feelings with the person with whom she is presently upset she feels more loving – and is able to recover more quickly.
- When a woman expresses her feelings she is processing and discovering. For a woman, feelings are not facts.

- Women tend to shut down and "give up" communicating if they consistently have no success in being heard.
- Women assume men need what they need.

4. WHAT WOMEN NEED TO UNDERSTAND ABOUT MEN

- A man's coping strategy is to sort out his thoughts, clarify his priorities, and then develop a plan of action – all of which is done without necessarily speaking a word.
- When a man can put his feelings into action – finding a solution – he feels more in-control of his life.
- Men cope by problem solving and implementing/offering solutions.
- When a man seeks intimacy, he wants to be appreciated and needed.
- When a man talks with someone with whom he is upset, his general goal is to get the listener to agree with him, to correct the problem.
- Men use communication as a means to pass along information or solve a problem.
- Men feel challenged – even threatened – when questioned.
- Men think an emotional woman is inflexible, has reached a conclusion, and is expressing fixed opinions.
- Men communicate only after determining what they have discovered.
- When a man is upset and talks with a person who upset him, he will remain upset until that person agrees with him. Simply listening to him and nodding sympathetically is not enough.

> **Emotional Wisdom**
>
> Men typically enter into a relationship as provider and protector – wanting a supportive and understanding partner. They seek sexual fulfilment in order to establish and secure emotional intimacy and trust.

- A man expresses his feelings like a fact – they are something he believes to be true.
- Men assume women need what they need.

Emotional Leadership Practice
ELP 2.2   Communication differences between men and women

Effective communication is the key to special relationships. Think of situations in your relationships with the other sex where you didn't feel understood or affirmed. Give examples of when your partner exhibited the typical male or female behaviour previously described.

_____

_____

_____

_____

EMOTION FAMILIES

1. LABELLING EMOTIONS

With the development of language, the sensations we experience were given names or labels; anger, fear, disgust, sadness, surprise and enjoyment, for example. These allow us to communicate to others how we feel. Because our perceptions or subjective experiences are different, there is no uniformity of terminology used to describe emotions. Therefore the terms; affect, feelings, and emotions, are used interchangeably.

Some definitions;

Affective states: Generically denotes events experienced as feelings or emotions.

Feelings: Affective states that have a longer duration – causing less intensive experiences – with fewer physiological repercussions on the body, and lowered interference on reasoning and behaviour. For example; impatient, startled or bored.

Emotions: An emotion is a feeling with a thought. From the Latin "emovere" – meaning moving, displacing. Emotions are manifest reactions to affective conditions that – due to their intensity – move us to some kind of action, response or behaviour. Emotions are characterised by a disruption of affective balance, and can have long-term physiological effects on the body. For example; angry, humiliated, rejected, depressed, betrayed or taken-for-granted.

Positive or negative energy states: A person will experience both positive emotions (pleasure) and negative emotions (pain) throughout their life. These two energy states have a strong impact on emotional health. We can think of positive emotions as adding energy (energising) and negative emotions as subtracting energy (draining).

2. SIX EMOTION FAMILIES

Paul Ekman (1992) has given us generic labels for all basic emotions or emotion families. Each emotion family is a grouping of related states or variations. The basic level emotions, according to Ekman are; anger, fear, sadness, enjoyment, disgust, and surprise.

Throughout *Emotional Leadership* we use the generic terms anger, fear, sadness, happiness, disgust, and surprise. Other possible basic emotions include contempt, shame, guilt, awe, embarrassment, and excitement.

Ekman identifies nine characteristics that define basic emotions;

1. Distinctive universal signals. For example, distinctive universal facial expressions for anger, fear, enjoyment and sadness.
2. Presence in humans and other primates.
3. Distinctive physiology. Distinctive expressions, imagery, memories, expectations and other cognitive activities.
4. Universal antecedent events. For example, the antecedent for fear is physical or psychological harm.

5. Coherence in response systems – automatic responses and expressive changes are not disconnected.

6. Quick onset. We are mobilised to respond with little time required for consideration and preparation.

7. Brief duration. Response changes will not last long unless the emotion is evoked again.

8. Automatic appraisal mechanism. As the gap between stimulus and emotional response is sometimes extraordinarily short, it must be automatic.

9. Unbidden occurrence. Emotions can occur with great speed, happening to – not chosen by – us.

 Emotional Leadership Practice

ELP 2.3   Recognising feelings

What emotion is depicted on each face? Use the worksheet to describe what you feel when you look at each face. Does your neighbour agree with your descriptions? Note if each face signals a sensitive or reactive person.

_____

_____

_____

_____

_____

_____

_____

_____

_____

_____

_____

_____

_____

_____

 Emotional Leadership Practice

ELP 2.4   Categorising feelings

One effective way of developing "feeling" words is to categorise them according to whether they are of a low, medium, or high intensity. Then you can discern both the feeling category, and the level of intensity that you wish to use. Develop your word list – add to it. It will help you to respond accurately to your own feelings and the feelings of others.

LEVEL OF INTENSITY

High Intensity Emotions

Anger	Fear	Sadness	Happiness	Disgust	Surprise
betrayed	scared	crushed	alive	appalled	aghast
furious	intimidated	distraught	energetic	rejected	flustered
resentful	threatened	vulnerable	overjoyed	unwanted	shocked

Medium Intensity Emotions

Anger	Fear	Sadness	Happiness	Disgust	Surprise
angry	anxious	alone	content	awkward	amazed
frustrated	panicky	depressed	full of life	guilty	irritable
irritated	pressured	miserable	happy	unloved	puzzled

Low Intensity Emotions

Anger	Fear	Sadness	Happiness	Disgust	Surprise
mad	afraid	down	good	tense	baffled
fed-up	shaky	lethargic	aglow	insecure	bothered
annoyed	worried	solemn	joyful	unattractive	mixed-up

Emotional Leadership Practice
ELP 2.5   Past dealings with life-tasks

Ekman has argued that what is unique in distinguishing basic emotions, is that when they occur we are dealing with life-tasks that are continually evolving. It is our past dealings with life-tasks, that influence how we respond to, and appraise, a current event, that marks an emotion.

What past dealings with life-tasks have influenced how you respond to, and appraise, a current event? Could your perceptions of future events effect how you respond to, and appraise, a current event?

PAIN TIMELINE

1. EMOTIONAL CONSTIPATION

Emotional constipation – or emotional distress, is "dis-ease" – an illness of how you think. You are what you think. How you feel depends on how you think. If you are experiencing emotional pain, you need to move from anger to assertion, or from fear to appreciation. The pain timeline helps you understand your emotional constipation, and the physiological impact of negative emotions felt, on your body. In chapters three and four, we teach you how your emotions are generated. And how you can change how you think, using a four-step cognitive framework. This cognitive technique will put *you* in control of your reaction to events – not the other way around.

2. PAIN IS FELT IN THE PRESENT

All pain is felt in the present – today. You cannot physically feel something yesterday or tomorrow. You can remember the pain of the past, and perceive a pain in the future, but you can only feel pain in the present (Chopra, 1993, p.187).[7] Deepak Chopra says, "We all want to avoid pain and experience pleasure. Therefore, all the complicated emotional states we find ourselves in are because we are unable to obey these basic drives." Quoting Psychiatrist David Viscott, Chopra explains the cycle of emotions that begins in the present (reality) – where only pain and pleasure are felt – and ends in complex emotions centred exclusively in the past – such as guilt and depression (perceived reality).

The cycle that gets repeated countless times in everyone's life is as follows;

■ Pain in the present is experienced as hurt.

■ Pain in the past is remembered as anger.

■ Pain in the future is perceived as anxiety – a lessening of mental relaxation, associated to the alert reaction.

■ Unexpressed anger – redirected against you and held within – is guilt.

■ The depletion of energy that occurs when anger is redirected inward, creates depression.

The cycle of emotion tells us that stored hurt is something we all have experienced to some degree, and is responsible for a wide range of emotional constipation. "Buried hurt disguises itself as anger, anxiety, guilt, and depression" (Chopra, 1993 p. 186). To live in the present we need to learn to avoid the easy emotion – anger, and deal with the hurt that is more difficult to confront. Unresolved anger will only grow worse, feeding on itself.

Sometimes you can cause another person pain by what you do or say. This external event may be intentional or unintentional, and may also create a pain for you; guilt, remorse, shame, and regret – that is, stress. For example, people who use ineffective communication (discussed in chapter six) often drag up "history" in arguments to hurt their partner. Their perception is that their partner has hurt them or is blaming them in some way. They are using a conditioned response, to ease their own pain felt in the present – not realising the physiological impact their behaviour is having on their own body.

3. PAIN FELT IN THE BODY

All emotion is felt in the present at various levels of intensity; low, medium and high. Pain felt in the body can be depicted on a pain timeline (see figure 2.1).

Negative emotion is felt in the body as stress. Each time you experience a negative emotion, such as a hurt in the present, anger or resentment from memory, or fear and anxiety from perceived pain in the future – you are adding to your store of stress. The accumulation of negative emotion in the body is stress – emotional constipation. The stronger you feel an emotion in your body, the greater the amount of stress that is accumulated in your body.

4. EFFECT OF STRESS FELT IN THE BODY

The body manages well with an optimal level of stress. Adrenalin generated to the optimal level of stress, is needed for alertness and clarity, and for being on guard – fight or flight. For example, when your thoughts focus on pain perceived in the future, the resulting negative emotions of fear and anxiety could increase stress beyond the optimal level. Thus causing the body to produce adrenalin, in excess of what the body needs.

Figure 2.1. Pain timeline

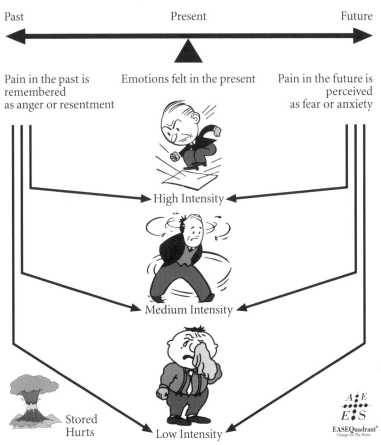

Past   Present   Future

Pain in the past is remembered as anger or resentment

Emotions felt in the present

Pain in the future is perceived as fear or anxiety

High Intensity

Medium Intensity

Stored Hurts

Low Intensity

EASEQuadrant®
Change for The Better

Similarly, thoughts focused on memory of pain in the past will increase stress beyond the optimal level. The body's ability to manage stress can be depicted graphically (see figure 2.2).

Higher levels of adrenalin in the body from increased stress – that is, accumulated negative emotion – will begin to affect the body. The chemicals adrenalin and noradrenalin are released by the body's involuntary nervous system (see chapter four) and take time to be eliminated from the body. Physiological effects on the body from accumulated stress include;

1. A breakdown in the immune system. Making a person more susceptible to colds and flu, skin eruptions, and other ailments.

2. An interruption to the autonomic nervous system that copes with digestion, bowel function and evacuation, reproduction, and recovery from stress.

3. A decrease in the level of serotonin – the chemical in the brain that elevates feelings of well-being – so that a person has mood swings. Often feeling flat, despondent, depressed – a loss of joie-de-vivre. This depression usually manifests as lethargy and "I can't be bothered".

   A decrease in the level of serotonin also significantly impacts a person's thinking. Serotonin is the chemical required to assist the electrical impluses in the brain (thought) to jump across the gaps between the neurons. Lowered serotonin results in thinking that is inaccurate, irrational and anxious. This then results in a lowering of personal self-esteem.

   Anti-depressant medication is used to elevate serotonin levels which effects both mood and thinking. (see Appendix D on the "Common Misconceptions about Antidepressants".)

4. A lowering of personal esteem – through a louder inner voice. Which may lead to depression and/or nervous suffering.

Figure 2.2. Stress graphs

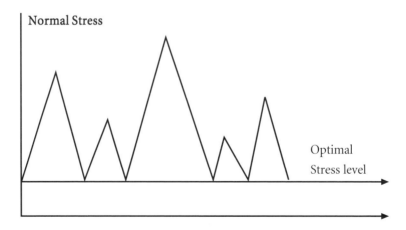

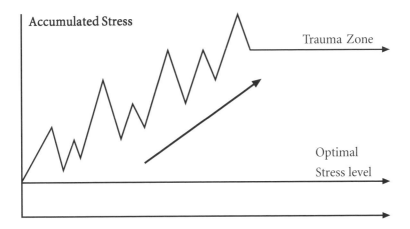

The events that cause stress – the stressors – are outlined in chapter three, where you discover and affirm your EAR-Identity – whom you choose to be, and how you choose to process emotion in your body.

The additional adrenalin produced by excess stress may cause physical, cognitive, and emotional symptoms of a stress or trauma reaction in some people (see table 2.1). The amount of additional adrenalin experienced in the body, will depend upon whether you are a reactive or sensitive person – and the nature of the trauma.

A psychological effect of accumulated stress – emotional constipation – is lowered self-esteem. When negative emotions are held within and not experienced, the cycle of mind-body sensations can lead to lowered self-esteem – and ultimately, depression.

BALANCING EMOTION

In the course of a day, if you experience a balance of good and bad feelings, it is unlikely that you will feel stressed. Sensitive people are more prone to stress as they feel each emotion with a greater intensity. But because a sensitive person similarly feels positive emotion with more intensity, if there is a balance of good feelings – if the person feels secure and loved, nurtured and understood – on a "bad" day, then the balance is restored readily. And the person copes with their stress.

Table 2.1. Common signs and symptoms of a stress reaction

PHYSICAL	COGNITIVE	EMOTIONAL
▪ Nausea, poor appetite	▪ Slowed thinking	▪ Anxiety
▪ Upset stomach	▪ Difficulty in making	▪ Fear
▪ Flatus (gas)	decisions	▪ Guilt
▪ Diarrhoea	▪ Difficulty in problem	▪ Grief
▪ Profuse sweating	solving	▪ Depression
▪ Tremors (lips, hands)	▪ Confusion	▪ Feeling lost
▪ Feeling uncoordinated	▪ Disorientation	▪ Feeling abandoned
▪ Dizziness	(especially to place	▪ Feeling isolated
▪ Chest pain (should be	and time)	▪ Worrying about others
checked at hospital)	▪ Difficulty calculating	▪ Wanting to hide
▪ Rapid heartbeat	▪ Difficulty concentrating	▪ Wanting to limit
▪ Rapid breathing	▪ Memory problems	contact with others
▪ Increased blood	▪ Difficulty naming	▪ Anger
pressure	common objects	▪ Irritability
▪ Headaches	▪ Seeing the event	▪ Feeling numb
▪ Muscle aches	over-and-over	▪ Startled
▪ Sleep disturbance	▪ Distressing dreams	▪ Shocked
▪ Increased frequency	▪ Poor attention span	
of passing urine		

1. WOMEN TALK OVER THEIR PROBLEMS

Typically, women use the left-hand side of their brain to talk and listen. If they have a problem, they communicate their feelings in order to process the problem and devise a solution. In fact, women don't mind having a problem – provided they receive emotional support, whilst they work out what to do about it.

If women don't receive emotional support they get upset. If women are allowed to be upset, then they won't *be* so upset. And so, they continue to talk and listen, until they have established an opinion about how to solve the problem. This may well be a different opinion than what they started out with.

A woman won't mind whom she talks to, provided there is a level of trust. That she won't be judged or scorned, as she talks her way through the process – thereby receiving emotional support. She may turn to her partner, friend, sister, mother or neighbour. If her partner will not listen, typically, a female is selected.

2. SENSITIVE PEOPLE ARE PRONE TO STRESS

A lot of stress is built-up internally when people either as give themselves permission to feel certain feelings, or consider themselves as weak and pathetic for feeling a certain way. Or, because they recognise that they have certain feelings – particularly hurt feelings – and can't let them go.

Sensitive people are therefore prone to stress. Sensitive people interpret their whole world through feelings. They often take things personally, and hold onto hurt feelings. These might be feelings of being overwhelmed, or overlooked, annoyed, frustrated, and guilty or misunderstood. Interaction by interaction, at home or at work, hurt feelings can build up.

Once you have accumulated a mountain of hurt feelings, your body interprets these as stress – even if your mind hasn't quite recognised it yet. You may have an upset stomach, heart palpitations or a racing chest. Your body may experience nausea, sleep disturbance or generalised anxiety. These highly uncomfortable feelings are present long before your brain has consciously decoded what is going on. Talking this through, and understanding the cause of the stress that you are under, often wins half the battle. Only then, can you work out what to do about it.

3. MEN WITHDRAW TO THINK THROUGH PROBLEMS

Men will typically retreat or withdraw to think through their problems – using the right-hand side of their brain. They will sort out solutions before announcing them. Although increasingly, some men are discovering that talking things out is better than thinking things through.

When you only think, your thoughts can be distracted. They can race off to other areas of anxiety before you've even finished the first line of thought. It's a bit like praying with your head on the pillow – you fall asleep before you're done. When you talk, there is a social courtesy to at least finish your sentence – and so you inevitably complete your thought process.

4. COUNSELLING – AN EFFECTIVE REMEDY FOR STRESS

In counselling you come to understand what stressors – situations or factors that stress you out – are affecting you. You then learn effective strategies to manage the destructive effects of stress.

Summary

Men and women need to understand each other, and how sensitive and reactive people experience emotion, to minimise the effect of negative emotion on their body. Men need to be understood – just as women do. But to understand men, a woman must think like a man – and vice versa. Men and women must learn from *each other* if they are to maintain fulfilling relationships.

Following Paul Ekman, we classify basic emotions into six categories; anger, fear, sadness, happiness, disgust, and surprise. Emotions fulfil vital life functions. They arouse only two impulses – pain or pleasure. The build-up of negative emotion in the body causes emotional constipation – the precursor for stress. Stress is negative emotion felt in the body, brought on by how you think. You experience emotion in the present, but events from which emotions come are often in your memory of the past, or are perceptions of the future. You need to experience a balance of good and bad feelings each day, to manage stress effectively and **evaluate** a life of EASE.

EMOTIONAL LEADERSHIP CHECKLIST

Use this emotional leadership checklist to understand sensitive and reactive people, differences between men and women, develop your emotional language, and accurately perceive emotion.

- Do I know my emotional style?
- Have I created new emotional language?
- Can I apply my new emotional knowledge?

EMOTIONAL LEADERSHIP POINT 1:
Do I know my emotional style?

A sensitive person interprets his or her whole world almost totally through feelings. They often take things personally, and then hold onto these hurt feelings.

When a sensitive person experiences negative emotion they internalise. An avoidance of others, addiction, or onset of depression may occur as a means of dealing with the pain.

☐ A reactive person interprets his or her world through events and activities. They will often cope with hurt feelings almost immediately, through brief and extreme displays of behaviour.

Anger expressed by a reactive person in this way can be ineffective.

☐ Men and women need to understand each other.

Men need to be understood – just as women do. It's just that to understand men, a woman must think like a man – and vice versa. Men and women must learn from each other if they are to maintain fulfilling relationships.

EMOTIONAL LEADERSHIP POINT 2:
Have I created new emotional language?

☐ With the development of language, the sensations we experience can be given names or labels such as; anger, fear, sadness, happiness, disgust, and surprise.

Emotional language allows us to communicate how we feel to others. Because our perceptions or subjective experiences are different, no uniformity of terminology is used to describe emotions.

☐ Labelling emotions.

With the development of language, sensations were given names. Some generic groups of emotions are; anger, fear, sadness, happiness, disgust, and surprise.

☐ **Categorising feelings into different levels of intensity.**

Categorising feelings into generic groups and levels of intensity – low, medium or high – helps you respond accurately to your own feelings, and the feelings of others, by developing an emotional vocabulary.

EMOTIONAL LEADERSHIP POINT 3:
Can I apply my new emotional knowledge?

☐ **Emotional constipation is "dis-ease" – an illness of how you think.**

Emotions fulfil vital life functions. They arouse only two impulses – pain or pleasure. A build-up of negative emotion in the body causes emotional constipation – the precursor for stress. Stress is negative emotion felt in the body, brought on by how you think. The goal of negative emotion is to lower self-esteem.

☐ **The physiological effects on the body from accumulated stress.**

Accumulated stress causes; breakdown in the immune system, interruption to the autonomic nervous system, decrease in the body's levels of serotonin, and lowered personal esteem – which may lead to depression and/or nervous suffering.

☐ **You need to experience a balance of good and bad feelings in order to manage stress effectively.**

You experience emotion in the present. But events from which emotions arise, are often in your memory of the past – or are perceptions of the future. You need to experience a balance of good and bad feelings each day, in order to manage stress effectively.

Talking about emotions using your new emotional knowledge, definitely helps to reduce your levels of stress. Adrenalin is released from your body and a calm state is restored.

Applying your new emotional knowledge.

Apply your ability to perceive emotion with your increased awareness of emotional knowledge, to **evaluate** your life of EASE.

Notes

1   Averill, J R 1994, "In the eyes of the beholder" in Ekman, P & Davidson RJ (eds) 1994, *The Nature of Emotion, Fundamental Questions*, Oxford University Press, New York, p. 12.

2   Ekman, P 1994, "All emotions are basic" in Ekman, P & Davidson RJ (eds) 1994, *The Nature of Emotion, Fundamental Questions*, Oxford University Press, New York, p. 15.

3   Ekman, P 1992, "An argument for basic emotions", in *Cognition and emotion*, 6, 3/4, pp. 169-200.

4   Aron, EN 1997, *The Highly Sensitive Person*, Broadway Books, New York.

5   McKay, M Rogers, P & McKay, J 1989, *When Anger Hurts: Quieting The Storm Within*, New Harbinger Publications, CA.

6   Adapted from John Jolliffe – "What men and women need to understand about the other sex", Public Seminar – The Enabling Centre, Singapore, January 2001.

7   Chopra, D 1993, *Ageless Body, Timeless Mind,* Harmony Books, New York.

CHAPTER 3

EMOTION
GENERATION

THE MISSION OF NEGATIVE EMOTION (STRESS) IS TO
LOWER PERSONAL ESTEEM. STRESS AND PERSONAL ESTEEM
OPERATE AS COUNTERWEIGHTS.

INTRODUCTION

Emotional pain derives from present hurts, memory of negative experiences, and perceptions of the future. Lowered self-esteem will negatively affect your view of yourself, and your relationships with others. It can cause you to experience ongoing emotional pain. Your inner voice judges and rejects you. It sets you up to relive the pain of the past and fear the future. The inner voice causes immense emotional constipation that can lead to depression and victim-hood. Come to grips with the cognitive distortions[1] and "shoulds" in your life. Regardless of the opinions of others, you have the capacity to define who you are.

In this chapter you will learn to recognise lowered self-esteem, identify your inner voice, understand and evaluate the components of your EAR-Identity, and identify the emotions that can arise from you judging and rejecting yourself.

Events in your life – such as memory, thoughts, beliefs, values, expectations, and the actions of others – can be appraised positively to generate emotional and physical responses that **affirm** your life of EASE.

UNDERSTANDING SELF-ESTEEM

In chapter one – Emotional Landscape – you learned that the mass of electrochemical pulses, or neuron connections, swirling around your brain is your brain's most significant quality – "mind" or "consciousness" – with all its great powers and uniqueness. Consciousness is your total thinking, personality, emotion, and warmth. Consciousness emerges from all the activities of the cerebral network as an independent entity that is influenced by subjective human values. By impacting on consciousness, human values become an underlying key to change. It is in your consciousness, your "mind", that the identity you create for yourself, your inner view of self, is formed.

1. YOUR INNER VIEW OF SELF

As the first three levels of your needs (physiological needs; safety and security, affection and belonging) are met, you will look for a little esteem from others. You cannot begin to have a need for the esteem of others unless, and until, you first feel safe and loved. Receiving love from your parents, family and friends ensures that your inner view of self – your self-esteem – has a solid grounding. But without self-esteem you won't necessarily feel loved.

In describing the nature of self-esteem, Mackay and Fanning (2000, p. 1) write;

> One of the main factors differentiating humans from other animals is the awareness of self – the ability to form an identity and then attach a value to it. In other words, you have the capacity to define who you are, and then decide if you like that identity or not. The problem of self-esteem is this human capacity for judgment. It's one thing to dislike certain colors, noises, shapes, or sensations. But when you reject parts of yourself, you greatly damage the psychological structures that literally keep you alive.

Self-esteem is the inner view you have of yourself. Others may hold you in high esteem and think well of you, nonetheless you may have low self-esteem – that is, you reject yourself.

2. THE COUNTERWEIGHT

Self-esteem and stress – negative emotion, see chapter two – operate as counterweights. As stress rises self-esteem decreases, and vice versa.

Your identity consists of the events, appraisals and responses, that keep you alive. The psychological structures that support and drive your identity can cause you emotional distress and/or psychological problems – or they can offer you a life of EASE. You choose. The choices you have made so far have led you to where you are today. Are you a victim or victor? Are you ready to affirm an identity for yourself without judgment, without rejecting self, without an inner voice?

CASE STUDY 3.1 – BANISHING LOW SELF-ESTEEM

Barry, a 37 year-old in senior management, came to counselling to explore his mood swings. He had been married for nearly six years to a "warm and wonderful person" who worked for the same company. They had arrived in Singapore only six months earlier. They were yet to have children, and Barry described himself as fairly conservative – certainly not a risk taker. Sometimes he couldn't believe he'd accepted a job in Singapore, as he'd never lived abroad before or visited Asia. Barry's good feelings often gave way to incredible depression and feelings of hopelessness and despair. He often felt "not good enough", "not worthy", and "not the person I thought I would turn out to be."

Karen's Assessment: Barry's critical view of himself had escalated since arriving in Singapore. He was in a senior position and on a good salary – which he felt was too high for the work he was actually doing. He admitted that he occasionally felt suicidal. Karen identified that Barry was suffering from lowered self-esteem. Identifying the problem was an important first step in dealing with his destructive negative emotions.

Work done in Counselling: Barry recognised that his negative feelings were not constant. They seemed to present themselves at unpredictable times – during both work and social situations. Karen helped Barry to identify the disturbing judgmental and critical thoughts he had about himself, which were giving rise to his negative feelings. By teaching Barry strategies to cope with these negative thoughts as they arose, he was soon able to identify them and control their devastating impact.

Outcome: Barry became confident of his own abilities and recognised that indeed he was the most competent and suitable person for his job. He resumed his post-graduate studies completing a master's degree successfully within the first year of his appointment. He continued to use the self-esteem resource book suggested by Karen, as a reference tool whenever his critical inner voice arose. Most of all he felt in-control of himself, his thoughts and his well-being.

Moving forward: Negative emotion can have a debilitating effect on an individual. A person will present physical, cognitive and emotional symptoms of a stress or trauma reaction. When negative emotions that arise from our critical inner voice are held within and not experienced, we can suffer lowered self-esteem and ultimately, depression. The inner voice is always negative and destructive and appears louder and more vocal when a person is vulnerable and feeling stressed. Reversing the mission of negative emotions is assisted through counselling. Precipitating thoughts are identified and reframed to create feelings of well-being that lead to raised self-esteem and self-confidence.

Emotional Leadership Practice

ELP 3.1   Banishing low self-esteem

Read case study 3.1, "Banishing Low Self-esteem". How often have you, like Barry, thought – "I'm not good enough", "I'm not worthy", or "I'm not the person I thought I would turn out to be"?

_____

_____

_____

RECOGNISING YOUR INNER VOICE

1. INDICATOR OF LOW SELF-ESTEEM

If you have experienced a lot of negative emotion in your life you will find that your stress rises as your negative emotion increases. As your stress increases you experience lowered self-esteem. It is the mission of negative emotion to lower self-esteem. But how does this happen?

Negative emotion is a response to stressors. The inner voice is a significant stressor and the **indicator** of low self-esteem. You experience lowered self-esteem as your stress – negative emotion – rises. No matter who you are, no matter your starting point of self-esteem.

We all have an inner voice – even children. Some people think that low self-esteem comes from parents who put you down or didn't praise you. This can be true and sometimes is. But people, regardless of how their parents treated them, experience lowered self-esteem when they are highly stressed. Once their stress level decreases their normal level of self-esteem is restored.

The inner voice has the task of setting you up to fail. Your inner voice judges and rejects you. It sets you up to relive the pain of the past, and experience fear of the future. As your self-esteem is lowered you hear your inner voice the loudest of all – you seem to be in a no-win situation.

2. WHAT IS THE INNER VOICE – THE VOICE IN YOUR HEAD?

The inner voice is the voice in your head, the monologue of negative thoughts.

When you are stressed your internal voice – or critic/chatterbox – gets louder. You know the one, the one that says;

"Don't do it, it may be the wrong decision", or

"You are such a hopeless organiser, you'll never get this finished…and you promised the kids", or

"You wanted children, and now you have two beautiful kids and still, you are not happy. Now you want to go back to work and leave them to be brought up by...", or

"You're always letting people down."

Sometimes your internal voice gets so loud it can feel like it has taken over. You find it difficult to differentiate between the critic and your rational thoughts. The critic fills you with self-doubt. You seem unable to trust your own judgement. It successfully maintains your stress levels, and you can't get the feeling of being in-control back. You feel vulnerable. And this exacerbates the stress.

 Emotional Leadership Practice
ELP 3.2   Conquer your inner critic

An exercise adapted from "The Self-Esteem Companion", 1999,
Matthew McKay, Patrick Fanning, Carole Honeychurch & Catharine Sutker.
New Harbinger Publications, Oakland, CA 800/748-6273
www.newharbinger.com/SEexer1.htm

Essential to understanding self-esteem is the concept of the Pathological Inner Critic. This is the name given to the "voice" we all hear in our heads from time to time – the critical monologue that reminds you of your weaknesses and failings. It may remind you of your own voice, or of one of your parents' voices. It may consist of isolated words, brief mental images, or long diatribes. In any case, it is this inner critic that destroys self-esteem.

This section will teach you how to identify your inner critic's messages, silence or refute them, and create an alternative, healthy, self-affirming voice of advocacy within yourself.

Meet your critic

Don't worry if you hear voices inside your head. Everybody does! It's called self-talk, or your internal monologue. It's the natural, everyday mental commentary that helps you interpret what's going on, avoid danger or pain, seek out pleasure or gain, and make choices and decisions.

Critical thinking is an essential faculty – you have to make critical judgments to survive. However, if you have low self-esteem, you often apply too many critical judgments to yourself. These can then get out of control and will take on a life of their own. This "out of control" critical voice in your head is called the pathological critic.

Your pathological critic is the negative inner voice that says, "I'm fat, I'm ugly, I'm incompetent." The critic blames you for things that go wrong. The critic compares you to others and finds you wanting. The critic expects you to be perfect. It constantly reminds you of your weaknesses and failures, but never once mentions your strengths and successes. The critic reads your friends' minds and tells you they are bored and turned-off by you. The critic makes absolute statements such as, "You always screw up. You never finish anything on time."

This voice may sound like a man or a woman, like your mother or your father, or like your own voice. For many people it doesn't sound like a separate voice at all – self-critical "truths" or "facts" just pop into their minds. That's a key feature of the pathological critic – no matter how outrageous its statements are, they seem true. You believe them without question.

To raise your self-esteem, you have to start noticing and questioning your pathological critic. To start, think of the one negative truth about yourself – that is, something that you view as negative – that you believe without question. What is your major vice, weak point, disability, or lack – the one that is obvious to you and anyone who knows you? This can be something as obvious and factual as "I'm short, "I dropped out of high school," or "I'm single."

For the rest of the day, and all day tomorrow, simply notice how many times this fact enters your mind. Carry a pen and paper around and tally how many times you think about it. If you actually hear the words in your head, jot that down too. It's good practice for later exercises.

But for now, just notice how much this fact is on your mind. Seems like a lot, doesn't it? That's the pathological critic. Keeping the spotlight on the negative and constantly reminding you of your faults and misfortunes. Once you've observed how present the belief is in your life, you can begin the other exercises in this section.

Catching your critic

You've seen it a hundred times in the movies. The CIA agents in the fake plumber's van, clutching their earphones, listening in on conversations being held over a tapped phone line. The private eye using the voice-activated tape recorder. The suspicious person picking up the extension to hear their partner planning a secret rendezvous with a lover.

The origin of the critic

The pathological critic begins with your parents' forbidding gestures, their negative reactions – such as scolding or hitting – when you did something dangerous, wrong or annoying. These forbidding gestures told you that you were bad, that there was something wrong with you. When you're a kid, your parents' disapproval is a life and death matter, since they are the sole source of your physical and emotional nourishment. You retain conscious and unconscious memories of all those times when you were punished and felt wrong or bad. These are the unavoidable scars that growing-up inflicts on everyone's self-esteem.

When your pathological critic starts pointing out how you've made a mess, fallen short of a goal, or made a stupid mistake, it sounds perfectly believable because it harks back to your earliest memories of punishment, shame and fear. The nastiness of your pathological critic depends on how frequent, rejecting, consistent, moralistic and blaming, your parents' forbidding gestures were.

The more "yes" answers you have to the following five questions, the more likely you are to have a loud and vicious internal critic;

1. Did your parents scold or punish you frequently?   Yes   No
   It takes many repetitions of "You always screw up.
   What's the matter with you?" before it sinks in and
   becomes part of your pathological critic's repertoire.

2. Did your parents reject you by anger or withdrawal?   Yes   No
   Children can tolerate a fair amount of criticism without
   damage to their sense of worth, if the criticism is
   delivered in a calm, supportive way. Damage is done
   when parents yell and hit or withdraw emotional support.

3. Did your parents have inconsistent rules?
   When parents don't enforce the rules consistently, it   Yes   No
   makes it hard for you to figure out what is expected of
   you. When you're punished, you are more likely to
   assume it's because you're bad by nature – not because
   you've broken a clear rule.

4. Did your parents make everything a moral issue?
   If your parents considered being noisy, getting a low   Yes   No
   grade, or breaking something a mortal sin, you are more
   likely to have low self-esteem than if they expressed
   their rules in terms of preferences, tastes, personal
   needs, or safety issues.

5. Did your parents blame you, not your behaviour?   Yes   No

A child who hears a stern warning about the danger of running into the street will have better self-esteem than a child who only hears that she's a "bad girl" when she runs into the street. Careful parents make a clear distinction between their child's inappropriate behaviour and the basic goodness of their child.

We refer to your inner voice as your "pathological critic". Answer the above five questions. Can you identify the origins of your inner voice? Your answers to these questions can help you identify the origins of your critic. It is important to remember that you can alter and control your critic – even if you answered yes to all of these questions.

Also note that a sensitive person will have a louder and more vocal inner voice – regardless of whether the messages from the parents were positive or negative. The sensitive person produces more adrenalin which effectively lowers self-eestem even when the parents are wonderful.

 Emotional Leadership Practice

ELP 3.3   Stress and the inner voice

Are you stressed? Is your inner voice setting you up for failure by telling you, "You don't measure up?"

What is your inner voice saying to you right now?

_____

_____

_____

_____

CASE STUDY 3.2 – TELL YOUR INNER VOICE TO "CHECK OUT!"

Robert felt uptight and out of control. He felt trapped and unable to escape the stress in his life. He hated his job. He felt bored, restless and under utilised. At work he was unfulfilled as his skills weren't acknowledged or used. Nevertheless, he worked longer hours to avoid his wife Laura, who was always unhappy and nagging him.

At home, Laura felt she managed the children on her own. The more decisions she made, the more Robert left her to it. When they arrived in Singapore she assumed that her strong relationship with Robert would see them through the stresses of a new environment. Yet Robert now seemed withdrawn and quiet, he wouldn't talk to her about his work, or what she was going through. She felt resentful, frustrated, unsupported and insecure. Laura knew of many couples with marriage problems, and she felt that it was only a matter of time before they too were just another statistic.

Karen's Assessment: Both Robert and Laura had a loud inner voice that was feeding them negative, irrational and anxious thoughts. As neither was communicating well with the other, their inner voice allowed them to believe whatever they wanted to believe. They each felt the growing distance between them, and were worried about where their marriage was headed. In the absence of effective communication, their inner voices had taken control.

Work done in Counselling: Karen explained that the inner voice attacks, judges or minimises. The inner voice is negative and destructive – and louder when a person is feeling vulnerable and stressed. Both Robert and Laura saw clearly how their own respective unhappy feelings escalated into anxiety about the marriage, as their inner voice got louder.

Outcome: Robert and Laura used their counselling sessions to reaffirm how they felt about each other and also learnt to communicate their insecurities so that a similar situation didn't arise again.

Moving forward: Everyone has an inner voice – it's the conversation you have with yourself. It accompanies you wherever you go, making its presence felt – even when uninvited. The inner voice may be a thought, or a feeling without any *real* thought attached to it. Often you believe this feeling to be true because it's so apparent to you. For example, "my partner doesn't appreciate me – he takes me for granted." When your head is full of anxious and irrational thoughts not checked against reality they become your new truth. Thereafter, anything you observe or hear will reinforce the new truth in your head. Tell your inner voice to "check out". Seek counselling to help overcome its negative message.

Emotional Leadership Practice
ELP 3.4   Tell your inner voice to "check out"!

Read case study 3.2. What were Robert's and Laura's inner voices telling them? What is your inner voice telling you right now?

_____

_____

_____

_____

_____

_____

3. TOO MUCH CHANGE

Your inner voice is not your conscience. Conscience knows right from wrong. Your inner voice tends to beat you up about whatever decision you make, about whatever you do. For example, upon leaving the supermarket, you realise you have been given too much change. Your conscience immediately directs you to return the overpayment. But as you turn to do so, your inner voice questions, "Why? You didn't steal it! Pocket it! This store has often overcharged you anyway!" Yet, as you put the money in your wallet guardedly, the inner voice reprimands you, "You thief! You hypocrite! You pride yourself as being honest and trustworthy, yet here, you are stealing from the supermarket, you should take the money back."

As your inner voice becomes louder – stronger – you feel immobilised, stuck. It seems that you are unable to make decisions, and no longer trust your own judgement. Your inner voice takes over and becomes your reality, your present identity, your "shoulds".

4. COGNITIVE DISTORTIONS AND YOUR "SHOULDS"

Recall from your study of the pain timeline in chapter two, that you are what you think. Emotional distress is emotional constipation; "dis-ease" or an illness of how you think, because how you feel depends on how you think.

A cognitive distortion is a conditioned form of thinking that you have traded for reality. Cognitive distortions are the tools the inner voice uses to achieve its goal – to lower self-esteem.

McKay and Fanning (2000, p. 61) hold that cognitive distortions are actually bad habits – habits of thought that you consistently use to interpret reality in an unrealistic way. Distortions are not beliefs themselves. They are habits of thinking, that often get you into trouble.

Bad habits of thought include overgeneralisations such as; "I'm so lazy", "I'm really helpless", "I'm always putting things off", "I'm never going to be happy". As well as global labelling; "All men are hopeless", "All women are stupid", and "Successful people are definitely part of the establishment".

Your "shoulds" are what you have been conditioned to believe from parental, cultural and peer expectations. For example;

- You should work hard, be persistent, and endure hardship.
- You should never feel hurt. You should always feel happy.
- You should not say anything if you have nothing nice to say.

- You should never make mistakes or be afraid.
- You should never show emotions such as anger or jealousy.
- You should achieve to create status, wealth and success.
- You should stay with the same employer to show you are stable.
- You should always finish your chores before watching television.

The "shoulds" of your life are the habits you have created – built on years of conditioning. Let's call them your "auto-responders". Auto-responders are behaviours that occur automatically – without thinking. No two people experience their bodies in the same way. Each person interprets

Emotional Wisdom

"Whatever is flexible and flowing will tend to grow, whatever is rigid and blocked will wither and die." – Lao Tzu, Tao Te Ching

experiences according to their own personal memories, values, beliefs, expectations, attitudes or assumptions (thoughts). Your auto-responders, or habits, fill the gap between the need of the moment, and the solution from the past. It's often not until you've had an "Oh shit!" experience – when you are denied your wants and needs – that you begin to see the damage and emotional wounds in yourself and in others, that your auto-responders have caused. Your challenge is to choose the behaviour you want to be, to reframe the "shoulds" in your life to generate positive emotion.

As adults, we often deny ourselves the immediate experience of an emotion. Our appraisal puts up a screen of words in our mind – a map of how we should act, throwing us into the emotions of hurt, anger, or anxiety that are mostly destructive. Stephen Covey (1989) describes these maps in our head;

Each of us has many, many maps in our head. These can be divided into two categories; maps of the way things are (realities), and maps of the way things should be (values). We interpret everything we experience through these mental maps. We seldom question their accuracy. We're usually even unaware that we have them. We simply assume that the way we see things is the way they really are – or the way they should be. And our attitudes and behaviours grow out of those assumptions. The way we see things, is the source of the way we think and the way we act.[2]

The danger of the "shoulds" is that they become absolute and fixed beliefs. An unbending sense of right and wrong.

Recognising the inner voice and challenging its message is to learn to be flexible, adaptable, and develop a greater tolerance for ambiguity. To rise from your point of view, to your viewing point. Regardless of the opinions of others, you have the capacity to define who you are.

EMOTION GENERATION

1. EMOTIONS EXPERIENCED AS AROUSAL

Emotions represent bodily feelings that you experience as nervous arousal – or an arousal of the nervous system. No one else can experience your feelings in the same way that you do. An implication of this fact is that you have to be responsible for your feelings. They're not happening to anyone else.

Shweder (1994) says that emotion states represent affective experience, "…not simply as a feeling – as tiredness or tension or a heartache, but as a perception – for example, betrayal by trusted allies, and a plan – for example, retaliation, realignment, withdrawal, and so forth."[3]

Emotions are generated to signal a need. But how are states of emotion generated? Can emotions be controlled?

Research provides arguments for and against what comes first – a feeling or a thought. Joseph Ledoux (1994) has argued;

The amygdala can … be activated by the thalamus at about the same time that the cortex can be activated by the thalamus… this may account for why we are not aware of why we respond emotionally, the way we do.

To the extent that the emotional stimulus is one that the species has developed specific response strategies to cope with, the initial reaction – reactions that have been perfected through evolutionary experience – will be automatic and the secondary reaction – specific to the individual, reflecting past experience, judgment, and prediction – will be voluntary.[4]

Phoebe Ellesworth (1994) says;

I think emotion is usually provoked by appraisals – including remembered appraisals – of the environment, and one's self in relation to the environment…[5]

Carroll Izard (1994) believes that there are four types of information-processing or emotion-activating systems; two non-cognitive (cellular and organismic) and two cognitive (biopsychological and cognitive). She argues that both non-cognitive and cognitive process activate emotion.

Yet there seems to be a need for some conceptual distinctions between such seemingly different processes as those that occur in genes, and those that require complex neural networks in the brain.[6]

Many researchers recognise the minimum for cognitive activated emotion as appraisal. The appraisal mechanism operates rapidly, but is not always automatic – as when there is a slow, deliberate and conscious evaluation of the event that triggered the emotion state. In a discussion on appraisal, Ekman (1994) says,

Automatic appraisal does not simply and solely operate on what is given biologically – dealing only with stimulus events that exactly fit what is given. Individual differences in our experience allow for enormous variations in the specifics of what calls forth emotion that are attributable to personality, family, and culture.[7]

We now turn to appraisal – your arousal "trigger" – to begin a cognitive-behavioural explanation of the role emotions play in your well-being.

2. EAR–IDENTITY: A COGNITIVE-BEHAVIOURAL PROCESS

From the foregone discussion on emotion experienced as arousal, you learned that emotion states are brought forth both biologically and consciously, in response to an event. Emotions are brought forth biologically when bodily feelings of hunger and lack of sleep, or allergic reaction to certain food substances such as gluten and wheat, act as stimuli to change one's internal chemistry. Emotions are brought forth consciously again and again in the drama of life. Reinforcing this, Chopra (1993, p. 21) says;

> **Emotional Wisdom**
>
> The key point in *Emotional Leadership* is EAR-Identity (figure 3.1) – how emotions are generated cognitively and experienced behaviourally, as event (stimulus), appraisal (perception), and response (behaviour).[8]

...emotions are not fleeting events isolated in mental space; they are expressions of awareness, the fundamental stuff of life... We, however, are not stuck in our life cycle; being aware, we participate in every reaction that takes place inside us. The problems arise when we don't take responsibility for what we're doing.[9]

Your EAR-Identity (event, appraisal and response - figure 3.1) arises from self-interaction. You experience this as internal dialogue generated by your memory, beliefs, values, expectations and assumptions, in response to a stimulus, facilitated through the amygdal/thalamus/cortex interaction in your brain. EAR-Identity is the identity that you have created for yourself.

Figure 3.1. EAR-Identity

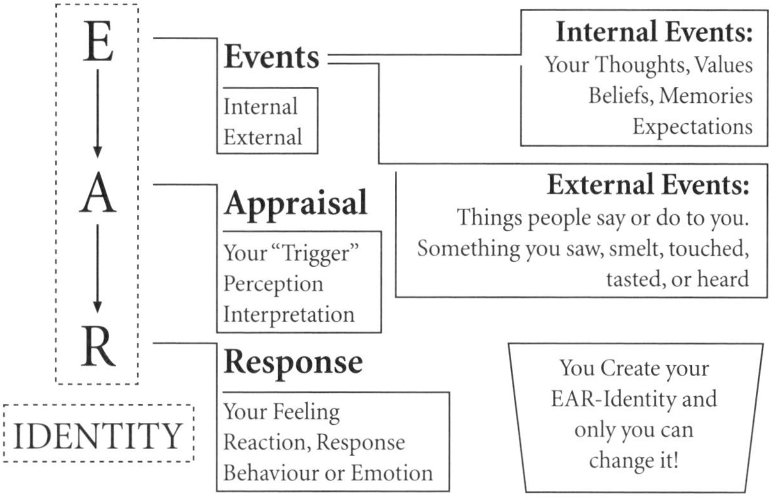

E ──── Events ═══════ Internal Events:
│   Your Thoughts, Values
│   Internal   Beliefs, Memories
↓   External   Expectations
A ──── Appraisal   External Events:
│   Things people say or do to you.
↓   Your "Trigger" Something you saw, smelt, touched,
          Perception   tasted, or heard
          Interpretation
R ──── Response   You Create your
                      EAR-Identity and
IDENTITY Your Feeling   only you can
          Reaction, Response change it!
          Behaviour or Emotion

Central to EAR-Identity is appraisal – your perception of how you know the world. From chapter one, recall that the key to knowing yourself, the world, and understanding change, is to recognise that it is your perception (appraisal) of events that causes emotional constipation and behavioural problems ("dis-ease") – not the events themselves. Winefield and Peay (1980, 1991) describe perception as a process;

Perception is the whole process by which information about the outside world impinges on the sensory organs, and is then decoded and interpreted by the brain – resulting in a conscious experience. It is one aspect of cognition – all the mental activities that enable you to know and make decisions about the world. [10]

Our assumptions here are that event (internal or external information) precedes response (behaviour), and emotion is thought plus feeling – where thought precedes feeling. This is necessary in order to understand how you are able to change your appraisal (perception) of an event using the 4-step cognitive framework described in chapter four, thereby mitigating your behaviour to enjoy a life of EASE.

EAR-Identity is your strategy to always be the person you want to be. To always behave the way you want to behave. EAR-Identity is your strategy to be predictable with each response to an event, because you are choosing to behave in a particular way, that does not give away your power. And you retain responsibility for your response. You cannot then say to someone, "You made me do this", "You made me feel this", or "See what you did to me". Other people will be able to predict or anticipate a certain response from you whenever they approach you to talk. For example, they may not get agreement but they will get kindness, wisdom, honesty, non-judgment and a listening ear, rather than sometimes getting kindness, sometimes being dismissed, sometimes getting irritability, and sometimes being put-down.

Using EAR-Identity your response now becomes a new conscious response, replacing a former negative auto-response. After a period of time and practice, your conscious response will in itself become a conditioned positive auto-response, displaying the behaviour you want to be. As a consequence, EAR-Identity allows you to feel in control of your behaviour, and thereby enables a formerly stressful event to be experienced as exhilaration – rather than as anger or anxiety.

The positive feeling that is generated when using EAR-Identity reinforces the benefits of using the strategy for reducing stress and enjoying a life of EASE. The good feelings you get from using EAR-Identity validate that using emotion to facilitate thought to choose the right response, puts you back in control of your behaviour. This is the behaviour of an emotionally intelligent person using his or her ability to facilitate thought, the second branch of the MSCEIT ability model of emotional intelligence.

3. LEARNING

Before discussing appraisal, perhaps a few words about learning – the bridge between cognition (thinking) and behaviour (emotion). Winefield and Peay (1980, 1991, p. 80) hold that;

> Learning – how behaviour is shaped and modified by experience – holds the key to any attempt to change behaviour for the better. Whether it is getting people to eat more healthily, control their anxiety, or grow up happy, loving, and capable.

In addition to your genetic ability to manage emotion, your behaviour is affected by your environment. Behaviour is a product of your learning and your environment. Russian psychologist Pavlov, found in 1903, that he could induce dogs to salivate by consistently ringing a bell whenever they were given food. Eventually the sound of the bell on its own was sufficient to cause the dogs to salivate. Other researchers applied Pavlov's findings to human behaviour. They believed that if behaviour is the product of learning and environment then it is possible to change behaviour, by behaviour modification.

The way you think and the way you feel have been influenced strongly from birth – perhaps before birth. And this continues throughout your life. Conditioned learning was discussed in chapter one. Your learning experiences to date have set the way your body operates now, affecting your current state of well-being.

There are many forms of learning including; classical conditioning, operant conditioning, and observational learning. As forms of learning is not the subject of this book, it is suffice to say that you are capable of learning new behaviour – involuntary and voluntary responses from events or stimuli – by drilling down to find the thought (event) plus appraisal (trigger), that gives you an often unhealthy response (emotion), and reframing the thought to generate your desired behaviour. You learn new behaviour by reframing your thoughts and by selecting new appraisals in the Gap (figure 3.2). You learn to do this using the 4-step cognitive framework described in stage four.

4. APPRAISAL

Appraisal involves interpretation of events – both internal (body) and external (world). You create your emotional health. Your mind and body are inseparable. They are bound together in a field of energy and information known as awareness – your feelings, thoughts, beliefs, memory, assumptions, expectations, and preconditions. You need to use your mind to build the body you want – to reprogram outdated triggers (appraisals).

Reality is experienced by your body through your senses; sight, hearing, touch, taste and smell. Your body's nerve endings are an extension of your brain.

In the **old paradigm**, your five senses reinforce the message that things *are* what they seem. Appraisal is experienced as the feelings from thoughts, judgements and predictions, racing around in your mind;

- You determine if something is pain or pleasure depending on how it fits your beliefs, values, rules and expectations.
- Beliefs are something you accept as true about reality.
- Values are your principles or standards. Your judgement of what is valuable and important in life.
- Rules are how you want to influence other people, things, and events, to be what you want.
- Expectations are your internal assumptions based upon your beliefs, values, or rules, about how someone or something should behave in response to you – but of which the other person is unaware.

In the **new paradigm**, reality is dictated by how you have learned to perceive it, in present-moment awareness. When you change your perceptions through creating your new EAR-Identity, by changing your learned triggers, or pattern of beliefs, values, rules, and expectations, you change the experience of your body. You change your reality. Chopra (1993, p. 36) believes, that "In the new paradigm, control of life belongs to awareness."

5. THE GAP BETWEEN EVENT AND RESPONSE

The problem with creating emotional health is that there is a gap between event and response, where impulse happens – usually from the amygdala. It is within this space that meaning is formed through appraisal. It is in the gap that the trigger (conditioned response) occurs, and you experience the response in your body. For example, your first experience on a roller coaster may be exhilarating, or terrifying. The memory will be stored as such, and be recalled any time the words roller coaster are mentioned.

Emotional Wisdom
The key to both your emotional growth and happiness is how you use the gap (see figure 3.2), how you apply meaning to each event in your life.

It is the perception you give to your experience that forms new meaning, that you store as memory. Chopra (1993, p. 41) again;

> The great enemy of renewal is habit. When frozen interpretations from the past are applied to the present, there will always be a gap. A mismatch between the need of the moment and the solution from the past.

Figure 3.2.
The "Gap" between event and response

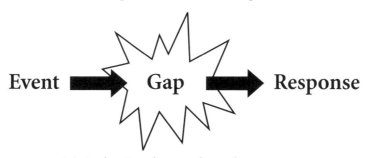

It is in the Gap that you have the power
to choose behaviour you want to be!

Your responses or reactions (behaviours) are generated by impulse – through amygdala/thalamus/neocortical interactions – from external or internal events. An external event may be physical – something someone said to you, or something you saw, touched, smelt, or tasted. An internal event may be a thought (including memory), expectation, belief, value, or prediction. Behaviour may be a controlled or uncontrolled, physical or passive, verbal or non-verbal response, experienced in the body as anger, fear, sadness, happiness, disgust or surprise.

When you respond to your two basic impulses – pain or pleasure – as an emotionally healthy person, your responses are free of negative appraisal. Your responses are effective in reducing stress from pain, and enjoying pleasure. Your body will recognise feelings of natural anger in the present, and use positive assertiveness to express your experience. Your body will respond to natural positive comments about you with joy and thanksgiving. You will live in a state of ease, without fear or rancour. You are emotionally healthy.

When you respond to your two basic impulses as an emotionally unhealthy person, your responses are laden with negative appraisal. Your memory is full of pain – hurt, anger and anxiety. You are ineffective in reducing stress from pain and have an inability to enjoy pleasure – as you have attached meaning to the event from a similar event in the past that is not intended. You'll live in a state of stress, full of bitterness, despair, guilt, shame, imagined fear, and a need for vindication. You are emotionally unhealthy – emotionally constipated.

Pain and pleasure are your natural response – your reality. But because you attach thoughts to them they become unnatural, or perceived reality. In the gap between event and response you are free to choose whether to respond naturally to stimuli as an emotionally healthy person – a victor, or to respond as emotionally unhealthy person – a victim, displaying all the symptoms of your self-inflicted "dis-ease".

When you ignore what happens in the gap, your body must rely on past conditioning – past memory – to trigger your response. This may not be how you want to behave. When you get to work on what happens in the gap you get to change or create the memory of your experience. Armed with renewed stored memory you can respond naturally to your impulse, and trigger the response of your choice. You get to control the impulse. The emotional response that is aroused is your natural response – how you want to be. Your willingness to let go of the old is the key. That is the secret.

You ignore the gap at your peril and miss the immediate experience of an emotion. You embrace the gap and raise

> **Emotional Wisdom**
>
> Like a river, my body changes as the moment changes. And if I could do the same, there would be no gaps in my life. No memory of past trauma to trigger new pain, no anticipation of future hurt to make me contract in fear. (Chopra, 1993, p. 39)

your emotional well-being. You use what happens to you to become fully emotionally aware. To change your body, you need to first change your awareness. Deepak Chopra expresses this concept very well (see box).

6. GET SMART AT NOTICING EMOTIONAL CONSTIPATION

You don't ignore your needs. That's one reason why you've chosen to read this book! Some people ignore their needs. They live in pain and may die from this. Others notice their need, but wait until the discomfort gets more uncomfortable – or even painful – before they act. Then they endure an "Oh shit!" experience, when their wants and needs are not met.

Sometimes you find that you do not have enough energy to deal with your feelings, because your body is attempting to deal with wants and needs that lie hidden deep inside of you. When trying to deal with these deep emotions our bodies become depleted of energy – sometimes leading to depression.

Don't wait for the "Oh shit!" experience. Get good at noticing emotional constipation – the very first feeling of discomfort. Avoid emotional "dis-ease" by taking care of your needs at the first sign of emotional distress, by creating an EAR-Identity centred in reality – not perceived reality (fantasy).

Live in present moment awareness, where you experience your emotion in the present from events in the present. Discover your true identity and evaluate the role it plays in creating your emotional distress.

Emotion is a state "triggered" by an event or stimulus. The stimulus may come to you through your senses. If you can see it, hear it, taste it, smell it, or feel it on your skin or in your body, then it is real.

Perceived reality is all mental or cognitive activity, including thoughts, memories, dreams and ideas. Perceived reality doesn't come to you. It comes *from* you. You create it using your own brain (mind). If you only think it, it may be true or it may be false – but it's not real.

Emotions that are triggered in your mind rather than by your senses, are unnecessary or optional. If you create painful emotions by thinking negative thoughts in your mind, you will need to change how you think in order to feel better. If you create pleasurable feelings, that's great – as long as you remember that you are only using your imagination.

Sometimes you create emotions that are so strong that they cover real feelings from your senses. When you do this you are "out of touch" with reality, and in danger of making serious mistakes.

7. MAKING A MISTAKE

A mistake is an event. It is anything you do, that you later – upon reflection – wish you had done differently. This also applies to things that you didn't do, that you later – upon reflection – wish you had done. "Mistake" is a label you always apply in retrospect – when you realise you could have done something differently, although the decision you made was right at the time.

Louise Hay (1984) says, "Learning is making mistakes until our subconscious mind can put together the right pictures."[11] The view of McKay and Fanning (1992, 2000, p. 136) on mistake is;

> Allow a quota for mistakes. A rule of thumb for most people is that between one and three decisions in every ten are dead wrong. And several others may be in a doubtful grey area.

Mistake is a label you apply to your behaviour at a later date when you have changed your awareness. "Mistake" is a function of limited awareness.

You will make the same mistake again and again until you develop emotional self-awareness. Self-esteem is rooted in your unconditional acceptance of yourself as an innately worthy being – regardless of mistakes. Because you made a mistake, it doesn't make you

> **Emotional Wisdom**
>
> Life is a series of events. Every event is an opportunity to learn. It is from the most painful events that you learn the most.

unworthy. Circumstances change and so will you.

Feelings that start in your senses are natural responses to the real world. When you notice real anger – or sadness, or dread – you are noticing that something is wrong in your body. When you notice real joy or excitement, you are noticing that something is going well in your body. You can always trust natural feelings – your intuition. Learn what your natural feelings are saying to you. Use them well.

Emotional leadership facilitates successful transformational change, motivating individual transition, including change management, revitalisation, and renewal. In chapter four we explore how you can convert responses to events experienced as negative emotion, to responses that generate positive energy flows using your EAR-Identity.

 Emotional Leadership Practice

ELP 3.5   Accurately identifying emotions

Imagine yourself listening to each of the people below. Discuss the emotion felt by the person in each example. Comment on where the emotion has "come from". That is, what was the inner voice of each person saying.

1. Young woman aged 25:
    "Sandra and Jenny showed up at the party in mini skirts with dates, and there I was in slacks!"

Emotion felt _____

Inner voice message _____

2. Trainee in a counselling training programme, aged 21, to a fellow trainee: "I know he's going to select me to role-play a counselling situation with someone before the whole group. I can't imagine myself up there in front of everyone! I'm determined to miss the class. I feel like telling him I'm sick."

Emotion felt _____

Inner voice message _____

3. Woman, aged 30, talking about her job: "It's not a big thing, but it's the second time this week that I've been asked to swap shifts with her. It certainly shows who is more favoured here. Why does it always have to be me that defers to her?"

Emotion felt _____

Inner voice message _____

4. Sales Manager, aged 26, talking about his boss: "I thought she was really going to get stuck into me. I was afraid she was going to tell me that I had to go. But we just sat in her office and talked over our differences."

Emotion felt _____

Inner voice message _____

 Emotional Leadership Practice – Individual Exercise

ELP 3.6   Recognising your EAR-Identity.

Recall the EAR-Identity idea? Events – internal and external stimuli – happen to us in reality, present moment awareness. We appraise the events happening to us that trigger a feeling, response, reaction, or emotion.

Identify the events in your life that are likely to trigger a conditioned response from you.

Event	Response

What can you do to remind yourself of the gap that exists between event and response? So that you can begin to change your EAR-Identity.

Emotional Leadership Practice – Individual Exercise
ELP 3.7 – Applying emotional intelligence[12]

Lena, an e-commerce project leader, sought executive coaching to assist her in dealing with the many difficulties surrounding her project. Project members were used to functioning independently in their individual domains. Lena relentlessly drove others to get things done on time, and some members were anxious about her leading the group. She did not have hierarchical authority over all areas of the project as project members came from various functional groups in the organisation. Aside from the usual office politics, there was a high level of finger pointing and a lack of accountability amongst the team members. Lena was not the cause of these problems, but it seemed that strong leadership was required to turn things around. Lena's results in the MSCEIT™ are shown as;

Branch	Score
Perceiving emotion	Strength
Facilitating thought	Consider improvement
Understanding emotion	High
Managing emotion	High average

How do you think Lena's low Facilitating Thought score supported the executive coach's observation that she had difficulty motivating and supervising people?

 Emotional Leadership Practice – Small Group Exercise
ELP 3.8 – Applying Emotional Intelligence.[13]
Using emotion to facilitate thought – empathy

Do you take the time to actively listen to others? Are you able to respond accurately to their expressed emotion, and level of intensity of emotion? Can you generate a certain emotion and then compare and contrast its sensations with that of emotions being experienced by other people? Do you have an ability to empathise?

Below are comments made by two different people. From the list of comments decide which responses are an empathic response and which are not.

1. Ben, a 38-year-old father of two, is describing his current work predicament to his wife, "I feel quite trapped in this job. I enjoyed it at the beginning, but with so many staff changes over the past two years, I feel isolated now and no longer valued. I think about moving on, but where to? I'm not good for anything else. And with the kids' school, fees and our living expenses, I can't just quit and have a holiday!"

To these comments you reply;

a. "I can go back to work if you want to do some further study."

b. "I know it's become hard for you since your best friends left. But moaning and groaning about it only makes you feel worse."

c. "Don't worry, this is just a down time you're going through. You'll get over it. I'm still here for you."

d. "It must be pretty awful for you, knowing that you'd like to move on but really can't. Sort of a 'stuck here for life' feeling. Especially when we are so financially committed at the moment."

2. Debbie, a 26-year-old woman says to her friend at dinner, "I was so upset today. First I got caught in the rain, then I missed the bus into the city and was late for lunch with Linda, then I had to leave early to attend a meeting with my boss. So nothing went according to plan. And because I was so upset, I forgot to ring my niece for her birthday."

To these comments you reply;

a. "Oh your niece will be disappointed you forgot her birthday."

b. "Why didn't you take a taxi when you missed the bus. Then you would have had more time for lunch with Linda."

c. "What a frustrating day! And you were so looking forward to your lunch with Linda."

d. "I am really sorry that your day was so awful."

e. "I'm sure Linda would have also been upset that your time together was so short."

f. "I'm sure you'll be able to spend longer with Linda next time."

Summary

The mission of negative emotion is to lower self-esteem. Self-esteem and stress (negative emotion) operate as counterweights. As stress rises self-esteem decreases, and vice versa. Your inner voice judges and rejects you, and sets you up to relive the pain of the past and fear the future. You all have an inner voice, even children. Learn to recognise your inner voice and tell it to "Check out!" whenever it begins its task of setting you up to fail.

Emotion is a state triggered by an event. Your appraisal of events generates a response felt in the body. Your EAR-Identity – event, appraisal and response – arises from self-interaction. You experience this as internal dialogue generated by your beliefs, values, expectations and assumptions, in response to a stimulus, facilitated through interaction of the amygdala/thalamus/cortex in your brain. EAR-Identity is the identity that you have created for yourself. How you transform your EAR-Identity can mean the difference between emotional health and emotional illness.

Emotional leadership is about recognising the old habits and changing your appraisals. Developing your emotional abilities to question and reframe your interpretations, evaluations and expectations, so as to control your body's impulsive reactions to events. Gradually, free from self-imposed conditioning, you will learn to allow events to unravel around you, and react to them spontaneously – without suppressing your emotions.

Life is a series of events. Every event is an opportunity to learn. It is from the most painful events that you learn the most. It is through experiencing your emotions that you move on, and learn to create a new identity and **affirm** your life of EASE.

EMOTIONAL LEADERSHIP CHECKLIST

Use this emotional leadership checklist to understand self-esteem, recognise your inner voice, and your EAR-Identity.

- Do I know what emotion generation is?
- Have I recognised my EAR-Identity?
- Can I apply my emotional abilities to facilitate thought?

EMOTIONAL LEADERSHIP POINT 1:
Do I know what emotion generation is?

☐ It is in your consciousness – your "mind" – that the identity you create for your self, your inner view of self, is formed.

Emotions derive from the identity you create for yourself. From present joys and hurts, memory of past experiences, and perceptions of your future.

☐ Emotion generation is felt in the body.

Emotions represent bodily feelings that you experience as arousal. No one else can experience your feelings in the same way that you do.

☐ Self-esteem and stress operate as counterweights.

As stress rises self-esteem decreases, and vice versa. So it is with your emotions.

☐ Negative emotion.

The goal of negative emotion is to lower self-esteem. Reversing negative emotion creates a feeling of increased well-being.

☐ What is the "inner voice"? What's its role?

The "inner voice" is the voice in your head – the monologue of negative thoughts. It has the task of setting you up to fail. Your inner voice judges and rejects you. And sets you up over and over again to generate negative emotion, to relive the pain (negative emotion) of the past, and experience fear of the future.

EMOTIONAL LEADERSHIP POINT 2:
Have I recognised my EAR-Identity?

☐ Your EAR-Identity arises from self-interaction.

You experience your EAR-Identity as internal dialogue generated by your thoughts, memory, beliefs, values, and expectations. You experience EAR-Identity as (E) Events, (A) Appraisal, and (R) Response.

☐ Central to EAR-Identity is perception.

Your perception (appraisal) of events causes emotional distress and behavioural problems ("dis-ease") – not the events themselves.

☐ The key to EAR-Identity is the gap.

The problem with creating emotional health and a life of EASE is that there is a gap between event and response – where impulse happens (emotion is generated). It is within this space that meaning is formed from appraisal.

The key to both your emotional well-being and happiness is how you choose to use the gap – how you apply meaning to events in your life.

.

When you ignore what happens in the gap, your body must rely on past conditioning (past memory) to trigger response.

EMOTIONAL LEADERSHIP POINT 3:
Can I apply my emotional abilities to facilitate thought?

☐ **Relevance of emotions (empathy) to performance, productivity and teamwork.**

Individual coaching focusing on communication techniques, beliefs, and behaviours can assist you to generate emotions others feel (empathy) and how you want them to feel.

☐ **Your mood and its impact on others.**

By generating a different mood and emotional style, you can assist cognitive activity and change the impact you have on others.

☐ **Don't wait – become adept at noticing your emotion generation.**

Become attuned to noticing your very first feeling of discomfort. Create an EAR-Identity centred in reality – present moment awareness.

A stimulus may come to you through your senses or cognitive activity. If you can see it, hear it, taste it, smell it, or feel it on your skin, or in your body – that's reality!

Perceived reality and pain remembered in the past is fantasy. Emotions generated this way are unnecessary or optional. You don't want to create painful emotions, but you do want to generate pleasurable or positive feelings.

Emotional Leadership Practice – Individual Exercise
ELP 3.7 – Applying Emotional Intelligence
Using emotion to facilitate thought

Suggested Answer

Lena did not see the relevance of emotions to performance, productivity and teamwork. Individual coaching focused on team interactions, beliefs and behaviours. Lena was encouraged to discuss how each of the team members felt, and how she wanted them to feel.

Together with her coach, Lena developed strategies and tactics to overcome negative feelings and build on positive emotions. She called each team member after the monthly meeting to determine how they felt about what had taken place in the meeting. As issues arose, Lena addressed them.

The emotional intelligence assessment provided Lena with an objective overview of her emotional leadership style. Whilst she perceived, understood and managed emotions well, she was initially not able to generate emotions or create a certain mood during meetings to motivate team members to meet project goals. With the help of her executive coach she was soon on her way to managing many disparate elements, and brought them together to collaborate and achieve meaningful outcomes for her organisation.

Notes

1   Terms and insight from McKay, Matthew & Fanning, Patrick (1992, 2000) *Self esteem*, (3rd Ed.), New Harbinger Publications, Oakland, CA. Chapters 5 and 7.

2   Covey, S R (1989) *The seven habits of highly effective people*, London: Simon & Schuster, p. 24.

3   Shweder, R (1994) *You're not sick, you're just in love: Emotion as an interpretive system*. In Ekman, P & Davidson R.J (Eds.) *The Nature of Emotion, Fundamental Questions*, Oxford University Press, New York. pp. 39.

4   Ledoux, J.E (1994) *Cognitive-Emotional Interactions in the Brain*. In Ekman, P & Davidson R.J (Eds.) *The Nature of Emotion, Fundamental Questions*, Oxford University Press, New York. pp. 216-223.

5   Ellsworth, P.C. (1994) *Levels of Thoughts and Levels of Emotion*. In Ekman, P & Davidson R.J (Eds.) *The Nature of Emotion, Fundamental Questions*, Oxford University Press, New York. pp. 192-196.

6   Izard C.E (1994) *Cognition Is One of Four Types of Emotion Activating Systems*. In Ekman, P & Davidson R.J (Eds.) (1994) *The Nature of Emotion, Fundamental Questions*, Oxford University Press, New York. pp. 203-207.

7   Ekman, P (1994) *All emotions are basic*. In Ekman, P & Davidson R.J (Eds.) (1994) *The Nature of Emotion, Fundamental Questions*, Oxford University Press, New York. pp. 15-19.

8   See "Stages of stress" in Chopra, D (1993) *Ageless body, timeless mind. A practical alternative to growing old*, Harmony Books, New York, p. 154 and "The components of your emotional system" in Weisinger H (1998) *Emotional intelligence at work*, Jossey-Bass, California, Ch. 2, for two learned explanations of emotion generation and adrenalin arousal felt in the body.

9   Chopra, D (1993) *Ageless body, timeless mind. A practical alternative to growing old*, Harmony Books, New York, p. 21.

10 Winefield, H.R & Peay, M.Y. (1980, 1991) *Behavioural Science in Medicine*. Department of Psychiatry, The University of Adelaide, South Australia. p.53.

11 Hay, L. L. (1984) *You can heal your life*. Specialist Publications, Concord, Australia. p. 114.

12 Adapted from Mayer, JD, Salovey, P & Caruso, DR 2002, *Mayer-Salovey-Caruso Emotional Intelligence Test (MSCEIT) User's Manual*, Copyright ©1999, 2002. Multi-Health Systems Inc. All Rights Reserved. pp. 27-28.

13 Adapted from Mayer, JD, Salovey, P & Caruso, DR 2002, *Mayer-Salovey-Caruso Emotional Intelligence Test (MSCEIT) User's Manual*, Copyright ©1999, 2002. Multi-Health Systems Inc. All Rights Reserved. p. 26.

CHAPTER 4

4 STEPS

EMOTION
CONVERSION

THE 4-STEP COGNITIVE FRAMEWORK IS THE KEY TO
DEALING WITH UNPLEASANT SENSORY AND
EMOTIONAL EXPERIENCES.

INTRODUCTION

Live positively by recognising the events that cause you stress, and changing your reactions to them. Know the difference between angry talk and positive assertion – both involve sticking up for your rights. Recognise that panic felt from intense fear and anxiety will die down, enabling you to enjoy greater receptivity to arousal.

Use the 4-step cognitive framework to raise your well-being. Learn to notice your feelings, and identify and challenge facts for and against, automatic negative thoughts. Learn to reframe negative thoughts and focus on thoughts more helpful. If a value or belief causes you unhappiness, change it. Make successful transitions from anger to assertion, from fear to appreciation.

In chapter four you learn to live in present-moment awareness. You experience growing self-confidence and self-esteem as you tell your inner voice to check out! You are ready and equipped to construct your new identity – to **affirm** your life of EASE.

TEACHING EMOTIONAL KNOWLEDGE

1. LET'S REVIEW AND UPDATE SOME DEFINITIONS

Event – Any internal or external stimuli that occurs to or within the body.

Appraisal – The "trigger" for the emotional response. Appraisal is a source of autonomic arousal, as the emotional response is mediated by the autonomic nervous system.

Response – Any feeling, reaction, behaviour, or emotion felt in the body.

Auto-Response - A pre-conditioned autonomic response from a "trigger" or appraisal (thought plus perception). For example, a perceived threat to a person's integrity (appraisal), such as being asked a question, could generate a pre-conditioned response of anger.

Feeling feelings – Feelings are experienced spontaneously in the present. Being hurt is real and puts you in the present where you can accept reality. In the present you can trace your emotions back to their source. We cannot be in the present without a willingness to feel hurt. It is in the present that we are free to love and be loved. This is reality – this is present moment awareness.

> **Emotional Wisdom**
> Emotional knowledge can be learned. You are not stuck with what you were born with, or have been conditioned with to date. Emotional intelligence can be nurtured by applying emotional knowledge to conditioned habits.

Feeling emotions – Emotions are felt in the present, but are derived from emotional patterns from events in the present, past conditioning, and future predictions. An emotion is a sensation (feeling) linked to a thought. The sensation is in the present, but the thought (value, belief, expectation, assumption, memory or prediction) is most often about the past or future.

True feeling – Laurence (1990) says that true feeling expands your clarity and awareness.[1]

Values – Morality – right or wrong. The worth, desirability or utility of one's principles, standards, or judgement, of what is valuable or important in one's life.

Beliefs – Our perspective of the truth. The accepting of a principle, statement, system, or fact, as true.

Expectation – Your conditioned pattern of wants. Your view of what should happen based upon your values and beliefs. We often assume – adopt the attitude (see below) – that other people have expectations like our own.

Thoughts – One aspect of cognition – all the mental activities that enable us to know and make decisions (appraisals) about the world (our environment).

Attitudes/Assumptions – Your your settled mode of thinking. You can use emotions to improve thinking. Cognition can be disrupted by emotions – for example, when experiencing anger or fear – but emotions can prioritise the cognitive system to attend to what is important.

Mood – Your state of mind or feeling. For example, fits of melancholy or bad temper.

Rule – Principle to which an action or procedure should conform. A dominant custom or norm.

An open person – To be an open person is to be flowing and sensitive to the present. To live in the present, "…is to feel an emotion fully and completely, to experience it and then release it." Deepak Chopra (1993)[2] provides four steps to feel in the present:
1. Realise that hurt is the most basic negative feeling.
2. Be with your sensations.
3. Say what you feel to the person who caused your hurt.
4. Resolve your emotion and move on.

A closed person – Closed people hold onto emotional patterns that cloud current reality. For example, you may interpret someone as criticising or ignoring you, and respond with anger. Your response of anger often disguises deeper feelings in you, such

> **Emotional Wisdom**
>
> A closed person sees in others what he fails to see in himself.

as feeling; unloved, unworthy, rejected, disappointed, betrayed, fearful, or self-loathing.

Revisit chapter one for another look at "The Johari Window", for different views of self.

2. GET READY FOR EMOTION CONVERSION

Just as words are the mode of the rational mind, non-verbals are the mode of emotions. Non-verbals are emotions you express or have, that are triggered by impulses generated deep inside of your brain in the amygdala/thalamus/cortex interactions.

Impulses are formed from your fields of energy and information conditioned from childhood. Even verbal cues fed to you by your parents amount to over 25,000 hours of pure conditioning (Chopra, 1993, p. 52). You add to or change these fields, holding your attitudes, values, and assumptions, throughout your lives.

As you get older you develop convincing stories to justify your attitudes to life. This is the work of your rational mind. You become entrenched in your "point of view" (your interpretation of events), rather than rising to your "viewing point" (reality). When your attitudes and values are questioned, you feel personally affronted and threatened, and become sidetracked into validating preconceptions and past programming about how life *should* be (see **Cognitive distortions and your "shoulds"** in chapter three).

Emotion conversion is;

- Being ready to practise acceptance. Permitting events to unravel around you, reacting to them spontaneously and freely. Experiencing your emotions fully. Being ready to let go of childhood conditioning and emotional blocks.
- Recognising your "shoulds" and learning how to change your auto-responders using the 4-step cognitive framework. Enabling you to reframe your beliefs, values, assumptions, and expectations, to control your body's impulsive reactions to internal and external events.
- Developing and nurturing your emotionally intelligent abilities to use emotion to facilitate thought. For example, using anger to assist you in attending to problem-solving or happiness to change your viewpoint.
- Moving from anger to assertion, and fear to appreciation.

PAIN PERCEPTION AND AROUSAL

1. PAIN – A PERCEPT OF THE BODY AND MIND

Before we introduce you to the 4-step cognitive framework – the key to emotion conversion – we need to develop your understanding of pain perception, and how appraisal triggers arousal (emotional response) in your body.

9/11 and pain perception

Where were you, what did you feel, and what did you do when you first heard the news of the September 11, 2001 disaster in New York, USA? The October 12, 2002 bombing in Bali, Indonesia, or the train bombing in Madrid, Spain on March 11, 2004?

What did you feel over the next two to three days after each event? Did your body feel normal?

In chapter two we introduced the pain timeline. Appraisal arouses only two impulses – pain or pleasure. We all want to avoid pain and experience pleasure. Therefore, all the complicated emotional states in which we find ourselves are because we are unable to obey these basic impulses. Pleasure seems to be managed well by most people. In *Emotional Leadership* we focus on resolution of pain from negativity or emotional constipation – a major reason why people seek counselling.

Emotional Wisdom

Emotions are an affective experience with a mission. The mission of negative emotions (pain) is to lower self-esteem – the identity we create for ourselves.

Pain is any unpleasant sensory and emotional experience. Acute pain is a normal sensation triggered in the central nervous system (see page 129) to alert you to a possible injury. Chronic pain refers to discomfort relating to injury, disease or emotional distress. Chronic pain persists and may exist in the absence of any past physical injury or body damage. Examples of chronic pain include; arthritis pain, cancer pain, headache, lower back (coccyx) pain, and pain from damage to the central nervous system itself.

Although pain affects your body's responsiveness, its overall impact on you lies within. Your perceptions are crucial in pain management. Treatment for pain includes; medications, acupuncture, surgery, relaxation therapy, yoga, psychotherapy, and behaviour modification using your EAR-Identity.

Pain is communicated to others through language, posture, withdrawal, and abuse – physical, emotional, and sexual abuse. In an integrated model of the cognitive, affective, and physiological aspects of emotion, pain is manifested as negative emotion (accumulated stress) and can lead to nervous illness.

The physiological effects of accumulated stress felt in the body were described in chapter two – see **Effects of stress felt in the body**. These effects included;

1. A breakdown in the immune system.
2. An interruption to the autonomic nervous system.
3. A decrease in the level of the hormone serotonin in the brain.
4. Lowered self-esteem – which may lead to depression.

In the discussion on EAR-Identity in chapter three, we revealed;

The problem with creating emotional health is that there is a gap between event and response, where impulse happens (usually from the amygdala). It is in this space that meaning is formed through appraisal. It is in the gap that the trigger – the conditioned response – occurs and you experience the response in your body. For example, your first experience on a roller coaster may be exhilarating or terrifying. The memory will be stored as such, and will be recalled at any time the words roller coaster are mentioned.

Appraisal, through the operation of the thalamus, hypothalamus, and limbic system, is the trigger for emotional response. Appraisal is a source of autonomic (involuntary) arousal, as the emotional response is mediated by the autonomic nervous system.

2. THE AUTONOMIC NERVOUS SYSTEM (ANS)

Our central nervous system is comprised of two parts – voluntary and involuntary. We use our voluntary nerves to direct our muscles within our body to move, more or less, at will. The involuntary nervous system helps glands control the functioning of organs, such as; our heart, lungs, bowels, and digestion. The involuntary nerves consist of two types – sympathetic and parasympathetic. The sympathetic nervous system provides adrenalin. The parasympathetic nervous system has a moderating influence. It helps restore the balance, once the threat has passed.

When our bodies are in a peaceful state, the two branches of the ANS are in check. However, when there is a stressful response – anger, fear, sadness, happiness, disgust, or surprise – the sympathetic (fight, flight) branch dominates the parasympathetic (calming, restorative) branch, and we are aware of our organs functioning. We may feel a racing heart, clammy hands, a tightening in our abdomen, and an urge to use our bowels. Sympathetic nerves react this way by means of a chemical called adrenalin, which is released at the nerve-endings of the organs concerned. For any task, there is an optimum level of arousal at which performance will be most efficient. On the whole, moderate levels of arousal seem to act as positive reinforcers, and extreme as negative (Winefield & Peay, 1980, 1991).[3]

3. SENSITISATION

In discussing the commonest kind of nervous illness, the anxiety state – often referred to as nervous breakdown – Dr Claire Weekes, best selling author of *Peace from nervous suffering*, (1972, pp. 3-8), says

> **Emotional Wisdom**
>
> "The symptoms of so much nervous illness are no more than the symptoms of stress exaggerated by severe sensitisation." (Weekes 1972, p. 7)[4]

that the symptoms of sensitisation – a state in which nerves are conditioned to react to stress in an exaggerated way – are the symptoms of stress.

Normally when we're afraid, we accept our racing heart, rapid breathing – even the spasm of fear in our "middle" – because we know that when the cause of fear disappears, those reactions will also pass. Our feelings become calm because we change our mood. Changing our mood (attitude) is the only conscious control – other than medication – that we have over our involuntary nerves, and so, over our symptoms of stress.

Fear and its manifestation, anxiety, is a painful emotion caused by impending danger or an evil event. A state of alarm, dread of something, or anxiety (extreme worry) over life changes. Fear is pain perceived in the future. Fear arises from our thoughts – how we feel depends on how we think. Fear is a negative emotion felt as stress in the body.

The body manages well with an optimal level of stress. The adrenalin generated up to that level of stress is needed for flight or fight. When our thoughts focus on pain perceived in the future, the resulting negative emotions of anxiety and fear could increase stress beyond that optimal level. This causes the body to produce adrenalin in excess of what the body needs. The additional adrenalin produces physiological, cognitive, and emotional symptoms of a stress reaction. Higher levels of adrenalin in the body – from increased stress or negative emotion – will begin to affect the body's immune system, autonomic nervous system and serotonin level in the brain. This can lead to a person experiencing low self-esteem and/or nervous suffering.

In discussing the three pitfalls of nervous illness, Dr Weekes (1972, p.4) holds that, "Sensitisation is a state in which nerves are conditioned to react to stress in an exaggerated way; that is, they transport unusually intense feelings when under stress, at times with alarming swiftness." The symptoms of sensitisation are the same for stress, as nerves under stress always release the same chemicals, which act on the same body parts with the same results.

Dr Weekes (1972, pp. 7-8) writes on fear and anxiety;

The symptoms of so much nervous illness are no more that the symptoms of stress, exaggerated by severe sensitisation... Bewilderment and fear keep sensitisation alive. Bewilderment acts by placing a sensitised person constantly under the strain of asking, "What is wrong with me? Why am I like this?" The more he struggles to be the person he was, the more exasperation and tension he adds, and of course, the more stress.

While he feels, in his bewilderment, that he cannot direct his thoughts and actions adequately, he stands especially vulnerable to, and defenceless before, fear, which can overwhelm him before he has time to reason with it…The sensitised person puts himself in a cycle of fear-adrenalin-fear. In other words, his fear of the state he is in (that is, fear of the way he feels) produces the adrenalin and other stress hormones, which continue to excite his nerves to produce the very symptoms he fears. The fear-adrenalin-fear cycle is called an anxiety state.

People will often fear the way they feel when the "feeling" is a new experience. Many of the emotional, cognitive and physical symptoms will be unfamiliar. This causes a person to feel "out of control", or even fearful that their body is showing signs of an undiagnosed medical condition. Keep in mind that fear is pain perceived in the future. Thoughts that give rise to fear or anxiety can be changed. Changing the way we think and our mood (attitude), assisted by awareness or counselling, is the only conscious control – other than medication – over our symptoms of stress arising from fear.

Four very common signs and symptoms of a stress reaction are a heavy chest, nausea, a racing heart, and headaches. For a detailed list of signs and symptoms of a stress reaction see chapter two, Table 2.1.

Emotional Leadership Practice – Individual Exercise
ELP 4.1   Stress and anxiety checklist

Ask yourself the following questions;

1. Do you believe that your worry is excessively severe   Yes   No
    considering your problems?
2. Has your worry persisted for more than six months?   Yes   No
3. Does your worry relate to at least two everyday
    events or problems of life?   Yes   No
4. Do you worry for more than half of every day?
5. Does your inner voice (negative thoughts) intrude   Yes   No
    more than usual? Such as, "When will I ever be
    better?" And are the negative thoughts more difficult   Yes   No
    to drive out than usual?

If you answered yes to all of the above questions, then you may consider looking for help in learning how to handle stress from your doctor, psychologist, or counsellor. If you are prone to stress, do not suffer alone – seek professional advice.

 Emotional Leadership Practice
ELP 4.2   Fear and anxiety

Read again the section on sensitisation (page 129). Are you prone to excessive worry? Review the common signs and symptoms of a stress reaction in chapter two, Table 2.1. Note any that you have experienced yourself.

_____

_____

_____

One of the aims of this book is to help you affirm a life of EASE by assisting you in getting rid of negativity, by removing your pain through cognitive reframing, and changing the events (attitudes) that have control over your involuntary nerves and symptoms of stress – triggered by your amygdala/thalamus/neocortex interaction. Which are then mediated in your body through your autonomic nervous system.

5. ANGER AND FEAR-BASED REACTIVITY VERSUS ASSERTION AND APPRECIATION-BASED PRO-ACTIVITY

The drama of life is played out as states of emotion – either pain (negative emotion) or pleasure (positive emotion). Anger and fear-based reactivity versus assertion and appreciation-based pro-activity. Two emotion states – anger and fear – dominate either side of the pain timeline. These are discussed further on, as examples of why you need to convert these negative emotions into feelings of well-being.

In the drama of life, anger and fear based reactivity is;

Automatic – biological or conditioned responses.
Negative – a subtraction of energy.

Limited to:
- Fighting – Explaining and complaining, physically engaging your perceived arouser. Retaining a need for vindication.
- Fleeing – Taking drugs and/or having affairs. Not resolving issues.
- Freezing – Restricting displays of emotion and spiritual energy.

In the drama of life, assertion and appreciation based pro-activity;

Requires conscious no-lose decision-making.
Letting go of the outcome and seeing each choice as an opportunity to learn (see chapter seven).
Is *positive* – the addition of energy.

Is open to:
- Creativity – Recognising and optimising your potential.
- Approach (versus avoidance) – Willing to self-disclose and receive feedback, and take risks with emotions.
- Emotional growth – Developing self-awareness. Accepting change. Building and valuing special relationships.

FROM ANGER TO ASSERTION

1. THE FUNCTION OF ANGER

A lot is written about anger. Why is that?

Anger is more commonly displayed in reactive people. Whilst sensitive people can also express anger, they are unlikely to do so unless provoked strongly, as any form of arousal causes sensitive people additional stress – see chapter two for the discussion on sensitive versus reactive people.

> **Emotional Wisdom**
>
> The sole function of anger is to stop stress, to stop pain.

Anger is a way of releasing or blocking emotional awareness and projecting onto the other party one's anxiety, guilt, muscle tension, frustration – a perceived threat to physical well-being. Typically, a person will have learned that anger meets their need, from the behaviour of a parent or significant other, who treated them with anger to get what they wanted. Anger is a way of releasing pain for reactive people. Sensitive people block anger, as its expression causes further arousal or stress.

Anger used intentionally to hurt another actually gives your power away. Anger is only used effectively when it does not offend the other person directly. Seeking control over others through anger is a waste of energy.

> **Emotional Wisdom**
>
> No one makes you angry. Your anger arousal comes from within you – from your perception of events.

Anger is perhaps the most often recurring emotion, felt and displayed by many people. In the cycle of emotions (see chapter two – **Pain is felt in the present**), anger is pain in the past remembered. When the thought that is attached to your feeling is memory of a hurt, the emotion generated is anger. Anger displayed and anger withheld is a major cause of breakdown in relationships.

2. MOVING TO ASSERTION

Anger can be a natural, healthy emotion that allows us to be assertive. It can be a form of communication where an individual expresses his own thoughts, feelings and beliefs, honestly and directly, and with regard to the thoughts, feelings and beliefs, of the person to whom he is talking.

Anger talk: "Don't speak like that, you make me angry."
Assertive talk: "When you speak like that I feel angry."

Anger is present in assertion for a brief time, while we are galvanised to take any appropriate action. However, whenever we are blocked from something we want, a part of our energy goes into feeling anger. This is destructive anger and comes from our past experiences and attitudes towards life. Most of us are afraid of our anger. We have been conditioned as children to suppress angry thoughts.

"If you haven't got anything nice to say, don't say anything at all."

Anger is often disguised behind an outwardly agreeable manner, in order to hide the more complicated emotions of feeling unloved, unworthy or powerless. Owning your anger is about responsibility. Being unassertive/submissive puts your own needs on the shelf for other people.

So-called "righteous" anger is not the same as being assertive. It is unjustifiable and should not be used to intimidate others. In most cases, being angry is not an appropriate response. But it represents our negative conditioning and the prejudices that are triggered – that is, "pushing the wrong buttons".

In western European culture men are prone to respond with anger. Acting tough is seen as a means of retaining control, avoiding the vulnerability of intimacy and trust – "big boys don't cry". Women in western European culture will often cry when they are actually angry. Instead of experiencing their anger, they withdraw to cry on their own – leaving hurts unresolved.

Typically, a woman's tears result in the man having an emotional response – he may either feel compassion or as though he is being manipulated. Each response to a woman's tears will manifest in a different reaction from a man.

Assertion consists of standing up for your rights, and expressing your thoughts, feelings and beliefs, in direct, honest and appropriate ways, that respect the rights and feelings of others (Montgomery and Evans, 1984).[5]

> **Emotional Wisdom**
>
> You need to learn to catch your anger before it becomes entrenched as the natural response or reaction to an event or stimulus. Your anger at an external event, or the actions of someone else, teaches you about yourself.

Montgomery and Evans (1984, pp. 123-126) provide a six-step strategy for assertion. We summarise their effective strategy as follows;

1. Listen to the other person. You can listen to someone else's point of view without surrendering your own.
2. Think about the situation. Ask yourself, "Is it necessary to be angry?", tell yourself, "I don't have to rush in, I'll take my time."

3. Work out how you see the situation. Consider the rights of all the people involved and why you feel your rights are threatened.

4. Assert yourself. Enough thinking – now do it!

5. Use helpful self-talk. If the other person starts to get upset or angry, say to yourself, "Stay calm. I don't have to get upset. If she wants to that's her problem."

6. Review the situation afterwards. Remember that success means only to stay assertive – not change the other person's behaviour.

> **Emotional Wisdom**
>
> No one makes you angry. Your anger arousal comes from within you. From your perception of events. You see in others what you fail to see in yourself.

The essential point about assertion is to respect the feelings and rights of others. An angry person gives his or her power away, by not showing respect for another individual. Raging is an inappropriate use of anger.

CASE STUDY 4.1 – RAGE AGAINST THE MACHINE – KIDS IN CRISIS

Sally came to counselling desperate for help with her seven-year-old son Max who experienced frequent rages, "It's as though he's possessed", she explained. At unpredictable times Max would lose control, become hysterical and shout foul language at siblings, parents or even teachers. He also threatened to harm himself because he hated his life. Following each rage, Max would sob with remorse and seek comfort. Max realised his behaviour was inappropriate but was unable to control himself. Sally felt his behaviour was completely out of character.

Karen's Assessment: Max was a very sensitive boy, meaning that he felt his feelings with intensity. When Max felt a negative emotion he felt it strongly and if unable to resolve it or articulate it, the pain accumulated and resulted in intermittent rage – his reaction to stress. Rage is common in teenagers and is usually a result of the intense emotions and frustrations experienced during puberty.

Work done in Counselling: Karen urged Sally to not respond emotionally to Max but to detach herself and acknowledge his painful feelings. For example, "Max, you must be really angry that I'm asking you to help me when you want to watch TV". If Sally gets it right Max will probably agree and calm down, as he now feels understood – instead of annoyed. Karen explained that Max would yell how unhappy he is with his life when he feels completely isolated. When misunderstood by everyone around him it feels as if no one can comprehend the pain he is experiencing.

Outcome: Sally reported immediate changes in Max's frequency of outbursts. She watched for signs of agitation, and then acknowledged Max's feelings. In most instances, this diffused the situation. Sally shared this strategy with her husband and Max's teacher, and they all reported an improvement.

Moving forward: Parents often feel exasperated or bewildered when their child suddenly starts exhibiting anger or rage. They question what – as parents – they're doing wrong. Raging behaviour is usually a result of the child feeling a negative emotion – leading to stress – about a situation in their life that they are unable to analyse or articulate. The pain of the emotion is experienced with the outburst of behaviour. Children report that they are actually quite scared when they rage, as they feel out of control and the anger seems bigger than them. Parents can assist by thinking about what the child may be feeling and validating that feeling. As well as helping the child to feel better, they'll also learn an emotional language which will lead to improved communication.

Emotional Leadership Practice

ELP 4.3   Rage Against The Machine – Kids in crisis

Read case study 4.1. Parents often feel exasperated or bewildered when their child starts exhibiting anger or rage. In this instance, Karen gives some advice for moving forward. Note any point of interest.

3. RATIONALE FOR ASSERTION

Assertion is a form of communication where an individual expresses his or her thoughts, feelings and beliefs, honestly and directly, taking into consideration to the thoughts, feelings and beliefs, of the person to whom he or she is talking. Assertion theory is based on the premise that every individual possesses certain basic rights. Using assertion skills allows an individual experiencing a conflict situation to achieve a workable compromise – without sacrificing their self-respect or integrity. It allows them to say "no" with minimal feelings of guilt, anger and anxiety.

Table 4.1 sets out reasons why people are aggressive, submissive, and assertive, with the risks and costs associated with each style of behaviour.

Table 4.1

REASONS WHY PEOPLE ARE AGGRESSIVE	RISKS/COSTS
▪ Afraid they won't get what they want. ▪ Lack of self-confidence. ▪ It's succeeded in getting them what they want in the past. ▪ To gain attention. ▪ To demonstrate power. ▪ To release anger often set-up from unreal expectations. ▪ To manipulate others.	▪ Conflicts in relationships because others feel threatened. ▪ Loss of self-respect. ▪ Lack of respect for others. ▪ Being disliked. ▪ Increased stress. ▪ Possible violence. ▪ Often produces opposite of desired result.

REASONS WHY PEOPLE ARE SUBMISSIVE	RISKS/COSTS
▪ Fear of losing the approval of others. ▪ Fear of other people's reactions. ▪ May be seen as polite – the appropriate response. ▪ To avoid conflicts. ▪ To manipulate others.	▪ Loss of self-esteem. ▪ Feelings of hurt, anger and frustration. ▪ Encourage others in relationships to take control. ▪ Pent-up feelings may erupt later in an aggressive outburst.

REASONS WHY PEOPLE ARE ASSERTIVE	RISKS/COSTS
▪ Feel good about themselves and others. ▪ Mutual respect. ▪ Helps achieve goals as needs may be met. ▪ Minimises hurting others. ▪ Increases self-confidence. ▪ Feel in control. ▪ Honest to yourself and others.	▪ Not being liked by others for expressing your own feelings. ▪ Being labelled pushy. ▪ Possibility of changes in relationships.

Table 4.2 sets out aggressive, submissive, and assertive behaviours, with the messages the behaviours convey about themselves to others. The phrase "I'm OK, You're OK" is from the book of the same name by Thomas Harris (1967, 1995)[6].

Table 4.2 is to assist readers in identifying behaviours that they may currently be using as influencing styles, and recognise their impact on others. Individuals can then choose to use their emotion to facilitate thoughts that will generate right choices for the behaviour they want to be.

Table 4.2

AGGRESSIVE BEHAVIOURS	SUBMISSIVE BEHAVIOURS	ASSERTIVE BEHAVIOURS
▪ Stands up for own rights and ignores rights of others. ▪ Dominates and, in some cases, humiliates others. ▪ Does not listen to others. ▪ Makes decisions that do not consider others' rights.	▪ Ignores own rights and allows others to infringe own rights. ▪ Does not state own needs, ideas, or feelings. ▪ Is emotionally dishonest – actions and words are not in accord with feelings, leading to suppressed anger and resentment.	▪ Stands up for own rights and recognises rights of others. ▪ Expresses needs, ideas, and feelings. ▪ Relates confidently to others.
MESSAGES I'm OK, You're Not OK	**MESSAGES I'm Not OK You're OK**	**MESSAGES I'm OK You're OK**
▪ I think this – you're stupid for thinking differently. ▪ I feel this – your feelings don't matter. ▪ This is the situation. I don't care how you see it.	▪ Your thoughts are important – mine are not. ▪ Your feelings matter, mine don't. ▪ It's how you see the situation that counts.	▪ This is what I think. ▪ This is what I feel. ▪ This is how I see the situation. ▪ I would like to hear what you think and feel and perhaps we can both be happy.

Emotional Leadership Practice

ELP 4.4   Rationale for assertion

After reading section three, **Rationale for assertion**, review reasons why people are aggressive, submissive or assertive. Examine the behaviours exhibited and the messages given out by these traits.

4. PRACTISING ASSERTIVE BEHAVIOUR

Situation 1:   A person whom you don't particularly like asks you for a lift home. You were actually looking forward to some time alone to think something over.

Aggressive response
Self-talk:

"She always asks me for a lift home. I'm fed up with it. I want to be alone today. I'm not putting myself out for her. I don't like her anyway – having to put up with her all day at work is bad enough!"

Non-verbal behaviour:

Clenches fists, red in the face, speaks brusquely.

Verbal behaviour:

"No I can't give you a lift. Why don't you find someone else?"

Submissive response
Self-talk:

"There goes my time alone to think. I find her a real bore but I guess I had better give her a lift, otherwise she'll think I'm mean. I'm a real sucker."

Non-verbal behaviour:

Does not look at the other person, speaks in a muffled, uncertain tone of voice.

Verbal behaviour:

"Oh well, I suppose I could manage to give you a lift."

Assertive response
Self-talk:

"I don't find her particularly good company. Besides, I wanted to think about something by myself. I'll feel uncomfortable doing it, but I can calmly refuse her request."

Non-verbal behaviour:

Looks directly at the other person, using a calm but firm voice.

Verbal behaviour:

"I'm sorry, but I'm afraid I can't give you a lift home tonight."

 Emotional Leadership Practice

ELP 4.5   Practising assertive behaviour

Read and discuss the situation below and formulate responses, writing them on the sheet provided.

Situation 2:   Telling your superior that you can't stay back to work overtime.

Aggressive response
Self-talk:

Non-verbal behaviour:

Verbal behaviour:

Submissive response
Self-talk:

Non-verbal behaviour:

Verbal behaviour:

Assertive response
Self-talk:

Non-verbal behaviour:

Verbal behaviour:

FROM FEAR TO APPRECIATION

1. WHAT IS FEAR?

What is fear and anxiety – its physiological manifestation?

The basic emotion of fear described by Ekman[7] refers to a category of feeling words such as; scared, afraid, anxious, frightened, harassed, panicky, terrified, alarmed, worry, and dread. Fear is felt as a pain in the body – a body sensation. It can "hang around" for a very long time as anxiety. Fear is fed by self-pity – a desire for "victimhood".

A 35-year-old woman is going to hospital for a CAT scan. The doctor suspects a brain tumour. But nobody has told her exactly what kind of scan will be conducted. She is supposed to take medication and not eat anything before the test. She has heard rumours about what these scans are like, but she doesn't really know what to expect. Imagine yourself in this woman's position. Write down what you are feeling.

2. DEALING WITH FEAR PHYSICALLY

The body deals with fear in two ways;

Level 1 –   Fear in the present is felt as pain in the body – a feeling of scare (being scared).

For example: "I'll never be able to cross this busy road."

Level 2 –   Fear in the future is perceived as anxiety.

For example: "What if I get knocked over? I'll become disabled and won't be able to provide for my children?"

When people feel fear – that is, they are frightened or scared – it is usually because they are confronted with stressful situations that will bring change to their lives. There are several sorts of stressors.

Firstly, there are those short-lived unpleasant traumatic events – such as getting fired from a job, or being told of a new medical diagnosis – which confront people with a change in their life that requires them to adapt. Sudden and unpleasant life events appear to be particularly important in triggering the onset of certain psychiatric illnesses.

For example, the death of a relative may trigger depression or addictions that lead to obsessions. On the other hand, long-standing life difficulties seem to be important in maintaining disability and suffering in "victimhood".

Secondly, there are stressors that exert their effects in longer-lasting ways – the strain on a mother caring for a disabled child, or those living with a violent, alcoholic spouse. The type of coping required to endure these sorts of difficulties is different from the impact of a sudden traumatic event.

Thirdly, there are events such as getting married, having a baby, or sitting an exam, that generate fear because they lead to change in an individual's life – requiring an adjustment.

The ways in which different people react to these stressors (stressful events) varies widely. Each stressor has a different effect on different people – depending on whether you are a sensitive or reactive person.

3. FEAR AND THE SENSITIVE OR REACTIVE PERSON

A **sensitive** person interprets their whole world through feelings and will hold onto fear, leading to depression. When fear is not faced or dealt with by the sensitive person in the present, they will become unduly anxious and may develop a phobia toward an event. For example, a fear of flying may lead to a person being unable to accomplish their responsibilities in travelling abroad, leading to extreme anxiety about losing their job.

Sensitive people often deal ineffectively with fear. They anticipate pain in the future as they imagine the recurrence of an event that has previously caused them emotional distress. They become immobilised, often requiring anti-anxiety medication and antidepressants. Fear can create a state of emotional paralysis or immobility in a sensitive person.

A **reactive** person interprets their world through events and activities, and will usually experience fear almost immediately through displays of brief and extreme outbursts of behaviour. They will use facial expressions, acts of bravado, and physical actions such as facing up to their adversary, or precipitating an event. They are motivated to be in control of the situation through choice, energy, and action. For a reactive person fear is often irrelevant.

Reactive people need to understand that not everyone is able to deal quickly and effectively with fear. Comments such as, "Oh, don't be so silly. It's not going to hurt" or, "Come on, you'll get over it. Life goes on." don't usually allay the fears of a sensitive person. On the contrary, the sensitive person will feel more of an arousal over the perception that they are silly for feeling fearful.

4. FEAR AND TRAUMATIC EVENTS (CRITICAL INCIDENTS)

Extreme traumatic events such as an earthquake, rape or violent assault, may cause a psychiatric problem called post-traumatic stress disorder. After such events, the traumatic experience plays on a person's mind for many hours of the day. The person is preoccupied and may even recur the experience in nightmares – resulting in panic attacks, hyperventilation (rapid breathing), and heavy sweating.

Imagine you have experienced a traumatic event (critical incident), an injury, loss of a loved one or property, or a serious threat – any overwhelming emotional experience. Even though the event has passed, you may now be experiencing, or may experience later, some strong emotional or physical reactions. It is very common, in fact quite normal, for people to experience emotional aftershocks when they have experienced a horrible event.

Sometimes the emotional aftershock (stress reactions) appears immediately following the traumatic event. Sometimes it may appear a few hours or a few days later. And in some cases, weeks or months may pass before the stress reactions appear.

The signs and symptoms of a stress reaction may last a few days, a few weeks, a few months or occasionally longer, depending on the severity of the traumatic event. With understanding, and the support of loved ones or significant others, the stress reactions usually pass more quickly. Occasionally the traumatic event is so painful that professional assistance from a counsellor may be necessary. This does not imply craziness or weakness. It simply indicates that the particular traumatic event was just too powerful for the person to manage alone. For some very common signs and symptoms of a stress reaction see Table 2.1 in chapter two. Table 4.1 provides some helpful hints for recovery from a traumatic event.

Table 4.1. Helpful hints for recovery from a traumatic event

FOR YOURSELF	FOR FAMILY MEMBERS AND FRIENDS
▪ Try to rest more. ▪ Contact friends. ▪ Have someone stay with you for a few hours, a day or so, or even longer. ▪ Recurring thoughts, dreams or flashbacks are normal – don't try to fight them – they'll decrease over time and become less painful. ▪ Organise a daily routine. ▪ Eat well-balanced and regular meals – even when you don't feel like it. ▪ Try to sustain a reasonable level of activity. ▪ Fight against boredom. ▪ Physical activity is often helpful. ▪ Re-establish a normal schedule as soon as possible. ▪ Express your feelings as they arise. ▪ Talk to people who love and care about you. ▪ Find a good counsellor if feelings become prolonged or too intense.	▪ Listen carefully. ▪ Spend time with the traumatised person. ▪ Offer your assistance and a listening ear, even if they have not asked for help. ▪ Reassure them that they are safe. ▪ Help them with everyday tasks such as cleaning, cooking and caring for their family. ▪ Give the person some private time. ▪ Don't take their anger or other feelings personally. ▪ Don't tell them that they are "lucky it wasn't worse" – those statements do not console traumatised people. Instead, tell them that you are sorry such an event has occurred and you want to understand and assist them.

If the symptoms described above are severe, or if they last longer than six weeks, the person may need professional counselling.

Emotional Leadership Practice
ELP 4.6   Traumatic event (critical incident)

Refer to the section Fear and Traumatic Events on page 147. Have you experienced trauma? What were the physical, cognitive, and emotional signs and symptoms? Record your notes below.

_____

_____

_____

_____

5. UNDERSTANDING FEAR AND ANXIETY

There are two central issues involved in coping with fear and anxiety.

1. Ability to identify stressors

One of the major reasons people do not cope with stressful events is because they are unable to identify the stressor, or acknowledge the effect that it is having on their lives.

For example, a woman who suffers continual verbal abuse from her male partner may not recognise that this is not normal behaviour. She will not understand that the physiological changes to her body are due to stress, caused her by that abnormal behaviour. It is only when the nature of the problem is clearly defined that a person can set about solving the problem. Here is where a counsellor, relative, or friend can assist in defining the nature of the problem the individual is confronting.

2. Understanding the physical discomfort from anxiety

The physical discomfort of anxiety, the sensations of a racing chest and pounding heart, or feeling sick, can be so strong that a person stays focused on the issues, or event that caused the fear. This results in the person retaining their "bad feeling", the body continues to produce adrenalin and anxiety escalates.

For example, imagine being with a friend who is returning a purchased product that has broken, and he is complaining to the customer service staff. Voices are raised as your friend becomes angry, and the service staff says it is not their responsibility. You become embarrassed (aroused) and want to disappear (flight response).

This state of panic is described by Dr Claire Weekes (1972, p. 24) as "First Fear".

> Each of us experiences *first* fear from time-to-time. It is the fear that comes almost as a reflex in response to danger.

Your heart is pounding, your chest is racing, your head swims with anxiety – now recognised as arousal or *first* fear. Almost immediately you want to run away. This is "Second Fear".

> Recognising *second* fear is easier when we realise it can be prefixed by "Oh, my goodness!" and "What if …?" (Weekes 1972, p. 24)

You want to run away because the "What if's …" kick-in almost immediately, "What if my friend loses his cool? What if the situation gets worse and someone is offended? What if other people see us arguing?" The sensitive person withdraws instinctively for some time when he or she feels embarrassed by someone (a perception).

Anti-anxiety medication (herbal or prescribed) can help to reduce the discomfort of the physical symptoms of stress and anxiety. Alternatively, it can be very helpful to use specific techniques such as cognitive reframing, relaxation exercises or yoga, to contain the symptoms of fear and anxiety as a preference to relying on medication.

6. MOVING TO APPRECIATION

Phobias occur when a person has a "fear of the fear", or a fear of the anxiety that has been experienced on a previous occasion. For example, the person suffering from agoraphobia – phobia of an outside place – fears leaving home. This is because on some past occasion they have experienced an anxiety reaction or

> **Emotional Wisdom**
>
> The real issue is not fear itself, but how we hold onto fear. Feelings of fear surging through us (adrenalin surges) are of little consequence unless we hold onto fear and feed it.

panic attack in a certain place – perhaps in the supermarket, or whilst driving. The fear of this nasty sensation occurring again creates a phobia, and the person remains at home *in order to prevent* the possibility of a recurrence.

Fear and anxiety produces a negative feeling. Appreciation produces a warm positive feeling. We appreciate other people, or what they do for us, if we get a good feeling from them. For example, if in the presence of her partner, Sharon feels fearful, anxious, or on "egg shells", then she perceives that her partner is "making her feel bad". In Sharon's old paradigm this translates to resentment that he is not behaving differently so that she "feels better". She will perceive this as, "He doesn't care about my feelings" – the root of so many marriage problems.

In the new paradigm, Sharon will realise that her partner is not "making her feel" anything – she is. Her own appraisal, her unmet expectation, and fears of a relationship going bad resulted in her "feeling" that her partner didn't care about her. Often the partner is totally unaware of all anxieties being felt by their partner.

Your basic emotional need is to feel loved. To feel that you are loved, and that others need and accept your love. When you look outside of yourself to have your needs met by others, you become a victim of another person's level of emotional awareness and response to you. To be emotionally unaware and fear the actions of others or the problems in life is to be a victim. As a victim you are validating perceptions and past programming that limit you.

Choose to regain your power over your perceptions of the world, and responses toward you by other people. Choose assertion over anger and appreciation over fear. Choose to generate happiness and be open to new opportunities.

The writer Susan Jeffers (1987)[8] says, "Feel the fear and do it anyway."

Claire Weekes (1972, p.107) argues, "There is only one way out of our fears and that is through them."

A cognitive-behavioural approach to dealing with anger and fear is the 4-Step Cognitive Framework, a description of which follows. This approach is aimed at relieving specific symptoms you experience as anger and fear, associated with certain thoughts and events that produce negative arousal.

7. PRACTISING APPRECIATIVE BEHAVIOUR

Situation 1: You arrive at the airport to meet a friend.

Fearful response
Self-talk:
"I hate being here. I feel crowded and I want to escape. I wish that I had not said that I would come to meet her. I was so stupid."

Non-verbal behaviour:
Flushes, heart starts to pound, stammered speech, chest races, eyes dart everywhere, breathe rapidly.

Verbal behaviour:
"I'm quite disoriented. I don't know where I'm meant to be, and I'm late for my friend. Can you tell me where the plane from Sydney is coming in?"

Appreciative response
Self-talk:

"I love airports. This is a huge building with plenty of room for everyone. I'm looking forward to seeing my friend. She will be thrilled to see me waiting here for her. Even if I'm lost and a bit late, she'll wait patiently – she knows I'm coming."

Non-verbal behaviour:

Slightly anxious feeling in stomach, slight clammy feeling of hands, can focus on the Arrival Board and read the information, deeply and slow breathing.

Verbal behaviour:

"Excuse me, can you direct me to Gate 9 please."

 Emotional Leadership Practice

ELP 4.7   Practising appreciative behaviour

Read and discuss the situation below and formulate responses.

Situation 2:   You have to prepare and give a presentation at work.

Fearful response
Self-talk:

_____

_____

Non-verbal behaviour:

_____

_____

Verbal behaviour:

Appreciative response

Self-talk:

Non-verbal behaviour:

Verbal behaviour:

4-STEP COGNITIVE FRAMEWORK

1. THE KEY TO EMOTION CONVERSION

The 4-step Cognitive Framework is the key to emotion conversion and a life of EASE. It is primarily an exercise that, once learned and practised, will become automatic for you. The process is a psychological technique to reframe negative thinking through cognitive-affect-behavioural learning.

The reframed neurons in your cortex, standing watch over your pathways for information en route to the thalamus and limbic system, when called upon in the future to act as triggers for arousal, will mediate positive emotion leading to a reduction of adrenalin in the body. Thus restoring the balance between the sympathetic (fight/flight) and parasympathetic (calming/restorative) branches of the autonomic nervous system (ANS).

As information from your senses is filtered through the newly formed amygdala/thalamus/cortex interaction, the reframed neurons in your cortex moderate impulses toward negative behaviour, favouring positive responses that affirm you. This interaction generates positive emotion that leads to raised self-confidence and self-esteem.

2. THE 4-STEP COGNITIVE FRAMEWORK

Step 1 – Notice your feelings.
- Close your eyes and take some deep breaths.
- Relax your body.
- Notice where you feel depressed in your body.

Step 2 – Notice the situation.
- Where are you?
- Who are you with?
- What's happening to you?

Step 3 – Automatic negative thoughts – what are you thinking?
- Listen to the thoughts that correspond with the feeling in that depressed part of your body.
- Notice everything that you are saying to yourself.
- Try to remember how the feeling began.
  3a. **Distortions in thinking**
  FOR – List facts (evidence) **supporting** the negative thoughts?
  3b. **Challenging the distortions**
  AGAINST – List facts (evidence) **negating** the negative thoughts?

Step 4 – Focus on thoughts that are more helpful, that is, facts listed in Step 3b. Convert the facts in Step 3b to affirmations.

Emotional Wisdom

The 4-Step Cognitive Framework

To begin the 4-Step Cognitive Framework, think of a situation when you experienced a high intensity emotion. The four steps are to write down (1) your feeling, (2) the situation, and (3) your automatic negative thoughts – firstly facts **supporting** and then facts **negating** the negative thoughts, and (4) focus on thoughts more helpful. These become your affirmations.

EXAMPLE of the 4-Step Cognitive Framework

1. Notice your feeling.

   "I'm feeling anxious. I feel sick in my stomach."

2. Notice the situation. Where are you? Who are you with? What's happening to you?

   It's 3am and my husband hasn't come home. I'm alone and becoming increasingly alarmed. "I think he is having an affair."

3. Automatic negative thoughts – what are you thinking? Listen to the thoughts that go with the feeling in that part of your body. Notice everything that you are saying to yourself. Try to remember how the feeling began.

a. **For** – List facts (evidence) **supporting** the negative thoughts.

I'm hopeless. I'm always crying when I talk over issues.

I'm not as qualified as other women.

He isn't interested in talking to me, that's why he is out so late.

I'm so boring and never have anything intelligent to say.

I'm not a good cook, so he goes out to eat three nights a week. That's probably when he met her.

b. **Against** – List facts (evidence) **negating** the negative thoughts.

I'm a sensitive person and I get really emotional.

It's OK to cry, especially when I feel hurt.

I'm a confident and experienced accountant.

I feel that I have something to offer – I maintain a peaceful and harmonious home life.

I hold strong opinions about …

I love and trust my husband. We have built a strong marriage.

I know my husband has strong values about commitment and family.

4. Focus on thoughts that are more helpful in 3b. Convert the facts in Step 3b to affirmations.

 Emotional Leadership Practice

ELP 4.8   Practising the 4-Step Cognitive Framework

Think of a situation when you experienced a high intensity emotion. Complete the worksheet by writing down (1) your feeling, (2) the situation, and (3) your automatic negative thoughts. Next write down facts supporting and facts negating the negative thoughts, (4) focus on thoughts more helpful.

1. Notice your feeling

_____

_____

_____

2. Notice the situation. Where are you? Who are you with? What's happening to you?

_____

_____

_____

_____

_____

_____

3. Automatic negative thoughts – what are you thinking? Listen to the thoughts that go with the feeling in that part of your body. Notice everything that you are saying to yourself. Try to remember how the feeling began.

   a.   For – List facts (evidence) **supporting** the negative thoughts.

_____

_____

_____

_____

_____

b.   Against – List facts (evidence) **negating** the negative thoughts.

_____
_____
_____
_____
_____
_____

4. Focus on thoughts that are more helpful. Convert the facts in Step 3b into affirmations about you.

_____
_____
_____
_____
_____
_____

3. SELF-CONCEPT INVENTORY

The self-concept inventory (McKay & Fanning, 1992, 2000)[9] assists you to learn to perceive accurately your balance of strengths and weaknesses – your current identity. The 4-Step Cognitive Framework will assist you to reframe aspects of your inventory (your identity). In chapter five you will transform aspects of your self-concept inventory into affirmations, giving you the power to behave as you really want to be.

Emotional Leadership Practice

ELP 4.9   Self-concept inventory

Write down words or phrases that describe you under the following headings. Hold onto them until you have read all of chapter five.

1. *Physical appearance.* Include descriptions of your height, weight, facial appearance, quality of skin, hair, style of dress, as well as descriptions of specific body areas such as your neck, chest, waist and legs.
2. *How you relate to others.* Include descriptions of your strengths and weaknesses in intimate relationships and in relationships with friends, family, and co-workers, as well as how you relate to strangers in social situations.
3. *Personality.* Describe your positive and negative personality traits.
4. *How other people see you.* Describe the strengths and weaknesses that your friends and family see.
5. *Performance on the job.* Include descriptions of how you handle the major tasks at work.
6. *Performance of the daily tasks of life.* Descriptions could be included in areas such as hygiene, health, maintenance of your living environment, food preparation, caring for your children, and any other ways you take care of personal or family needs.
7. *Mental functioning.* Include here an assessment of how well you reason and solve problems, your capacity for learning and creativity, your general fund of knowledge, your areas of special knowledge, wisdom you have acquired, insight, and so on.

1. Physical appearance.
   (For example, likes jeans and t-shirts)

2. How you relate to others.
   (For example, good listener)

3. Personality.
   (For example, love to be busy)

4. How other people see you.
   (For example, forgetful)

5. Performance on the job.
   (For example, knowledgeable in field)

6. Performance of the daily tasks of life.
   (For example, lousy housekeeper)

7. Mental functioning.

   (For example, very creative)

Summary

Emotional knowledge can be taught. An **open** person is flowing, open, and sensitive to the present. A **closed** person holds onto emotional patterns that cloud current reality.

Emotion conversion is being ready to practice acceptance, recognising your "shoulds" and learning how to change them. As well as, developing your emotionally intelligent abilities to use emotion to facilitate thought.

Pain is any unpleasant sensory and emotional experience. It is mediated through the body by the autonomic nervous system. The pain of anger and fear can be brought under control through applying the 4-Step Cognitive Framework. This cognitive-behavioural technique will lead to reduced adrenalin in the body, thus restoring the balance between the sympathetic (fight/flight) and parasympathetic (calming/restorative) branches of the autonomic nervous system (ANS).

The 4-Step Cognitive Framework is the key to emotion conversion, the key to your new identity to **affirm** your life of EASE.

EMOTIONAL LEADERSHIP CHECKLIST

Use this emotional leadership checklist to see if you are ready to practise emotional freedom. Move from anger to assertion and fear to appreciation, and use emotion to facilitate thought.

- Do I know what emotion conversion is?
- Do I really understand the 4-Step Cognitive Framework?
- Can I use my emotions to facilitate thought?

EMOTIONAL LEADERSHIP POINT 1:
Do I know what emotion conversion is?

☐ The practice of acceptance, permitting events to unravel around you, reacting to them with emotional wisdom.

Appraisal (perception) is a source of autonomic (involuntary) arousal. Appraisal triggers impulses laid deep inside of you, that generate emotions such as anger and fear-based anxiety.

When you are appraising events from emotional freedom your autonomic impulses will be positive and life enhancing.

☐ Changing your mood and thereby your triggers through cognitive reframing.

Getting rid of your "shoulds" using the 4-Step Cognitive Framework to reframe your thoughts, memory, beliefs, values, expectations, and preconditions that control your body's impulsive reaction to internal and external events.

Changing to a positive mood (attitude) through cognitive reframing is the only conscious control you have – other than medication – over the sympathetic branch of your autonomic nervous system.

☐ **Moving from anger to assertion (reactive person).**

Anger used to intentionally hurt another gives away your power. Anger can be a natural healthy emotion that allows you to be assertive. "Righteous" anger is not the same as being assertive.

Assertion respects the rights and feelings of the other person.

☐ **Moving from fear to appreciation (sensitive person).**

Learn to recognise the state of panic that is *first* and *second* fear and use specific techniques such as cognitive reframing, relaxation exercises or yoga, to contain the symptoms of fear and anxiety as a preference to relying on medication.

Appreciation of life's goodness, emotional freedom, friends, family, and workmates empowers you to overcome fear.

EMOTIONAL LEADERSHIP POINT 2:
Do I really understand the 4-Step Cognitive Framework?

☐ **The key to emotion conversion and a life of EASE.**

Once learned and practised, emotional conversion using the 4-Step Cognitive Framework will become automatic.

☐ Get hold of the 4-Step Cognitive Framework.

Step 1 – Notice your feelings.

Step 2 – Notice the situation.

Step 3 – Automatic negative thoughts – what are you thinking?

    a. For – List facts (evidence) **supporting** the negative thoughts?

    b. Against – List facts (evidence) **negating** the negative thoughts?

Step 4 – Focus on thoughts that are more helpful. Convert the facts in Step 3b to affirmations about you.

☐ Self-concept inventory.

A valuable tool to help you formulate your affirmations. Necessary in step 4 of the 4-Step Cognitive Framework.

EMOTIONAL LEADERSHIP POINT 3:
Can I use my emotions to facilitate thought?

☐ Empathy (sensations) tasks.

The key is to be able to generate a certain emotion, in order to compare and contrast it's sensations within you, with the same sensations in other people. Look for ways to develop your ability to empathise with people (see chapter six).

☐ Mood (facilitation) tasks.

Different moods facilitate changes in behaviour. If you are in a bad mood, chances are that other people will pick up on it quickly, and your mood will impact on their state of well-being. You have the ability to generate a mood state that always has a favourable impact on you, and others you come into contact with.

☐ **Emotions are capable of organising cognitive activity.**

The positive effect of the cognitive framework is enhanced by you generating the emotion you want. Reframing the neurons in your cortex, standing watch over your pathways of information to the limbic system, **affirming** your life of EASE.

Notes

1   Laurence, AM 1990, *You've got what it takes. A Guide to self-discovery and effective living*, Lotus Publishing House, Sydney, p. 36.
2   Chopra, D 1993, *Ageless body, timeless mind. A practical alternative to growing old*, Harmony Books, New York, p.186.
3   Winefield, HR & Peay, MY 1980, 1991, *Behavioural science in medicine*, Department of Psychiatry, The University of Adelaide, South Australia. p.108.
4   Weekes, C. (1972) *Peace from nervous suffering. A practical guide to understanding, confidence and recovery*, Angus & Robertson, London. p. 7.
5   Montgomery, B & Evans, L 1984, *You and stress*, Thomas Nelson, Australia, p. 110.
6   Harris, T A 1967, 1995, *I'm OK – You're OK*, Arrow Books, London.
7   Ekman, P 1992, "An argument for basic emotions", in *Cognition and Emotion*, 6, 3/4, 169-200.
8   Jeffers, S 1987, *Feel the fear and do it anyway*, Random House, London.
9   McKay, M & Fanning, P 1995, 2000, *Self-esteem*, 3rd edn, New Harbinger Publications, Oakland, CA, pp. 46-49.

CHAPTER 5

CREATING
TRANSITION

INDIVIDUAL TRANSITION BEGINS WITH AWARENESS;
ACKNOWLEDGING YOUR NEED TO CHANGE.

INTRODUCTION

In this chapter we discuss chains and blends of emotions, and how emotions combine and progress through individual and relationship transformations. For example, a chain of feelings – including loss, sadness and guilt – may follow a major upset or change in your life. Anger can change into rage. Feelings of acceptance, joy, and warmth combine to form the blended emotion of contentment. Interpret these feelings accurately and learn techniques to move on, in spite of pain and confusion. Understanding emotions is an ability expressed by emotionally intelligent people.

Emotional change embraces change in your identity, your personality. Creating individual transition begins with awareness – acknowledging your need to change and making a choice to do so. What motivates a particular individual to change may be something idiosyncratic to that individual. Unfortunately, change is often sought following a crisis – an "Oh Shit!" experience – that has caused a person to become aware of unacceptable behaviour and its cost, and the barriers he or she has erected against change. Far better that you recognise your need for change and embrace it *before* emotional arousal.

Change is a process. It often begins with shock or disbelief and continues through several stages before you reach acceptance. Change is facilitated through unpacking your negative jigsaw, practising visualisation, and constructing affirmations – truths about yourself. When you choose to change aspects of your behaviour and personality, the impact this decision will have on you and others will be felt immediately.

Creating transition leaves you thinking and feeling that you can **seal** your life of EASE.

UNDERSTANDING CHANGES AND BLENDS IN EMOTIONS

1. DESCRIBING EMOTIONAL AROUSAL

Understanding emotional information is crucial to sealing a life of EASE. Emotions combine, progress and change in intensity, through individual and relationship transitions. Being able to label emotions and understand their different combinations, is important in developing your personal awareness – and in your dealings with other people.

How can you know that another person is describing the same experience you describe, using the same emotional language? You can't. But more intense forms of emotion state are distinctive. Because we all experience emotions in different ways we need to use Table 5.1 (Adapted from Winefield & Peay, 1991)[1] as a framework to distinguish emotional arousals and help us understand what someone else is experiencing. The framework can assist us in examining the common antecedents of emotional arousal, and the experiential and behavioural consequences.

For example, let's look at enjoyment:

Antecedents – Affirmation and positive reinforcement (approval and attention). When you affirm someone or remove your negative behaviour toward him or her, they receive a good feeling. Physical – including sexual – contact with others. Knowledge of results, money, and familiar objects associated with happiness in the past. Enjoyment can be experienced in intensity from contentment to ecstasy.

Behavioural signs – Verbal and non-verbal signs of enjoyment include laughing, smiling, clapping, jumping and embracing.

Consequences – Enjoyment has a non-problem status. A consequence of enjoyment is happiness. However, windfalls of money that may induce enjoyment can have negative consequences for health. Happy events may involve readjustments.

Table 5.1 – Describing the six emotion families

Use the framework below for an understanding of some antecedents, behavioural signs, and consequences of the six emotion families; anger, fear, sadness, enjoyment, disgust, and surprise.

EMOTION	ANTECEDENT EVENT	BEHAVIOURAL SIGNS	CONSEQUENCES
ANGER	Pain in the past is remembered as anger. Innate aggression – primordial drive of "fight". Frustration, temperature, change, crowding.	Frustration conditioned from childhood. Bullying tendencies. Blows and shouts. Self-hatred. Aggressive behaviour, demeaning oneself, or denying oneself pleasures. Also anger from grief over the death of a loved one.	In people brought up to "be nice", there is anxiety about devastating consequences. Resentment. Denied anger may be covertly expressed through dreams, fantasies, or sub-servient attitude toward the perceived source of the anger.
FEAR	Pain in the future is perceived as fear, the manifestation of which is anxiety. Primordial drive of "flight". Fear results from injury or threat of it and lack of information.	An anxious person may or may not admit it. Small movements in hands, eyes, mouth. Less smiling and torso to be held rigidly still.	Motivate avoidance of threatening situation. Someone who has been shamed or scolded may develop the habit of social withdrawal to avoid fear, so is unable to test reality.

EMOTION	ANTECEDENT EVENT	BEHAVIOURAL SIGNS	CONSEQUENCES
SADNESS	Extreme sadness is manifested as depression. Usually follows loss to individual of some source of gratification. Old age. Loss of self-esteem. Loss of control over environment.	Conscious feeling of sadness, hopelessness, and emptiness. Loss of interest and appetite. Dejection to despair to depression.	Health changes, sometimes requiring medication and counselling. Anger and guilt may follow sadness. Severe sadness or depression may result in suicide.
ENJOYMENT	Affirmation and positive reinforcement. Physical – including sexual – contact with others. Knowledge of results, money, and familiar objects associated with happiness in the past.	Laughing, smiling, clapping, jumping, and embracing. Often measured by low scores of distress rather than in its own right. For example, if you are not distressed then you must be happy!	Enjoyment has a non-problem status. A consequence of enjoyment is happiness, which derives from fine-tuning your identity. Enjoyment is experienced in life's tasks as you build emotional awareness for a life of EASE.

EMOTION	ANTECEDENT EVENT	BEHAVIOURAL SIGNS	CONSEQUENCES
DISGUST	Dislike of or opposition to a certain belief, value, attitude, or behaviour. Something that is repulsive, to the senses or to one's beliefs.	Curling of lips. Facial expressions reveal absolute disapproval. Entire body can reflect disgust including utterance of certain sounds of disgust, feeling sick, occasional vomiting.	Feeling of disapproval of the actions (behaviour) of an agent. Withdrawal from person or object. Longer term loathing or resentment of self and others. Nausea/ vomiting can occur at times of association.

EMOTION	ANTECEDENT EVENT	BEHAVIOURAL SIGNS	CONSEQUENCES
SURPRISE	Excited by something unexpected or unknown. Expectations of an occurrence or behaviour not yet met. Can be a positive experience, but also very negative.	Often a feeling of being taken aback or startled. Raising one's eyebrows with a widely opened mouth to see all around to discover the cause of something unexpected.	Positive feelings linger for a while, creating a feeling of well-being and often creativity. Negative feelings, if not managed, bring on resentment and depression.

2. EMOTIONAL CHAINS

An emotional chain describes when several emotions are experienced in succession as a response to an event. When you experience an emotional chain following an event, such as the death of a loved one or being retrenched, you will often experience a sequence of distinct emotions. Understanding emotional chains, or how emotions transition from one to another, is a critical part of your emotional intelligence.

Two examples of emotional "chains";

- The death of a loved one can lead to sadness, grief, anger, guilt, and depression.
- Drinking alcohol can cause you to feel distrustful, angry, and disgusted with yourself.

 Emotional Leadership Practice
ELP 5.1   Emotional chains

In the situation described below, identify the emotions felt by "A". Indicate whether the intensity of each emotion felt is low, medium, or high.

A1:   "Guess what! I auditioned for the new musical. I knew I would get into the chorus, but I felt it would be a good experience to audition for a lead part as well. I thought I may get a lead role next year, but to get one this year, on my first try, is unheard of!"

FEELINGS:

A2:   "Two days later I got these (shows teeth to reveal bands/braces). I just had to give up the part. I couldn't do it looking like "Jaws" and speaking through wired up teeth."

FEELINGS:

A3:   "I've had them on once before for over a year. But the orthodontist didn't take any teeth out, so when my wisdom teeth grew they all went out of line again. You'd think he'd know! It's his job – and he charges enough. It's bad enough having to go through it once, but having to go through it again and missing an opportunity to play lead …"

FEELINGS:

3. EMOTIONAL BLENDS

Your ability to analyse blends of emotions into their parts and conversely, to assemble simple feelings together into compound emotions, is part of your emotional intelligence. If you are a reactive person it is likely that a low level of annoyance will combine with irritation to build into high intensity rage – experienced as outward signs of inappropriate behaviour. The complex emotion we label contentment is comprised of feelings of security, happiness and relief, and when experienced by a sensitive person will promote a rapid depletion of built-up adrenalin (stress) from the body.

Two examples of blends of emotions;
■   A feeling of concern combines the emotions of anxiety, caring and anticipation.
■   Acceptance, enjoyment and warmth combine to form contentment.

 Emotional Leadership Practice
ELP 5.2   Emotional blends

What is the overall emotion felt by "B" in each situation described below? Identify the feelings/emotions that blend and combine to form the overall blended or compound emotion you have chosen. Indicate whether the intensity of each emotion felt is low, medium, or high.

B1: "I just don't know what to do. I've been going out with this really great guy. He's bright, intelligent, and fun to be with. He's helped me discover a whole new dimension to my life. I've been able to share my feelings with him because he listens to me. And I've really liked being able to do that – you know, talk about my feelings and all that. I've realised that I've never really been able to do that before with other men."

FEELINGS:

B2: "Well! He was everything I've ever dreamed about. He always seemed to know just what I needed. We had made plans together. We both seemed to want the same things. And then, all of a sudden, it was over. He said he wanted space – that I was crowding him. "Go to Hong Kong for a couple of weeks, and let me have the apartment to myself", he said. But everything seemed to be so good. I just wanted to be with him all the time. I can't understand that he didn't want to be with me."

FEELINGS:

B3: "Yes, his demand for space really hurt. What's the matter with me anyway? Am I so dependent on him? I find this great guy and then I've got to go and spoil it. I know that I've got to give him space if our relationship is ever going to work, but I just can't stay away. I keep driving past his office, his apartment. I go to all the places we used to go together. Can't he see what he's doing to me?"

FEELINGS:

When you have developed knowledge of emotional chains and blends, and can correctly perceive how another person processes emotion – either as a sensitive or reactive person – you can employ these abilities to enhance your thinking or cognitive ability. You can become more empathic toward others and skilled at identifying emotional signals that reveal the other person's emotion state. This ability places you in the enviable position of being an effective "agent of change" to help others improve their emotional awareness toward a life of EASE.

AWARENESS

1. THE OLD AND NEW PARADIGMS

A paradigm is a pattern of established norms. Best selling author Stephen Covey (1989, pp. 24-29), describes a paradigm as follows;

> The word paradigm comes from the Greek. It was originally a scientific term, and is more commonly used today to mean a model, theory, perception, assumption, or frame of reference. In the more general sense, it's the way we "see" the world. Not in terms of our visual sense of sight, but in terms of perceiving, understanding, interpreting… Paradigms are the source of our attitudes and behaviours. We cannot act with integrity outside of them.[2]

In the old paradigm, health was the absence of disease. Winefield & Peay (1991, p. 1) state that the reductionist view of medicine implied that "… illness was simply a matter of bodily disorder." Emotions and awareness played no part in explaining the condition of a person's body.

In the new paradigm you control your health through awareness. Deepak Chopra (1993, p. 21)[3] says emotions are:

> "… expressions of awareness, the fundamental stuff of life."

"… being aware, we participate in every reaction that takes place inside us. The problems arise when we don't take responsibility for what we're doing."

Emotions are fundamental to awareness and health. Emotional "dis-ease" and psychosocial problems have a major effect on mental and physical health. Becoming aware of your emotions and accepting the role they play in nervous illness, is fundamental to "dis-ease" and at the root of living a life of EASE.

2. ACCEPTANCE VERSUS WITHDRAWAL

Awareness means you accept responsibility for what you do with what happens to you. You take ownership of the feelings and emotions occurring inside your body. You recognise that they are your feelings and no one else's, and you make choices about how to deal with them.

> **Emotional Wisdom**
> Awareness means you accept responsibility for what you do with what happens to you. This is the beginning of creating transition.

Acceptance means that you agree to open up to events happening around you and react to them spontaneously. Acceptance leads to emotional health, as you are able to clear stress as soon as it happens, and don't remain locked into old behaviour patterns that are familiar. By acknowledging your feelings you give yourself the opportunity to manage them productively.

The alternative to awareness, or acknowledging your feelings, is withdrawal – trying to change events from what they really are, and responding to those events with familiar patterns. Blocked emotions can't be felt, but withdrawal will betray you. You are the one displaying the symptoms, the one resisting awareness by trying to retain control of your emotions.

Having control is rooted in withdrawal – the fear and threat of being exposed. The anxiety from fear and threat rooted in non-acceptance causes you pain which you block. Thereby causing you to exercise more control (to protect yourself), and so the cycle continues. Often with disastrous effects on the people around you and the ones you love. It is far better to experience fear and threat, and enter into awareness. For example, non-acceptance of being identified as a sensitive person will mean that you (Person A) continue to anticipate that someone who

> **Emotional Wisdom**
>
> We see in others what we fail to see in ourselves. We see other people as the cause of our anger, our anxiety. In blaming "out" we avoid taking responsibility for anger and anxiety created within. In blaming out we give away our power.

treated you with anger (Person B, a male partner) will continue to behave with anger toward you. Even though his reality has changed, and Person B has accepted ownership for his anger, and adapted his behaviour to that of not displaying anger toward you. Your non-acceptance of the change in Person B will continue to be a source of arousal for you, until you accept change in you (Person A).

People are our mirrors. We often see in others what we fail to see in ourselves. In this case, you (Person A) see anger in Person B. But you fail to experience your own pain through unawareness and non-acceptance. This builds up residual frustration and unmet expectations in you. You'll continue to experience emotional chains and complex emotions, until you fully experience your frustration (response) from your event (unmet expectation).

Experiencing emotion is processing emotion and taking ownership. Fully experiencing the thoughts and sensations associated with a better understanding of changes (chains and blends) in emotions.

The change process begins with awareness. Accepting responsibility for what you do with what happens to you, through information that is made available to you. Through your increased knowledge of the identity and nature of your problem, you experience the change process.

CHANGE FOR THE BETTER!

1. CHANGE MEANS CHANGING YOUR EAR-IDENTITY

Emotional change embraces change in your identity – your personality. We have learned that the human body is programmed to perceive change in the internal and external environment. Research in emotion, starting with Charles Darwin in 1872[4], has given us the idea that emotions signal meaning about individual and social needs. For example, the need for survival, love and affection. Personality characteristics such as empathy, warmth, social skills, motivation and persistence, are

> **Emotional Wisdom**
>
> Change is a process, a movement from one state to another. The path mandated is self-directed change for the better. From what is known and within your comfort zone, to values, goals, and dreams of what is possible for you as an individual.

influenced by the adaptive nature of emotional expression – changing your personality from within. Emotional intelligence (EI) has emerged from the field of personality to be studied in its own right "… as the capacity to reason about emotions, and as the capacity of emotion to enhance thought."[5] Emotional intelligence represents abilities to solve emotional problems that impact on personality – the id, ego, and superego.

2. STRUCTURE OF PERSONALITY

Sigmund Freud (1856-1939) developed a non-biological theory of personality that has dominated psychoanalysis. Freud's theory has been described (Winefield & Peay, 1991 p. 140) as follows:

> The psychic structure is conceived of as a three-part iceberg, most of which remains unconscious. The id, unconscious source of all energy

particularly through the biological drives of sex and aggression, seeks immediate satisfaction and is guided only by the pleasure principle. Derived from this in the course of development is the mainly conscious ego, which mediates between the id, and the demands of both society and of conscience. It operates on the reality principle, is rational, can delay gratification, and seeks safety. The superego or conscience, partly conscious and partly unconscious, is a watchful and critical moralist, which strives for perfection. The necessary conflict between these elements of personality, and how it is resolved, is seen as the source of personality.

To cope with anxiety engendered by the dramas of life – especially threats to self-esteem – and the need to control one's impulses, the ego develops various helpful coping mechanisms. These include; memory, judgement, logical analysis, concentration, empathy and tolerance for ambiguity. Each of these if used immoderately can have a harmful, rather than beneficial, result.

3. DEFENCE MECHANISMS

Defence mechanisms (Adapted from Winefield & Peay, 1991 p. 141) that your personality – your identity – uses to cope include:

- **Denial**
  The short-lived capacity to be selectively inattentive to external threats. Anxiety-provoking impulses or memories may be repressed, sparing the ego from dealing with guilt or threat.
  Example: Refusing to accept the reality of a life-threatening illness.
- **Objective rationality**
  Everything is rationalised. Intellectualisation or rationalisation that may cut a person off from reality to an artificial and damaging extent.
  Example: A man believes that his marriage is fine. "I know what to do," he says. Meanwhile his marriage is falling down around him.

■ **Projection**

Unrealistic attribution of your feelings onto someone else. For example, projecting our anger onto others. We see in others a feeling that we are really feeling ourselves. Conversely, you see in others what you fail to see in yourself.

Example: You are feeling quiet and awkward in room crowded with people you don't know, and you say to someone, "You're really quiet. Are you tense about something."

Example: You do not arrive for a scheduled interview. You ring up to apologise but feeling acutely embarrassed you say, "I can hear you are really mad at me."

> **Emotional Wisdom**
> Attachment by many people to defence mechanisms is based on fear, insecurity, and lack of awareness. Insecurity requires stepping into reality – into present-moment awareness – where emotions are fully experienced without conditioning.

■ **Displacement**

Choosing an inappropriate, rather than an appropriate, expression for an unacceptable arousal (over reaction).

Example: You are trapped in a lift. You start screaming to get out. But really you are safe and secure. You just need to wait to be rescued.

Example: You may be really angry about your workload, or feel overlooked because something you submitted to your boss has not been considered. So you target the boss, "He is a pig!"

Attachment by many people to these defence mechanisms is based on fear and insecurity. Typically, all of us rely on these defence mechanisms, as we do not know our true self, our identity. Paradoxically, a search for security is fruitless, as attachment to what is known (memory) and what may be (fantasy) generates negative emotion. Insecurity or uncertainty requires stepping into reality – into the present – where emotions are fully experienced without conditioning.

4. CHARACTERISTICS OF MENTAL HEALTH

Winefield & Peay (1991, p.141) point out our debt to Freud and those following him, for making explicit these characteristics of mental health:

a. Personality is the result of past experience – rather that predominantly of chance or inheritance.

b. Behaviour is not always rational in the face of anxiety. Except when defending against the anxiety from a major need – that is, in this circumstance it is rational.

— Example of a major need: A wife who is highly anxious about possible infidelity needs reassurance that there is none. Seemingly irrational behaviour exhibited may include spying, following her partner, taping conversations, and checking her partner's email, which is in fact rational behaviour to her.

— Example of a major need: You may need reassurance that you are doing a good job. If you are a sensitive person, anxiety produces irrational behaviour – you constantly seek feedback.
But if as a sensitive person you need repeated reassurance to settle your arousal, then your request for feedback is not irrational. It is normal for you.

c. The mechanisms by which we protect ourselves from anxiety can buy time and permit the development of better solutions – they can help us to cope. Or they can, if allowed to dominate behaviour, lead to maladaptive patterns that may need expert help to "unlearn".

— Example: The mechanism of withdrawing and avoiding helps someone experiencing anxiety to calm down.

Winefield & Peay (1991, p.142) promote a view on personality as "a set of behaviours acquired through learning." This is the behaviourist perspective where the focus is more on what people do, rather than on what people are like. For example, telling a child, "I don't like what you have done", not "I think you are stupid". This view of personality is adopted in this book, which provides the very necessary **experiential** and **strategic** emotional leadership to develop your personality – your EAR-Identity.

5. ANALYSIS OF IDENTITY

The outline of personality as above, the bio-psycho-physical interactions detailed in chapter one, our work with over 1,650 individual clients from 73 ethnic groups over six and-a-half years in our clinical counselling practice in Singapore, and 35 years experience in human support, academia and business, lead us to the following conclusion in the analysis of human identity.

- Sensitive people are prone to experiencing fear-provoking anxiety – leading to flight/withdrawal.
- Reactive people are prone to experiencing memory-driven anger – leading to fight/aggression.

Acceptance of this analysis of your identity means that you are ready for change. Ready to seal a life of EASE, where emotion is experienced in "present-moment awareness"[6] and energy is directed to achieving your life goals.

Change for the better! Reinforce your growing awareness by raising your knowledge of how pain is experienced in your body (chapter three). Use the 4-step cognitive framework (chapter four). Understand blends and changes in emotions (chapter five). Learn effective communication techniques (chapter six). Make no-lose decisions (chapter seven). And practise good intrapersonal and social management. Including, identifying how you give and receive love, and healing emotional wounds (chapter eight).

We now describe the *change process* itself.

THE CHANGE PROCESS

1. TEN STAGES OF CHANGE

The ten stages of the change process (Figure 5.1) follow what many people experience when they suffer a loss of any kind. For example; loss of a loved one through death, loss of a job, an incapacity through mental illness, physical harm or injury, the onset of old age, loss of regular contact with family and friends through relocation, and children leaving the family home.

Change may come as a shock and be totally unexpected. Change may be planned for in advance. When the reality of change sets in, people experience the stages within the change process to varying degrees. If you spend too much time in any one of the stages it may be a sign of "dis-ease" in which case you should seek professional help.

1. Shock/Disbelief
    You have been made to withstand pain, trauma, and even great tragedy.
2. Emotional Arousal
    Your feelings signal bodily needs. Terrible loss is felt as a surging of feelings within. You feel uncontrollable discomfort.
3. Physical Symptoms
    Intense arousal causes physiological responses to occur that affect your ability to sleep, eat or concentrate.
4. Guilt/Self-reproach
    You feel a sense of responsibility for the change, and begin to think about what you did or did not do, or what you should have done to prevent it.
5. Depression/Despair/Withdrawal
    You are preoccupied about the change and cannot concentrate on anything else. As you have probably not experienced some of these feelings before, you despair that something is happening to your mind. This causes you to withdraw from activities, family and friends, to hide your feelings. At the same time you feel isolated and alone.

6. Anger/Rage/Frustration

   Hostility and resentment take over as you have been holding back emotion. You blame "out" – the doctor, your partner, God, often someone who is closest to you.

7. Idealising The Past Situation

   You take solace in thinking about how it was in the past.

8. Reality Check

   You are beginning to approach acceptance of change. The unreality of your present position slowly begins to dawn on you.

9. Positive Attitude

   Mood changes in response to positive thoughts, during growing periods of acceptance.

10. Acceptance

    You are now your old self and are stronger emotionally because of your experience of change.

Figure 5.1. The Change Process

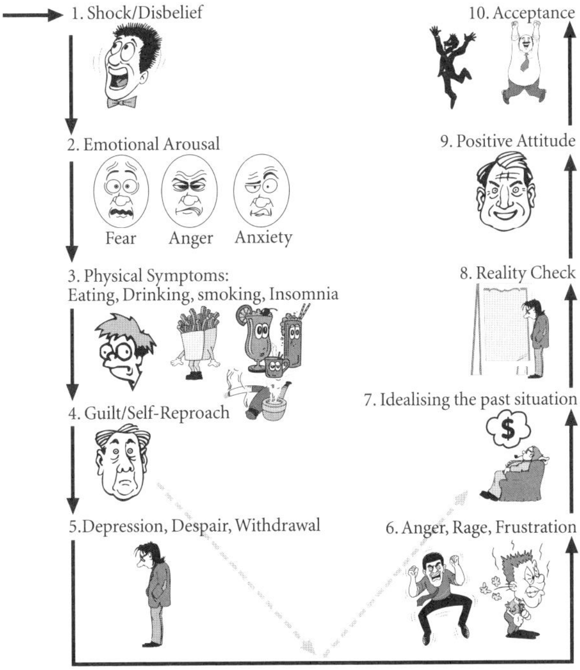

2. NORMAL GRIEF REACTIONS

Two primary ingredients in grief are (1) the experience of loss (including anticipated loss), and (2) emotional pain. See below the feelings, physical sensations, cognitions and behaviours, that are associated with grief.

FEELINGS	PHYSICAL SENSATIONS
Sadness, Anger	Hollowness in the stomach
Guilt and self-reproach	Tightness in the chest
Anxiety	Tightness in the throat
Loneliness (isolation)	Over sensitivity to noise
Fatigue, Helplessness	A sense of depersonalisation
Shock	Breathlessness
Yearning	Weakness in the muscles
Emancipation	Lack of energy ("can't be bothered")
Relief, Numbness	Dry mouth

COGNITIONS	BEHAVIOURS
Disbelief	Sleep disturbances
Confusion	Appetite disturbances
Preoccupation	Absent-minded behaviour
Sense of presence	Social withdrawal
Hallucinations	Dreams of the deceased
	Avoiding reminders
	Searching, calling out
	Sighing, Crying
	Restless over activity
	Treasuring objects
	Carrying objects

Depression and grief are different, although they may manifest similar characteristics (sleep disturbance, appetite disturbance, intense sadness). In a grief reaction there isn't the loss of self-esteem commonly found in most clinical depressions. That is, people who have lost someone do not regard themselves less because of such loss. If they do, it tends to be only for a brief amount of time.

3. THE FOUR TASKS OF MOURNING – DR J. WILLIAM WORDEN[7]

In grief not everyone experience the same responses. One can feel concerned that they are not passing through the right stage in the right order. Dr William Worden outlines tasks that must be accomplished in the grief process.

Task 1 – To accept the reality of the loss.

If you are able to talk in the past tense about events/people that belong to the past, even yesterday, you are accepting the reality. Talking about the event of loss means that you are not denying the fact that it has really happened.

Task 2 – To experience the pain of grief.

Allow your body to really hurt and weep. Your chest may feel tight and painful. You may feel restless or lethargic. Your muscles may ache. That's OK. It won't last forever. This signals that you are processing grief.

Task 3 – To adjust to an environment in which the deceased is missing.

This task is harder as we become familiar with routines and "old habits die hard". In the first weeks and month after a loss you may still think and act like the "old times". For example, setting the table for two and then realising there is only one of you now.

Task 4 – To withdraw emotional energy and reinvest in another relationship.

Withdrawing from a relationship – even from someone who has left or has died – may feel disloyal, and cause you to feel guilty. Initially there may be no desire at all to be in another relationship. This task may take many months.

4. SIX STAGES OF GRIEF – DR ELIZABETH KÛBLER-ROSS[8]

Psychiatrist, Dr Elizabeth Kûbler-Ross, is well known for her work in describing the process of grief. She speaks of the five stages of grief that a person will go through. However, it is important to note that not everyone experiences every stage, before arriving eventually at hope for the future and the possibility for recovery and renewal.

1. Denial
   Feeling of numbness and that what has happened can't be so.
2. Anger over the loss
   Some people experience anxiety rather than anger at this time. These are the feelings of arousal being experienced in the body resulting in restlessness – a need to keep busy, to do things, to move about. Anything to fight the feelings of awfulness.
3. Bargaining with God to reverse the loss.
   Making deals with God to do certain things if He eases your pain.
4. Depression
   Intense sadness, frequent crying, occasionally wanting to die – to be free of the pain. Sometimes experienced as a terrible wrenching in your body.
5. Acceptance
   Feelings of relief that you can perform daily tasks and think about the loss without intense emotional pain.
6. Eventually, hope for the future.
   You can see the possibility for recovery and renewal.

UNPACKING YOUR NEGATIVE JIGSAW

A jigsaw is a puzzle – a picture pasted on a board and cut into irregular shapes. The objective of the puzzle is to reassemble the pieces to view the picture. Creating transition is being motivated to **unpack** the negative jigsaw you have assembled through your life.

Imagine you are about to start a 1,000-piece jigsaw puzzle of your brain, but it's your black brain – the one with all the negative thoughts. When you start out in life – before you start your jigsaw – there is not much negativity. And the picture of the black brain is not even recognisable. But with every negative thought and feeling you experience you put in a few pieces. And gradually, your jigsaw starts to take shape.

When your jigsaw is half-done, there are still lots of gaps. Lots of places for positive thought and clear thinking, to come through. Even when the jigsaw is three-quarters complete, there is room for rational thought – a few gaps here and there.

However, one day you wake up after a period of negative experiences, and the picture of the black brain is complete. That is your new reality – the negative brain. There is no room for anything else. From that moment on, everything that happens outside of yourself seems to reinforce your negative jigsaw – the picture of your black brain that you have pieced together. External events confirm the negative picture – the self-fulfilling prophecy.

Many of us with stressful lives start out each day with a near-completed jigsaw, a negative picture of ourselves full of negative emotion from an active and loud inner voice. To create transition, if you live life with a negative jigsaw you must learn how to unpack it – **piece by piece** – so that some rational thinking then has a chance to shine through.

Unpacking your negative jigsaw is another form of the 4-Step Cognitive Framework. Each time you have a positive thought or revise a weakness (negative thought) you are removing one piece of the jigsaw. Continue to do this, one piece at a time, step-by-step, until your jigsaw is completely unpacked. As you unpack the negative thoughts in memory and fully experience the emotion associated with each thought, you are recreating your identity – your positive view of yourself.

Three ways to unpack your negative jigsaw:
1. The waterslide.
2. Repeating affirmations.
3. The compassionate response.

1. THE WATERSLIDE

One way of unpacking your negative jigsaw is to use the waterslide – a metaphor for allowing rational thinking to reframe negative thoughts.

Visualise yourself on a waterslide with a strong turbulent gush of water. Once you are on it, you don't really enjoy the experience – you get bashed again and again against the side, and dumped off your rubber ring. Even though you don't want to be there you can't stop until you get to the bottom, feeling washed out and exhausted. It's like that with negative thinking. You know it's happening, you don't like it, but you can't get off.

So when you're on the top of the waterslide, and realise you're going to board the "negative slide", you have to stop and say, "No, I don't want to ever start down here. I want to go down that positive water slide over there." Then cross over and go down the positive slide. The one that is smooth and straight, and a good experience.

To allow rational thinking to come through you have to choose which waterslide you want to be on. The negative water slide with the turbulent water, or the positive one that feels safe and calm.

How do you do this? By using your imaginary cupboard (visualisation).

Imagine a cupboard made from your favourite wood. There is no lock on your cupboard and the doors never stick – you are able to open them whenever you need to. Inside are several shelves. Some are labelled:

Personality
How others see me
Mental functioning
Achievements
Family Life

And there are others. On each shelf there are many notes, each with a statement of truth about you on it. It may be a positive comment, an acknowledgement of an achievement, or a revised weakness (see ELP 5.3). Whatever it is, whatever shelf it's on, you can take one of those notes from the cupboard whenever you need to – any time your inner voice is getting too loud. You can utilise this visualisation to choose the positive waterslide – to regain control whenever you start to feel negative.

2. REPEATING AFFIRMATIONS

Over time, affirmations, prayers, and mantras permit rational thinking to reframe negative thoughts. An affirmation is a statement of truth about you.

In *Ageless Body, Timeless Mind* (1993, p. 182), Deepak Chopra, quoting Hermann Hesse in *Siddhartha*, writes, "Within you there is a stillness and sanctuary to which you can retreat at any time and be yourself."

Chopra continues:

This sanctuary is a simple awareness of comfort, which can't be violated by the turmoil of events. This place feels no trauma and stores no hurt. It is the mental space that one seeks to find in meditation... you can approach this place of calm with the following exercise, write down this affirmation:

I am perfect as I am. Everything in my life is working toward my ultimate good. I am loved and I am love.

After you have read the affirmation above, shut your eyes and let your body respond. Your first thought may be of anger as you feel this affirmation does not reflect how your life has worked out. Continue to read the affirmation and wait for your responses to change. You are participating in cognitive reframing, eavesdropping on your inner voice and slowly but surely telling it to "check out!"

Here is a list of affirmations drawn from our life experiences and books we value, including: *Ageless body, timeless mind,* 1993 by Deepak Chopra; *You can heal your life,* 1984 by Louise Hay; *Real Magic,* 1992 by Wayne Dwyer; *You and stress,* 1984 by Montgomery & Evans; *Self-Esteem,* 1992 by McKay &

Fanning; and *The secrets of the rainmaker. Success without stress*, 1997 by Chin-Ning Chu.

I accept and love you exactly as you are.

I am a unique and valuable human being.

I am a capable person.

I am willing to change.

I always do the best I can.

I am a filial son (or daughter).

I forgive you for not being the way I wanted you to be. I forgive you and I set you free.[9]

I will keep sight of the big picture I have set out to achieve.

Everything in my life is working toward my ultimate good.

I am perfect and complete. I am the creation of that glorious perfection.[10]

I know I have the power within me to create a life of EASE.

I am perfect as I am.

Everything in life is working toward my ultimate good.

I am loved and I am love.

I am a unique and valuable human being.

I am at least as good as others of my age and occupation.

I like myself exactly as I am.

I am a successful and capable person.

I love myself, mistakes and all.

I love and accept myself exactly as I am.

Today I love myself more than yesterday – tomorrow I will love myself even more.

I know I have the power within me to create a life of fulfilment and joy.

I am a miracle, and therefore I am a creator of miracles.

My intention creates my reality.

I intend to heal myself of negative assertion.

I intend to manifest the necessary talent and intellect to become the kind of purposeful person I am destined to be.

As I think, so shall I be.

I love you. I will try harder to hear your concerns.

I will keep my mouth shut.

I am motivated by my inner awareness of having a heroic mission and staying with it, regardless of outcomes.

I will focus on purpose.

I possess all that need to fulfil my dreams.

I am limitless and a part of the perfection of this physical world.

I now move to a better place.

I am my own person.

I love my body.

I am filled with love and affection.

I am joyous and happy and free. I am totally healthy.

I'm basically alright as I am.

I approve of myself. I have worth because I struggle to survive.

I have legitimate needs.

It's alright to meet my needs as I see fit.

I am willing to release the pattern of self-worth within me that is creating the need to delay my good.

I am responsible for my life.

I accept the consequences of my actions.

I feel warm and loving toward myself.

I invariably do the best I am capable of at the moment.

"Mistakes" is a label I add later – I am free to make mistakes.

Everything I do is an attempt to meet legitimate needs.

I am expanding my awareness to make wiser choices.

I am letting go of unwise choices in the past.

I can do anything I want, but what I want is determined by my awareness.

Everything I do involves a price to pay.

Shoulds, oughts and musts are irrelevant.

In a moment of choice, I do only what my awareness permits.

It's foolish to resent other's actions – they also do only what their awareness permits.

I am willing to release the pattern in me that created negative assertion.

I am in the process of positive changes.

I have a happy slender body.

I experience love wherever I go.

I have the perfect living space.

I can now create a wonderful new job.

I appreciate all that I do; I love and approve of myself.

I trust the process of life to bring me to my highest good.

I deserve to have a successful career and I accept it now.

 Emotional Leadership Practice

ELP 5.3   Writing your own affirmations

Review to your self-concept inventory from chapter four, ELP 4.9. Completing the self-concept inventory helps you to feel better about yourself. Repetitive affirmations alter your internal perception of self.

Mark positive statements with "+" and negative statements with "-". Don't mark items that are neutral, factual observations about you.

Write out your affirmations. Positive (+ve) statements become affirmations. Negative (–ve) statements are revised into affirmations.

Examples:

Self-Statement		Affirmation
I've got fat thighs.	-ve	Convert to: I've got 16 inch thighs.
I've got dry skin.	Neutral	Convert to: I'm happy with my skin.
I've got nice eyes.	+ve	Remains same: I've got nice eyes.

Now try converting your own self-statements to affirmations. Use extra paper as required.

_____

_____

_____

_____

3. THE COMPASSIONATE RESPONSE

Creating transition requires you to be compassionate to yourself. When you feel compassion for yourself you begin to expose your sense of worth. Mother Theresa is reported to have said, "The fruit of love is service, which is compassion in action: understanding, accepting, forgiving."

Understanding
You have figured out how you operate. What you are likely to do in a given situation, and why you would do it. Understanding others begins with active listening. Active listening is discussed in chapter six.

Accepting
Acknowledgement of the facts with all your value judgments put on hold. You neither approve nor disapprove. You may not like it, but you accept it.

Forgiving
Flows out of understanding and acceptance. Forgiving does not mean approval. It does not mean condoning past actions. Forgiveness means letting go of the past, self-respect in the present, and looking forward to a better tomorrow. You rise from your point of view to your viewing point. (See "Forgiveness & the healing of emotional wounds" – Appendix C – by Dr David Benner, Distinguished Professor of Psychology and Spirituality, and

Director, Institute for Psychospiritual Health. His writing explains the perspective that forgiveness and forgiveness alone has the power to break the controlling influence of the bad things that can happen to people).

4. POSITIVE AND NEGATIVE ENERGY FLOWS – DO THEY MAKE A DIFFERENCE?

From Deepak Chopra (1993, pp. 15, 22-23) we learn that the sequence of events that transforms DNA into protein from coded intelligence involves energy and information at every point. How this process occurs and what form this energy and information takes is not the focus of this book, except where it may explain how awareness (energy and information fields) changes. Chopra says;

> **Emotional Wisdom**
> Creating transition ultimately involves you being motivated to recognise how your perceptions create positive and negative energy flows. And how positive energy flows create your transition.

> Perception is a learned phenomenon… No two people share the same perception of anything… The body is made of experiences transformed into physical expression… Your cells are constantly processing experience and metabolizing it according to your personal views. You don't just funnel raw data through your eyes and ears and stamp it with a judgement. You physically turn into the interpretation as you internalise it.

Summary

The pathway to strategic emotional leadership begins with understanding changes and blends in emotion and acknowledging the need for change in your identity.

In the new paradigm you control your health through expressions of your awareness – emotions. Personality is a set of behaviours acquired through learning. Awareness means you accept responsibility for what you do with what happens to you. Acceptance means that you agree to open up to events happening around you and react to them spontaneously. Acceptance leads to emotional health.

Change is a process – a movement from one state to another, requiring self-direction. The functional and adaptive – seemingly emotionally intelligent – nature of emotions, serves to motivate change in your personality – your predisposition to behave one way rather than another.

Creating transition involves you being motivated to unpack the negative jigsaw you have assembled throughout your life and stored in your black brain. Using visualisation, affirmations and the compassionate response, you can alter your internal perception of self and **seal** your life of EASE.

EMOTIONAL LEADERSHIP CHECKLIST

Use this checklist to unpack your negative jigsaw, understand chains and blends of emotions, and be realistic and true about you.

- Do I know how to create transition?
- Have I accepted my need to change?
- Can I apply my emotional intelligence in transition?

EMOTIONAL LEADERSHIP POINT 1
Do I know how to create transition?

☐ Awareness creates responsibility.

Awareness means you accept responsibility for what you do with what happens to you. This is the beginning of creating transition.

☐ Withdrawal is the stumbling block to transition.

The alternative to awareness is withdrawal – responding to events in old familiar patterns.

Blocked emotions you cannot feel, but withdrawal will betray you – you are the one displaying the symptoms!

☐ Other people are mirrors.
We see in others what we fail to see in ourselves. We see other people as the cause of our anger, our anxiety.

In blaming others we avoid taking responsibility for anger and anxiety created within.

EMOTIONAL LEADERSHIP POINT 2
Have I accepted my need to change?

☐ Unpack your negative jigsaw.
A black brain is like a jigsaw made with pieces of negativity.

To create transition, begin by unpacking your negative jigsaw and build a new EAR-Identity.

Through increased knowledge of your EAR-Identity and emotional style you experience the change process.

☐ The Change Process

Change may come as a shock and be totally unexpected. Change may be planned.

Engage in the change process and don't spend too much time in each stage, lest you become a victim.

EMOTIONAL LEADERSHIP POINT 3
Can I apply my emotional intelligence in transition?

☐ Understanding chains of emotions.

Understanding emotional information is crucial to sealing a life of EASE. Emotions combine and progress and change in intensity through individual and relationship transitions. Being able to label emotions and understand their different combinations is important in developing your personal awareness and in your dealings with other people.

Understanding an emotional chain, or how emotions transition from one to another, is a critical part in applying your emotional intelligence.

☐ Understanding blends of emotions.

Your ability to analyse blends of emotions into their parts and conversely, to assemble simple feelings together into compound emotions, is essential to applying your emotional intelligence.

☐ Applying emotional intelligence to SEAL your life of EASE.

Applying your emotional intelligence will rid your ego of unwanted coping mechanisms such as, denial, objective rationality, projection and displacement, to **seal** your life of EASE.

Notes

1   Adapted from Winefield, HR & Peay MY 1980, 1991, *Behavioural science in medicine*, The University of Adelaide, Adelaide, South Australia, Ch. 7.

2   Covey, SR 1989, *The 7 habits of highly effective people,* Simon & Schuster, London, p. 23.

3   Chopra, 1993, *Ageless Body, Timeless Mind*, Harmony Books, New York, p. 21.

4   Darwin, C 1872, 1998, *The expression of the emotions in man and animals. Definitive Edition.* Introduction, Afterword, and Commentaries by Paul Ekman. Oxford University Press, Oxford.

5   Mayer, JD, Salovey, PS & Caruso, DR 2002, Mayer-Salovey-Caruso Emotional Intelligence Test (MSCEIT). User's Manual. Multi-Health Services,Toronto, p. 6.

6   The phrase "Present-moment awareness" was first used by Deepak Chopra, 1993, *Ageless body, timeless mind. A practical alternative to growing old*, Harmony Books, New York, p. 172.

7   Dr J. William Worden, Professor of Psychology, Rosemead School of Psychology, Biola University www.rosemead.edu/faculty/worden.cfm

8   The stages and processes of grieving have become well known since psychiatrist, Dr. Elisabeth Kûbler-Ross published her world-famous book, *On Death and Dying* in 1969 (Simon & Schuster/Touchstone). Dr. Kûbler-Ross outlined five distinct stages in the grieving process. The time spent grieving and the specific stages any particular individual experiences may differ.

9   Hay, L. L. (1984) *You can heal your life*. Specialist Publications, Concord, Australia. Page 14.

10   Chin-Ning Chu (1997) *The secrets of the rainmaker. Success without stress*, Stealth Productions, Australia, p. 96.

CHAPTER 6

COMMUNICATING
CHANGE

CLEARLY EXPRESSING YOUR THOUGHTS AND FEELINGS
IS VITAL FOR BUILDING INTIMACY AND TRUST.
ADOPT LANGUAGE APPROPRIATE TO THE SITUATION.

INTRODUCTION

Clearly expressing your thoughts and feelings, by adopting language appropriate to the situation, is vital for building intimacy and trust in relationships. Through this chapter you will develop a checklist of what to do, and what not to do, for effective communication. We describe the "communication model" and reveal basic communication skills, which will help you to focus on the person, reflect content and feelings, and practise levelling, active listening and validating. Using leading responses and open-ended questions is a useful technique to continue a conversation. Always place acceptance before judgement. Use "I" statements and not "you" statements to disarm your critic, affirm yourself, and influence others. Use the "XYZ" formula to express your true intent. You will learn to interpret non-verbal signals, and develop greater awareness of self and others, enabling you to communicate easily, confidently, and effectively to **seal** your life of EASE.

COMMUNICATION IN MALE/FEMALE RELATIONSHIPS

In chapter two you learned what men and women need to know about communication differences between the two sexes. We now examine the different ways in which men and women release negative energy.

Typically, women release negative energy by talking through their experiences. This seemingly incessant need to "chatter" often drives men to despair – they feel exhausted by it and usually "tune out".

Men however, usually resolve issues in their own head – without any discussion with others. Typically, men release negative energy by reactive behaviour; anger – shouting or physical action, and withdrawal – going to play golf, spend time with a friend to discuss things other than feelings, or simply not interact with their partner. This behaviour can bewilder women – who generally have a need for quality conversation – and leaves them feeling not listened to, ignored, and even insignificant.

Take a moment to reflect on the behaviours used by men or women that you have experienced, which left you feeling exhausted or unheard.

Emotional Wisdom

Where hurts have occurred in the home, and ineffective communication rules, the "housemate syndrome" sets in. You move from; deepest intimacy, to keeping things to yourself, to indifference, to housemate.

As discussed in chapter two, relationships fail for three main reasons; unresolved hurts, ineffective communication, and a lack of awareness about how we each give and receive love. Most relationship problems start with the "hurts". An angry word is spoken, an action is misinterpreted, and a frustration is held within. Soon there is a "communication problem".

Where hurts have occurred in the workplace and ineffective communication reigns supreme, a simmering unspoken tension and "backstabbing" scenario sets in. Feelings of being overwhelmed, frustrated, irritable, and resentful dominate the working relationship, and your communication becomes superficial. You complain and explain, feel bitter, and push others away who try to help – precisely when you need their help.

1. THE HOUSEMATE SYNDROME

Level 1 – Deepest intimacy

Do you remember when you first got together? When you started your relationship, and were "in love"? Do you remember what you used to talk about? You talked about everything, right? You couldn't get enough of each other. You got together whenever you could. You talked long into the night and were forever on the phone whenever you were not together. You would talk about yourselves and your past relationships, your hopes and dreams, your disappointments and failures – everything! That was because you believed that your partner wanted to know everything about you. They hungered for more! "Tell me more", is what it used to be like, "I want to know more about you." You felt safe that no matter what you said your partner would love you and not judge you.

Level 2 – Shallower communication

Then something changed somewhere along the line. Love waned and it probably started like this:

The woman brings up a topic for discussion and her partner retorts, "Not tonight dear, I'm tired." The negative response is different to what she's used to. "OK", she thinks, "I'll leave this until another time, and we'll talk when it's not so late." But when she raises the topic again his answer is, "Oh, don't be so ridiculous". This second negative response causes her to decide not to raise that particular topic again. She decides that she will be more careful from now on. She will carefully choose what she says and when, so as not to get a negative response.

A few days later he notices a difference in her. "Are you OK?" he enquires. "Yes", she answers sharply. He persists, "Are you sure, you seem a bit different?" She barks, "I said, I'm OK!" He is now taken aback by her negative response and vows to become a bit more selective about asking – lest there is a negative response. And so begins a decrease in intimacy, in telling each other what is going on inside the other's head and heart – because now there is the risk of a negative response.

Level 3 – The bedroom

Soon difficulties in the bedroom begin. The woman is now harbouring resentment against her partner. Hurts that haven't gone away because of his earlier negative responses. He is also feeling some confusion and resentment. He notices that she is slightly distant. She is starting to snap and bicker more than usual. And her short, sarcastic responses *really* hurt. Of course they are intended to hurt. Both are starting to feel that their relationship is not as deep and connected as it used to be.

Soon he approaches her for sex, just to recapture the intimacy that he now feels is going astray. He is seeking reassurance that this relationship is still okay. He wants to feel close to her again in the best way he knows how. But she is also feeling the distance, and therefore is not responsive to his approach. She wants to sort out the issues as *she* knows how – through verbal communication. She wants to talk about the hurts. The way she feels when he snaps at her, before she feels ready for sex. So she says, "No, not tonight". Several more responses of, "No, not tonight", and he stops asking. He doesn't like to be rejected. She notices that he stops asking. And she starts to feel even more hurt – more rejected than she felt before. Now she feels as though she has the obvious evidence that he doesn't find her special any more. She interprets his avoidance of sex as, "He no longer finds me desirable or attractive." Soon her inner voice asks loudly, "What's happening? Is there someone else?"

Level 4 – Housemates

As housemates there is no longer any emotional intimacy in the relationship. Neither he nor she is talking about feelings. They only discuss things such as money, holidays – and the kids. It is no longer safe to talk about feelings, about themselves – as there's too much risk of a negative response. She feels that she is walking around him on eggshells. He rehearses things in his head that he would like to say to her, but then he never says them out loud – in case she becomes hysterical. There's a decreasing level of trust, and no sex. Resentments, suspicion and confusion are rising, as the petty arguments and bickering increases. The Housemate Syndrome has arrived.

Choose not to be a victim of the Housemate Syndrome

Partners need to recognise that they have become merely housemates when they start to feel insecure, unfulfilled and empty. Often they yearn to get back to that deep place of intimacy they had at the beginning of the relationship – but they don't know how to get there. This is where counselling can help. Counselling teaches an effective communication model enabling couples to talk to each other about the things that hurt. The model creates a safe environment where each person feels heard and understood by the other. Resentments disappear, and a reconnection is made. Counselling facilitates this process in only a few sessions, and insecurities about the relationship begin to evaporate as effective communication begins.

Do not fall victim to the Housemate Syndrome – get help for your relationship as soon as possible.

Emotional Leadership Practice
ELP 6.1   The Housemate Syndrome

Have you experienced the Housemate Syndrome? What is the style of communication used within this scenario? How do you think effective communication begins? What are the objectives and components of effective communication?

_____

_____

_____

_____

_____

_____

COMMUNICATION MODEL

Whenever there is communication between two people, one person is the sender of the message and one person is the receiver. The sender first has to encode a message. They then send the message – usually in words. At this point they also use non-verbal communication. The receiver picks up both the verbal and non-verbal components of the message and decodes them.

There are three areas where interference of the communication process can occur, often resulting in an inaccurate decoding of the message. These are illustrated in Figure 6.1.

Figure 6.1 - Communication Model

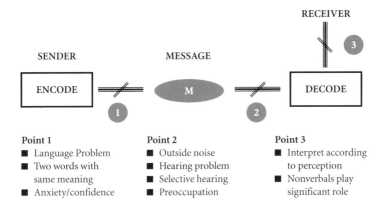

Point 1
- Language Problem
- Two words with same meaning
- Anxiety/confidence

Point 2
- Outside noise
- Hearing problem
- Selective hearing
- Preoccupation

Point 3
- Interpret according to perception
- Nonverbals play significant role

At **Point 1**, some of the inaccuracy of the communication process can occur through;

1. People speaking a different language,
2. Two words having the same meaning. For example, Mozart's Place or Mozart's birthplace, and
3. The sender experiencing anxiety, so that he doesn't complete sentences but only expresses half-sentences.

At **Point 2** interference of the communication process can occur through;

1. Outside noise affecting what is heard,
2. A genuine hearing problem,
3. Selective hearing. For example, when a person "tunes out" when the topic is not of interest to them, or
4. The receiver is preoccupied with something. For example, a person's attention may be diverted by the television. This can mean that words are heard inaccurately.

At **Point 3** even if the words are heard accurately, the receiver interprets those words according to his/her perception of their meaning. Thoughts in his/her head are often defensive if his/her perception of the message is construed as an order or attack. It is at Point 3 that the nonverbal actions of the sender play a big part in the interpretation. If their tone sounds sarcastic or irritated, if their voice is raised, if their hand gestures, or eye contact are not congruent with the words spoken, the nonverbal messages can have greater impact.

Research suggests that eight to 12 percent of communication received is through verbal means, and up to 90 percent through nonverbal means. If a wife sarcastically says, "I'm fine," the husband knows that is certainly not the case. Similarly, if a dad yells at his teenage son, "Okay go to your all night party, don't listen to me. Drink yourself stupid, your friends know best," the son will know that the actual "unspoken" message is the opposite of the words his dad is saying.

To be involved in effective communication, all parties need to be able to clearly construct (encode) their verbal messages. Most importantly, they need to listen, to make sure an accurate message is being received. That is, what was sent is being received.

HELPING MODEL OF COMMUNICATION SKILLS

The Helping Model of communication skills is included here to assist you in becoming familiar with skills used by counsellors. What follows is an outline of skills you can use in everyday life. What you will learn in chapter six are the basic skills taught to counsellors. You can use these skills when called upon to communicate better with a partner, family member, or work colleague in your personal and workplace relationships.

The nature of emotional distress and psychosocial problems that people experience can make heavy demands on friends, mentors, supervisors, managers, and professional counsellors. The Helping Model involves using skills of active listening, reflecting content and paraphrasing the senders' words and feelings.

It is important at the outset of any helping session to make sure that you are comfortable and relaxed, as well as mentally prepared. You may need to practise some relaxation techniques and/or breathing exercises before the session, to ensure that you are operating from a sense of balance and well-being. This will assist you in becoming a more empathic and effective listener.

The Helping Model is aimed at assisting someone in managing his or her problem. It is not a therapy for solving the person's problem. It is simply a way for you to improve your interpersonal communication, and apply communication skills to assist others you live and work with.

There are many "therapies" that apply techniques to assist people with emotional distress and psychosocial problems. For example, psycho-analytical (Sigmund Freud/Carl Jung), humanistic (Rogers), reality therapy (William Glasser), cognitive-behavioural therapy (Albert Ellis, Aaron Beck, & B. F. Skinner), and solution-focused brief therapy (Steven de Shazer and Insoo Kim Berg), to name a few.

Professional counselling is specialised work carried out by trained and experienced professionals, who are governed by a professional code of ethics that upholds respect for the individual, and a belief in their uniqueness, human capacity for change, and learning potential.

Ultimately the individual alone is responsible for changing his or her circumstances. To ensure the best care, a counsellor works in conjunction with corporate human resource personnel, doctors, psychiatrists, psychologists, and allied health professionals. This ensures that appropriate referral is made to other mental health professionals – to best meet the needs of the client. All counselling interviews are conducted in a professional manner where privacy and confidentiality are assured. Disclosure of confidential information may, in some cases, need to be reported to appropriate persons or agencies.

The Helping Model can assist you in developing a set of attitudes and communication skills which will help you, and people you come into contact with every day, to find out what is going on in other's lives – you help them tell their story.

The ABC of the Helping Model of communication skills can be summarised as:

A. Active listening – to build a relationship.

B. Boiling down the problem – looking at alternatives.

C. Challenging the person to act – encouraging them to take action.

In developing these skills you need to recognise that building a relationship with the person with whom you are communicating is the foundational basis for promoting growth. If you fail to establish a rapport with the person you are seeking to help, then you are unlikely to be of any meaningful assistance.

Most people want to jump to "B" and "C" as it is our natural response to want to "solve" the problems and get a result. In "A" you are finding out what the person is saying, thinking, and feeling – establishing their identity. "A" is foundational to the Helping Model – focusing on the person, not the problem.

To build up trust with the person you are helping, ensure that you;

1. Focus on the person not the problem.

2. Are accepting, not judging the person.

3. Counsel the person and not give advice.

What follows is a checklist for the Helping Model to assist you in developing your basic communication/counselling skills to strengthen your own identity and relationships, and enable you to assist people in your place of work, home and community. Of course, should someone require medical or psychological assistance you will help them the most by referring them to their doctor, allied health or counselling professional.

Your seven-part communication checklist

1. Active listening.

2. Continuing responses – attending skills.

3. Reflection of content – listening with understanding.

4. Reflection of feelings – empathy, the key ingredient.

5. Leading responses – An open invitation to talk.

6. Clarifying and summarising.

7. Attitude – warmth, empathy and genuineness.

1. ACTIVE LISTENING

Listening is the essence of any communication. Active listening is communicating acceptance, trust and respect, at a relationship level. By accepting another's feelings you are saying, "I understand that you feel such-and-such about a particular topic." Active listening encourages openness and a willingness to become engaged with a person. When you are recognised as an active listener you will find that people feel comfortable with you, and bring their problems to you.

■ Do not move too quickly
Move at the other person's pace. Observing and listening to the person (responding from their frame of reference) demonstrates that you are genuinely interested in him/her, and conveys respect – the foundations of a trusting relationship. An active

> **Emotional Wisdom**
> Active listening. A key behaviour that builds a feeling of long-term trust in business, professional, and social relationships.

listener is patient and aware of the communication model described above, and makes adjustments for it. For example, an expert active listener is aware when the sender is simply sending a message, without expecting anything but understanding.

■ Focus on the person
Observe the person's body language, eye contact and facial expressions, to assess how comfortable they may be feeling with you. Where there are two people in a joint interview or discussion, observe the interactions between them. Make adjustments to your posture, interviewing technique, and voice tone, to help the person feel more comfortable.

■ Be comfortable with silences
Allow time for the interviewee to sit, reflect and deal with emotion during times of silence. However, too prolonged a silence may become uncomfortable.

Communication of feelings

■ Content/Relationship Distinctions
Communication takes place at two levels:
1. The **content level** – the subject matter we are discussing.
2. The **relationship level** – what we communicate to the other person about how much we value them, or accept them.

The relationship level operates primarily on feelings: "I feel – valued, accepted, comfortable." If there is mutual respect and trust at a relationship level, it is possible to agree or disagree with equal comfort. However if the mutual respect and trust *does not* exist, then every issue can become a test of the relationship.

■ Acceptance of Feelings
One way we communicate acceptance, trust and respect at a relationship level, is by communicating acceptance of feelings as well as facts. If we only accept facts from people we are accepting them **conditionally**. That is, "I will accept only certain parts of you, I will accept you as long as you aren't expressing feelings." People, however, come fully equipped with feelings – it's a great part of what makes us unique! But when people express feelings and they are not accepted, they tend to push harder – as if to prove that their feelings are justified, or to prove to themselves that it is really all right to feel the way they do. On the other hand, when feelings are accepted they are then expressed in a less pressured, less accusatory and less defensive manner. In addition, once expressed, other deeper feelings can then flow in afterwards.

- Acceptance is Different From Agreement
We have been discussing accepting feelings. But let's distinguish acceptance from agreement. You express **acceptance** when you say, "I understand that you feel such-and-such a way about this topic." You express **agreement** when you say, "You couldn't be more right. I feel that way too." In the first you accept that the other person feels the way he does. In agreement, you *ally* yourself with the other person.

  One way we run into problems with feelings is to assume that if someone has a different feeling than ours, one of us must be right and the other must be wrong. But another way of looking at this is to consider than when two people react differently to the same situation, they are reacting within the rules of their own upbringing, training, experiences and values – that is, their own perspective. Because the training, experiences and values from our upbringing are unique to each person, the rules that govern feelings are also unique to each person. Since the rules are different for each individual, we cannot assume that just because we were disgusted by an event, doesn't mean that someone else is. It may be perfectly consistent within his/her individual reality. For example, one person may be terrified by a small earth tremor, another may be excited by the experience.

- Obliterating Other's Feelings to Prove Ours Correct
This proves nothing. It is a fact that people feel the way they feel. The only appropriate behaviour is to accept that others feel the way they feel, and begin to report the way *we* feel. We may not have the same reactions to the same experiences, but we can begin to share enough of our internal thoughts, beliefs and aspirations to begin to understand each other.

- Presenting Problems
Our culture has erected considerable barriers to the expression of feelings. The individual who expresses strong feelings is considered to be "over-emotional", or "overly sensitive". Read again our discussion in chapter one on **Traditional view of emotion in relation to cognition**. But

our feelings remain. So we learn to express feelings indirectly, through our content messages. Typically, unless one significantly trusts another, feelings become known only by implication.

One characteristic of this "communication by implication" is that people initially send presenting problems – small, relatively innocuous problems that if not rejected, can then lead to the sharing of more basic and deeply experienced problems. The pattern of descending levels of communication – proceeding from the presenting problem to deeper feelings – is typical of communication when there is an effective listener. But many of our conventional communication skills do not encourage this openness. Usually, people listen ineffectively, which then prevents the sharing of deeper feelings. In fact, unless the sender has strong feelings that can override our responses, we may never know about their problems.

Ineffective listening

The basis of much ineffective listening is two-fold. (1) Failure to distinguish those times when the sender is not expecting you to do anything except understand. (2) Failure to listen long enough, or with sufficient understanding of the sender's feelings, to really understand the definition of the problem.

Here are eight typical ways that people respond in a listening situation which communicate to the sender that their feeling is unacceptable.

1. Ordering, demanding. "You must try…", "You have to stop..."
    Don't have that feeling – have some other feeling.
2. Warning, threatening. "You had better...", "If you don't , then..."
    You'd better not have that feeling.
3. Admonishing, moralising. "You should...", "It's not nice to ..."
    You're bad if you have that feeling.
4. Persuading, arguing, lecturing. "Do you realise...?", "The facts are…"
    Here are some facts so you won't have that feeling.
5. Advising, giving answers. "Why don't you...?", "Let me suggest..."
    Here is a solution so you won't have that feeling.

6. Criticising, blaming and disagreeing. "You aren't thinking about this properly..."

   You're wrong if you have that feeling.

7. Praising, agreeing. "But you've done such a good job...", "I approve of..."

   Your feelings are subject to my approval.

8. Reassuring, sympathising. "Don't worry...", "You'll feel better..."

   You don't need to have that feeling.

When the sender perceives that he is getting one of these messages there is a risk that he will become defensive. He will then either justify the feeling further, or close off entirely – never allowing the listener to hear anything deeper than the Presenting Problem.

An alternative – Active listening

An alternative to the above type of responses is to acknowledge the other person's feeling by telling them what you understood them to be feeling and thinking. In active listening, the listener summarises in his own words, the content and feeling of the sender's message and states this to the sender to confirm understanding. They put aside their own frame of reference and take a look at the world from the sender's perspective.

The benefit of active listening

The benefit of active listening is that you can effortlessly communicate acceptance of the sender's feeling. In addition, active listening allows you to "double check" your understanding of the sender's message, and be corrected if you have misunderstood the situation in any way. Frequently, you will find that when you employ active listening, people feel more comfortable in bringing problems to you and in sharing deeper problems. You usually also find that when you use active listening, people are able to talk through their feelings and solve their own problems.

The HOW of active listening

When you listen to others you can listen passively, nod your head and say "Mm hmm" and "I see". At least you are letting the sender know you are there, and are not interrupting them. But they may wonder whether you really hear what they say. And at times, *you* may wonder whether you really understand what the sender is trying to say.

In order to make sure that you understand the sender – and also to let them know how well you understand them – you can restate what you think you *heard* them say.

For example:

Sender: "And as that has happened a number of times, I am about to leave the group."

Listener: "You are considering leaving the group?"

Sender: "Well, I am close to it. I just don't want to be criticised all the time."

Listener: "You are really tired of being criticised."

Sender: "Yes. I want them to stop criticising me – and I'm going to tell them that too! People always do that to me. They think I have no feelings and they can walk all over me."

Listener: "It happens at other times too. But this time, you are going to make them *stop* doing it."

Sender: "I sure will."

Active listening is encouraging the sender to come to their own conclusion of what they should do about the (perceived) problem. The listener makes no judgement about the sender's intended action.

In active listening there are different *levels* of listening.

1. You can just feed back the **content** to the sender – for example, "You are being criticised".

2. A richer kind of listening is when the listener also picks up on the sender's **feelings** as well – for example, "… and that annoys you".

You get to even more basic levels when you listen for sets or patterns – for example, "… and this always seems to happen to you this way". A "set" is a tendency to respond in a certain/typical way to particular situations. It is based on a rather pervasive continuous feeling that a person carries about himself, for example, "no one cares for what I think, I always do it wrong, I always lose, they never seem to notice me", etc. These feelings determine to a great degree how somebody is going to interpret – and therefore react – in a certain situation. If we can help the sender identify these patterns of responses, our contact becomes more meaningful.

When you feed back to someone what they've said and restate it, it is important to do this in a tone that indicates that you accept what they have said as being true for them. If you rephrase their statements in a challenging way you will cause them to be defensive – and stop their flow of thinking.

For example:

Listener: "Do you really believe they criticise you?"

Sender: "Of course they do. Yesterday even they…"

All the sender's energy goes into defending and proving your statement.

Active listening is not all there is to communicating, but it is a very powerful skill. Particularly when you go beyond the initial stage of parroting what was said, plus the feeling it brings out – and instead try to distil the **meaning** of what was expressed, and reflect that back to the sender.

Learning active listening

In the beginning when you try to actively listen you may want to use some helpful phrases to preface your feedback such as; "Let me see if I got you straight…", or "I hear you say…", or "As far as you are concerned…", or "You feel…".

Later on you'll become less mechanical. You'll catch the essence of what is said and inject your feedback in a way that minimally disrupts the flow of the person you are listening to, such as; "That upsets you", "She shouldn't have done that to you", "With hindsight you wish you had done that differently".

Feedback is always tentative. It is asking, "Is this the way you feel?" rather than telling, "This is the way you feel!" If you're unsure you can ask, "Is that right?" or "Does that fit for you?" If the person does not accept your feedback, do not put energy into proving that you were right, or explaining why you thought that this is what they meant. Instead, simply ask them to restate their feelings – what they mean – and **keep listening**!

The most important part of active listening is to find out what the other person's flow is, and to try to follow that to see where they lead themselves – rather than directing them. This is often difficult for beginners because as helpers they might feel that they are supposed to know where the conversation is going. But active listening is more like 'going with the flow of a river' – and the river always knows where it is going.

2. CONTINUING RESPONSES – ATTENDING SKILLS

It is important to listen accurately and respond relevantly to what someone is telling you. We call this "continuing responses".

Mm Hmm's	The simplest verbal response is "Mm, hmm". It communicates, "Continue, I'm listening and I understand." Some other examples of continuing responses include "Aha!" and "… so, go on – yes, I see …". These responses reduce the other person's anxiety by letting them know that they are being heard without judgment.
Echoing/mirroring	This is the listener repeating what the other person has just said. It is usually just one word or a phrase, or the last few words they said. Echoing/mirroring helps you to develop empathy with the other person.

Attending physically	Face the sender– this communicates your availability to them.
	Maintain an open posture – non-defensive.
	Maintain good eye contact – this facilitates deeper involvement.
	Eliminate distracting behaviour – any noise or distractions that may damage the flow of communication.
	Remain consistent and relaxed and remember, everybody wants to be heard.
Attending psychologically	Adopt a good posture, including facial expression, gesturing, and body movements.
	Don't smile when the other person is expressing sadness or talking of having suicidal thoughts.
	Use a warm tone of voice, inflections, spacing, and emphasise certain words.

3. REFLECTION OF CONTENT – LISTENING WITH UNDERSTANDING

Reflection of content – or paraphrasing – is feeding back to the other person the core material of what they have been saying. This helps both you and them to understand and clarify what has been said.

The way in which you listen and respond to others is crucial in order to build a fulfilling relationship.

Listen and respond in ways that make the relationship more distant and impersonal, or listen in ways that bring both the listener and the sender into a closer, more personal relationship. When listening it is crucial to convey to the other person that you have clearly heard and understood their story.

When you listen accurately and respond relevantly, you communicate to them, "I care about what you are saying, and I want to understand it."

It is important that you do not attempt to evaluate what the other person has communicated. A tendency to give evaluative responses is heightened in situations where feelings and emotions are deeply involved.

The most effective communication occurs when this evaluative tendency is avoided by giving understanding responses (paraphrases). An understanding response not only communicates a desire to understand the other person without evaluating their statements, it also helps us to see the expressed ideas and feelings from their point of view.

Although paraphrasing sounds simple it is often very difficult to do. Yet it has powerful effects. Many professional counsellors have found that listening intently to what a person says, understanding how it seems to them, is very helpful to the client.

When you paraphrase the other person's message, it tends to reduce their fears about revealing their thoughts. It decreases their anxiety about what they are communicating. The other person will feel safe, because they are not being judged. Paraphrasing facilitates their psychological health and growth.

For example, this response is an attempt to help both the listener and the sender understand what has been said. The focus of this response is for the listener to echo or mirror the content of what the other person has said.

Sender: "I'm not sure what to do. If I stay at school I will need to make up two courses, plus take two new courses and find a job. If I go home to junior college I could make up the two courses at night, and work for my father during the day."

Listener: "Let me see if I understand your problem (let me try and summarise what I hear the problem to be). You're not sure whether to stay here and be a full-time student, or go home and attend junior college at night and work for your father."

4. REFLECTION OF FEELINGS – EMPATHY: THE KEY INGREDIENT

Empathy is communicating to the other person; "I am with you, I can accurately sense the world as you are feeling and perceiving it." This is a communication of empathic understanding involving sensitivity to current feeling, and the ability to communicate this understanding in a language attuned to the other person's current feeling.

Empathy helps;
a. The listener to feel that they understand the problem,
b. The speaker to open up because they feel that their emotions are understood and accepted, and,
c. The listener has a more objective look at their feelings when the situation is being reflected accurately by the speaker's "mirror" (the listener).

It is not necessary for the listener to share the other person's feelings in any sense that would require the listener to feel the same emotions that the sender feels. It is instead an appreciation of those feelings, and a sensitive awareness of those feelings.

Empathy involves two processes;
a. Awareness and identification of the other's feelings, and
b. Reflection of feelings.

At a high level of accurate empathy, the message "I am with you" is unmistakably clear – the listener's responses fit in perfectly with the speaker's mood and content. Your replies not only indicate a sensitive understanding of the other person's obvious feelings, but they serve to clarify and expand their awareness of their own feelings or experiences. Not only the language appropriate to your exchange communicates this, but also the total voice qualities – which unerringly reflect seriousness and depth of feeling. The listener needs to shift their responses and correct language or content errors in communications, when they are not following what the speaker is trying to communicate.

At a low level of empathy, you may be "off on a tangent" of your own or may have misinterpreted what the other person is feeling. At a very low level, you may be so preoccupied and interested in your own intellectual interpretations that you are scarcely aware of the other person. You may be disinterested in them, or so focused on the intellectual content of what they are saying that you fail to sense their current feelings and experiences. You may be evaluating, giving advice, sermonising or talking about yourself!

5. LEADING RESPONSES – OPEN INVITATION TO TALK

The other person enters the discussion with something that they feel is a problem. Your initial task is to allow them enough time and space to find out how they see the situation. Most useful in determining this is the technique of providing limited structure, through the use of an "open invitation to talk".

An open invitation to talk is best understood when compared to a closed approach, for example;

OPEN: "Could you tell me a little bit about your marriage."
CLOSED: "Are you married? Do you get along with your wife?"

The open comments provide room for the speaker to express himself without the imposed categories of the listener. On the other hand, a closed invitation to talk often emphasises factual content as opposed to feelings. It demonstrates a lack of interest in what the sender has to say, and frequently attacks him or puts him in his place. Closed questions can usually be answered in a few words or with a "yes" or "no".

Crucial to open-ended questions is the concept of who leads the discussion. While the listener should ask questions when using this skill, the questions themselves are centred around the sender's concerns rather than the listener's concerns. The questions should be designed to help the sender clarify his problems, rather than provide information for the listener.

A typical problem with closed questions is that the listener leads the sender toward topics of interest to the listener. Too often a listener projects his or her own theoretical orientation to the information they are trying to gather – imposing artificial structure too early. If the listener relies on closed questions to structure the discussion, they are often forced to concentrate on thinking up the next question – and therefore fail to listen to the sender.

Open invitations to talk are extremely useful in a number of different situations. Here are some examples:

1. To help begin a discussion – "What would you like to talk about today?" OR "How have things been since the last time we talked together?"

2. To get the sender to elaborate on a point – "Could you tell me more about that?" OR "How did you feel when that happened?"

3. To help elicit examples of specific behaviour, so that you are better able to understand what the sender is describing – "Will you give me a specific example?" OR "What do you do when you get depressed?"

4. To focus the sender's attention on his or her feelings – "What are you feeling as you are telling me this?" OR "How did you feel then?"

Focus on feelings

If you are communicating with another person, ask questions about feelings and make sure you get feeling answers in return. Statements that begin with "I feel that …" or "I feel like …" are usually expressions of thought. It would actually be more correct for that person to say, "It seems that …" and, "It seems like …".

Statements that begin with "I feel …", will usually express feelings. If the person gives you a non-feeling answer, paraphrase it and then ask the 'feeling question' again. Don't assume that you know what it means when someone says, "I'm depressed, angry, scared, unhappy, bewildered." Enquire and clarify what their feelings, words, or expressions actually mean to them.

People need to take responsibility for their feelings. A useful definition of responsibility is "the ability to respond or react." Placing responsibility for your feelings on external events renders you powerless to change – unless the external event changes. It denies you the ability to respond or react. "She makes me feel dismissed", does not signify ownership of the feeling.

6. CLARIFYING AND SUMMARISING

It is necessary for the listener to respond for the process of communication to continue. Clarifying ensures correct understanding for you and the other person and helps them "hear" themselves. They then gain insight into their identity and this encourages them to delve deeper into their feelings.

A summary takes what has been said and puts it into a logical useable form. Forming a clear understanding –the total picture so far – occurs when you tie the thoughts and the feelings that represent an emotion state together.

A review of the total picture so far helps the other person to see where they have been and where they are headed. The more accurate you are in summarising content and feelings, the more helpful you will be.

7. ATTITUDES

Warmth	Ability to listen actively
Empathy	Ability to reflect content
Genuineness	Ability to make appropriate comments
Reliability	Confidence
Ownership of feelings	Maturity
Clear communication	Flexibility
Caring voice tone	Wisdom
Self-awareness	

REMEMBER YOUR ABC OF COMMUNICATION SKILLS ...

A. Active listening – Focus on the person not the problem.
B. Boiling down the problem – Accepting not judging.
C. Challenging the person to act – Communicating not giving advice.

LISTEN, REFLECT, EMPATHISE, CLARIFY, SUMMARISE.

 Emotional Leadership Practice

ELP 6.2   Reflecting of feelings

Complete the following record of your discussion by filling in your responses – as a listener – to the situation provided.

SENDER: I don't know what I'm going to do with Ricky. He's into everything! I can't take my eyes off him for a moment. He's on the go all the time, and when I try to stop him he puts on such a tantrum – kicking and screaming. I just can't control him.

YOUR RESPONSE:

_____

_____

SENDER: I'll say. I've just got to "screaming point". He works me up so much that I could...

YOUR RESPONSE:

_____

_____

SENDER: Yes – that's how I feel. I found myself screaming at him last night and I only just managed to stop myself before I really hurt him.

YOUR RESPONSE:

_____

_____

SENDER: I was terrified. What sort of a mother am i?

YOUR RESPONSE:

_____

_____

SENDER: I feel like I'm some kind of monster. But I love him – I really do.

YOUR RESPONSE (Summary):

_____

_____

 Emotional Leadership Practice

ELP 6.3   Reflecting correct intensity of feelings

Reword the reflections of feeling made at the wrong level of intensity with responses that reflect the feeling accurately.

SENDER: Thank you for seeing me at short notice. I'm almost at my wits end. I desperately need someone to talk to.

RESPONSE: So you're feeling a bit worried at the moment?

ACCURATE RESPONSE:

_____

_____

SENDER: A bit? I'm almost going out of my mind. I told you on the phone that my wife's left me, and she's taken our little girl!

RESPONSE: Yes, I sense that you were rather upset. Tell me more.

ACCURATE RESPONSE:

_____

_____

SENDER: Well, it happened following an argument. It was over such a stupid thing. I couldn't find the keys to the car, and we were late for dinner. My wife got upset, I blew my stack – and I hit her. I feel so ashamed.

RESPONSE: So you feel somewhat guilty about it?

ACCURATE RESPONSE:

_____

_____

SENDER: I feel terrible. I've never done anything like that before. Never. If only I knew where she was, I could tell her how sorry I am. But I haven't heard a thing from her since she left.

RESPONSE: You feel sorry that you can't find her?

ACCURATE RESPONSE:

_____

_____

✎ Emotional Leadership Practice
ELP 6.4   Open invitations to talk

Go through the examples of "open invitations to talk" again (that is the RESPONSES in ELP 6.3), and give some possible closed ended questions (wrong responses) in each case. Then change your closed questions to open questions.

_____

_____

_____

_____

_____

EFFECTIVE COMMUNICATION

Effective communication is essential for relationships of any nature – interpersonal, workplace, business, or even service relationships. The communication skills set out and practiced in the earlier sections of this chapter are fundamental to communication of any kind. What makes your communication effective is when you saturate your communication with empathy. When you project your emotional intelligence into your communication you are using your ability to empathise and understand changes and blends in emotion to make correct appraisals of messages received by you to help others to manage their appraisal. Your ability to empathise is communicated through levelling, listening, and validating – the XYZ of communication (Adapted from Montgomery & Evans 1984, 1995)[1]

SOME SIMPLE TOOLS ...

A formula for effective communication

Use the "X-Y-Z" formula to level about feelings and improve communication from inside a relationship.

Use either: "I feel X when you do Y in **situation** Z."

Example: "I feel very frustrated when you bring the car back to me with almost no petrol, just before I have to go out."

Or: "I feel X when you do Y, because the **effect** on me is Z."

Example: "I feel insecure when I see you looking at other women, because I then think that I'm inadequate."

An effective communication framework is:

( ) = optional steps

I feel / felt _____

When you _____ (make this specific, observable, and in the positive)

As / because _____

(It seems / seemed to me _____)

I'd prefer / I'd like _____

Example: "I feel angry when you use the phone in our office for personal calls, as I can't get my work done. I would prefer you used this phone only for genuinely urgent calls, please."

Example: "I felt really annoyed when you told me that you'd be home at 7pm and then didn't arrive home until 8:30pm because I kept the children up to see you. It seems to me that my scheduling doesn't matter at all. I'd like you to keep to your commitments please, or phone to tell me you've been held up at the office."

LEVELLING, LISTENING, & VALIDATING - LLV

Bob Montgomery & Lynette Evans (1995, pp. 133-147) provide "The three basic communication skills" – levelling, listening, and validating.

- **Levelling**
  Levelling means telling the other person clearly and non-defensively how you feel, or how you think about a particular issue, rather than trying to hide your feelings or misrepresent them.

- Listening

  By listening we mean actively trying to hear what the other person really says, rather than assuming you know what he is going to say, or listening to yourself, or interrupting. This gives the listener the opportunity to learn what is going on inside the head and heart of the other person talking. In a relationship, this is often the point where an

  > **Emotional Wisdom**
  >
  > Saturate your communication with empathy. Your ability to empathise is communicated through levelling, listening, and validating – the XYZ of communication. Drop the "YOU" word. Start your sentences with, "I feel…".

  argument starts – the listener perceives he is being criticised or attacked, gets defensive, and retorts with anger.

- Validating

  Validating means to accept as true what the other person tells you about her feelings – rather than denying her feelings, or insisting that she feels as you would, or as you think she should.

Emotional Leadership Practice

ELP 6.4   Practising effective communication

Read again the case study 3.2 presented in chapter three; Tell your inner voice to "check out"! Robert and Laura felt that it was only a matter of time before their marriage was another statistic. They seemed resigned to the fact that they would join the growing number of divorced couples.

Use the formula for effective communication above to appropriately express and validate the feelings of Robert and Laura.

Robert:

Laura:

Summary

Men and women must learn about each other's communication styles if they are to maintain fulfilling relationships in the workplace and the home. Whenever there is communication between two people, one person is the sender and one person is the receiver of the message. Be aware that there are three areas where interference of the communication process can occur, often resulting in an inaccurate decoding of the message.

When you communicate your needs with others, make sure that you prepare and look after yourself before any discussion. The "helping model" is aimed at helping the speaker manage his or her problem. It is not a therapy for solving the person's problem. Develop a checklist of communication skills to assist you in helping others in the home, workplace, or community.

Effective communication is essential for relationships of any nature – interpersonal, workplace, business, or service relationships. Use your knowledge of emotional chains and blends to practice empathy and communication skills – communicate change and **seal** a life of EASE.

EMOTIONAL LEADERSHIP CHECKLIST

Use this emotional leadership checklist to improve your communication by adopting language and techniques to disarm your critics, affirm yourself, and influence others.

- Do I know how to communicate in relationships?
- Have I dropped the YOU word?
- Am I doing the best I can to communicate effectively?

EMOTIONAL LEADERSHIP POINT 1
Do I know how to communicate change?

☐ **Communicating in relationships.**

Business and professional relationships fail through unresolved hurts and ineffective communication. Social relationships fail for these two reasons plus one other – not giving and receiving love according to each other's needs.

Typically, women release negative energy by talking through their experiences. Typically, men release negative energy by reactive behaviour – anger and withdrawal.

Take a moment to reflect on the behaviours you have experienced – by men or women – that left you feeling exhausted or unheard.

☐ **Build a long-term feeling of trust.**

Expressing your thoughts and feelings clearly is vital for building long-term trust in your business, professional, and social relationships.

Emotional leadership is applying emotionally intelligent behaviour to gain trust in relationships.

☐ **Saturate communication with empathy.**

Saturate your communication with empathy. Project your EAR-Identity into your communication with language grounded in a sound understanding of blends and chains of emotion.

EMOTIONAL LEADERSHIP POINT 2
Have I dropped the YOU word?

☐ **The XYZ mode of effective communication.**

Use XYZ statements: "I <u>feel</u> X when you <u>do</u> Y, because the <u>effect</u> on me is Z."

☐ **LLV – Levelling, listening and validating.**

<u>Tell</u> the other person clearly and non-defensively how you feel.

<u>Actively</u> try to hear what the other person really says – instead of assuming you know what he or she is going to say.

<u>Accept</u> as true what the other person tells you about his or her feelings.

EMOTIONAL LEADERSHIP POINT 3

Am I doing the best I can to communicate effectively?

[ ] **Communication model.**

> Eight to 12 percent of communication is verbal, and up to 90 percent non-verbal. Clearly construct verbal messages and listen to make sure an accurate message is received.

[ ] **Your ABC of communication skills.**

A. Actively listen – focus on the person, not the problem.
B. Boil down the problem – be accepting, not judgmental.
C. Challenge the person to act – communicate, don't give advice.

[ ] **Your seven-part communication checklist.**

1. Active listening
2. Continuing responses – attending skills
3. Reflection of content – listening with understanding
4. Reflection of feelings – using empathy
5. Leading responses – open invitation to talk
6. Clarifying and summarising
7. Attitude – warmth, empathy, and genuineness

[ ] **"I" Language.**

When you communicate using "I" language, your understanding of emotion chains and blends, LLV, your ABC communication skills, and your seven-part communication checklist, the person you are communicating with will become engaged with you.

Applying your understanding of changes and blends of emotions with effective communicating strategies is communicating change to **seal** your life of EASE.

Notes

1   Adapted from Montgomery, Bob & Evans, L. (1984, 1995) You and Stress, Penguin Books: Victoria, Australia, Ch 5.

CHAPTER 7

THE POWER
OF CHOICE

IN SHOWING EMOTIONAL LEADERSHIP YOU ARE CHOOSING
TO GIVE TO OTHERS IN A WAY THAT HONOURS THEIR RIGHT
TO BE HEARD, VALIDATED, AND RESPECTED.

INTRODUCTION

To enjoy a life of EASE you must learn to sow emotional leadership. Develop your emotional abilities to empower you to make no-lose decisions that will serve you, your partner, family, workmates, and community. No-lose decisions such as, "Who do I want to be? How do I want to behave?"

These questions are fundamental to your identity as an emotionally intelligent person. You are free to choose awareness over ignorance, assertion over anger, appreciation over fear, and joy over victim-hood. Without conscious choice you will not discover your true vocation in life – your potential for self-actualisation and fulfilment of your life goals.

Motivating yourself to deal with the difficult emotions you experience is the point of transformation for you. It is through dealing with what happens to us that we are empowered to **enjoy** a life of EASE.

EMOTIONAL LEADERSHIP - THE ONWARD PATH

1. SOWING EMOTIONAL LEADERSHIP

You will have heard the expression, "What you sow, is what you reap." This biblical admonition is often interpreted as if you "sow" well – work hard, invest prudently, and achieve in life – you will be successful and "reap" rewards in life. Go all out hard for something you really want – with or without regard for others – and in return you will receive the benefits. That may happen.

In the Judeo-Christian tradition, the intent of "What you sow, is what you reap" is spiritual poverty – in sowing spiritual poverty you will reap rewards in heaven. Spiritual poverty means you are called upon to show deference to

God, whose example teaches you to forget self and provide for the well-being of others. Act always with compassion. The rich must give to the poor. Be free of bigotry and prejudice. Serve your fellow human beings – then you will have riches in heaven.

Sowing emotional leadership is trusting in your emotional abilities and competencies to make no-lose decisions that will serve you and all those with whom you come into contact. Sowing emotional leadership is behaving with emotional intelligence. In sowing emotional leadership you are choosing to give to others in a way that honours their right to be loved, respected, empowered, and treated with dignity.

In *The seven spiritual laws of success*, Deepak Chopra (1996), in describing his Law 3, the *Law of Karma*, says;

Karma is both action and the consequences of that action. It is cause and effect simultaneously –because every action generates a force of energy that returns to us in like kind. There is nothing unfamiliar about the *Law of Karma.* Everyone has heard the expression, 'what you sow is what you reap.' Obviously, if we want to create happiness in our lives, we must learn to sow the seeds of happiness. Therefore, karma implies the action of conscious choice making.

Whether you like it or not, everything that is happening at this moment is a result of the choices you've made in the past. Unfortunately, a lot of us make choices unconsciously, and therefore we don't think they are choices – and yet, they are.[1]

How often have your unconscious choices led you on the wrong path in your life? Paradoxically, sowing emotional leadership for a life of EASE – making right choices – will reap for you an abundance of love, gratitude, and respect. Thereby meeting your need for these things and setting you on the right path to fully realise your life goals.

2. DEFINE YOUR PATH

The place to begin is to define your path. Lawrence (1990) says most people would choose an onward path, if only they knew how.

> Most of us have had a childhood of some confusion, misconception and insecurity. We either withdrew from, conformed to, or rebelled against life as we saw it. And we carry those patterns of behaviour and thinking into our adult lives. For the most part, we are living as a reaction to our childhood experiences and decisions. Our parents had their childhood influencing them! Round and round it goes unless we are freed from our past so that we can live freely in the present. It is ultimately our choice whether to stand still, or move forward in life. I sense that most people would choose an onward path – if only they knew how.[2]

Emotional leadership is the onward path – the path to reshaping and reprogramming your thinking, to heal emotional wounds. Emotional leadership is to develop and apply that rare skill, as Aristotle put it, "to be angry with the right person, to the right degree, at the right time, for the right purpose, and in the right way."[3]

First you must give in to self. Give in to awareness, give in to your point of view, and give in to the old patterns that have not worked for you and have brought you negativity and pain. Give in to loving yourself – only then you will begin to receive, your pain will ease, and you will experience emotional freedom and a life of EASE.

3. POWER OF CHOICE

Conditioning has you trapped in fixed patterns of thoughts, feelings, and actions. Events – people and circumstances – trigger automatic appraisals in you that have not served you well. You have been programmed into making choices automatically. Responding automatically to events. You are what you are today because of the choices you have made.

Whether you choose to go skydiving by jumping out of a plane at 10,000 ft, deep sea diving, travelling to exotic or dangerous places, or watch a love-story at the movies, you feel an emotion that has a positive or negative effect on your body. When you interpret something that is said to you as a manipulation, it will generate a different emotion in you than if you choose to accept it as a compliment.

Emotional arousal creates awareness of your defence against change. How you react when change is placed in front of you will depend upon whether you are a "sensitive" or "reactive" person. The emotion that is generated in you by change, or the thought of change, will vary from person to person. If you are a sensitive person, change will create arousal in you that will linger much longer than if you are a reactive person. This is true whether the arousal brings a positive feeling – for example, a sense of excitement about a trip overseas – or a negative feeling, such as anxiety.

Positive emotions will reduce your stress and help relax you physiologically.

Negative emotions raise your stress levels and harm you physiologically. The resulting emotional constipation will stick with you as you hold your emotions in – refusing to experience them and let go. You will hold onto a sense of being stuck and unhappy with your life's direction.

Power of choice is about regaining control over your EAR-Identity. Reframing your current thoughts, memory, values, beliefs, expectations, and predictions, in a way that your appraisal of them produces the response or reaction you want. Power of choice means deciding to fully engage your emotional abilities to perceive, use, understand and manage your emotions intelligently.

Power of choice is about you empowering you. *You* have the power within you to make right choices in life. You choose who you want to be. You get to be whatever you choose to think. If you choose to think angry thoughts you will suffer negative emotion (stress) in your life. If you choose to have happy thoughts you will enjoy positive emotion. You need to choose the behaviour you want to be.

A word of caution. You can become trapped and stifled by the anxiety of wanting – which drives you further from what you want. In fact, you get to want what you want, instead of achieving what you want. This anxiety of wanting is based on attachment to your fear of survival and fear of death – your need to achieve something before you die. The more you cling to the fear of not surviving, the more you cling to past conditioning. To achieve success you need to incorporate a life of EASE into everyday living where you are detached from the need to survive and the anxiety of wanting. Only then will you be free to exercise and enjoy the power of choice!

MIKE'S JOURNEY – ANGER TO ASSERTION

1. FREE OF CONDITIONING

"Who of you remembers much about the events in your lives between the ages of zero and eight? As a child growing up in the Fijian Islands in the South Pacific, I was fortunate to have an abundance of friends, a pristine environment in which to play, a wonderful Grammar school and school chums, and a guiding morality from Protestant religious instruction. The Fiji coat of arms extolled us to 'Fear God, and honour your King'. Exposed at an early age to a wide variety of cultures, I grew up with an appreciation, love and respect of Fijian, Indian, Chinese, Australian, American and English, cultures and values. I can recall the loving care I received from my mother and father, family, relatives, and the family house girl and her family. The games I played were wholesome, outdoors, and filled with challenges – sailing, fishing, climbing, cricket, hockey and rugby. Swimming in crystal clear streams and the coral-filled sea were everyday events.

But did growing up in the South Pacific – my childhood conditioning – make me emotionally wise, so that later in life I could deal with the effects of alcohol disease within me? Did my childhood conditioning prepare me to handle the hurt, loss, grief and trauma, of a totally unexpected rejection and divorce from my former wife, and a lifetime separation from my two infant daughters? Did my conditioning help me in 1992 at the age of 43, to understand betrayal, further rejection, raging anger, and a sense of unworthiness? No. Not at all.

Have you reached the age of 20, 30, 40, or even 50, and felt completely stupid – even overwhelmed? That even though you knew intuitively that an understanding of emotions was important – and felt you were prepared for anything – when called upon to manage your emotions, you were left wanting, and did not know what to do?

You may ask, "Surely we are equipped from childhood to deal with the emotional traumas that life deals us?". Sadly – and what every eight-year-old should know – many adults have not been taught about the emotions that run (or ruin) our lives!

It wasn't until I reached my late 20's, then my early 40's, that I began to fully understand what it meant to be emotionally literate. The realisation that I was not totally adequate or knowledgeable in this area of life was difficult for me to accept. It is only now in my 50's, that I am becoming free of my conditioning. Free of the pain from past mistakes, secure to live life's uncertainty as a source of growth and understanding."

2. MIKE'S STORY

"I am a **reactive** person. My journey of awareness didn't really start until I was an adult and already married. At 25-years of age my first wife left me – taking our two-year-old twin daughters with her. It was a traumatic and painful experience for all concerned that endures to this day. Today I have no contact with my daughters. You can learn to manage your pain, but you never forget the painful experience. You can manage memory – you can't remove it.

The rejection and loss of my family was a point of transition for me, my 'Oh Shit!' experience. But not in time to save my marriage and retain the love and support of my former wife.

After the separation I received counselling from a lady attached to the

Catholic Cathedral in Adelaide, South Australia. It was there that I learnt for the first time about awareness, and the parent, adult, child ego states in transactional analysis. Sadly, I do not recall the counsellor's name. But 30 years ago she set me on a path of learning. I discovered that alcohol abuse and angry, violent behaviour is offensive and not appropriate behaviour. That severe lesson cost me my marriage to a woman that I loved but abused. It also caused me the loss of my daughters' love – who grew up without me.

I met and married Karen Alm some years later. We have enjoyed 27 years together and have two wonderful sons. We spent our first six fantastic years living on a 30-hectare sheep property in Wistow, South Australia – approximately 45 kilometres from the city – where we 'farmed' 120 ewes and lambs on weekends. In 1984, as a mature-age student, I graduated with a degree in Accountancy from the University of South Australia. Karen and I threw caution to the wind. We sold our farm and set off immediately on an 18-month odyssey to 38 countries on four continents. From the bustle of Bangkok to the majesty of the Annapurnas in Nepal; from the Kandian dancers of Sri Lanka to the stillness of the Dal Lake in Kashmir, Northern India. From Table Mountain in Cape Town, to the inner chamber of the Great Pyramid of Cheops in Egypt. From Galway Bay in Ireland, to Hull, Yorkshire in the UK – where my grandfather as a young man, had set out in the 1890's to become a Master Mariner settling in the Fijian Islands.

In September 1985 on returning to the Gold Coast in Queensland, Australia, I was accepted into the state civil service as a Corporate Inspector. Instead, I chose to set up a take-away food shop – one of those forks in the road of life. I love to cook. But after three years, the grind of cooking hamburgers, and fish and chips 12 hours a day, seven days a week, lost its appeal and we sold up – losing a lot of money in the process. We started out as nice guys trying to be tough – we ended up as tough guys trying to be nice!

By 1989 I felt a growing call to serve in the public ministry of the church. We moved back to Adelaide, and I completed a four-year degree in theology."

3. EXPERIENCE IS WHAT YOU DO WITH WHAT HAPPENS TO YOU

"From 1989 until 1992 I studied full-time at a seminary in Adelaide, South Australia. Karen was employed full-time and supported my decision to prepare for the public ministry of the church. We were ably suited for the roles of pastor and pastor's wife – Karen being trained as a social worker and I with considerable life experience. We had the support and best wishes of pastors and friends throughout the church, having been active members for some 15 years.

Whilst I had given up permanent secular employment to study full-time, I remained troubled by my father's admonition to "get a job" and my own value of being the "provider". Our first son was born in 1990. And as we were financing my study in the seminary, the lack of income was also a concern.

During those four years I examined myself closely to see if this was my right calling – my vocation. I saw my time at the seminary as a time for reflection. A chance to challenge past behaviours and explore my suitability for the role of public ministry. My inner voice was particularly strong at the time – telling me that I didn't measure up in various ways. For a start, I had divorced and remarried – something that at the time was tolerated, but not really accepted in the church Karen and I attended.

Early in 1993, after successfully graduating with a Bachelor of Theology degree, and in anticipation of continuing to complete two final years of post-graduate study in pastoral ministry, I received a letter from the principal of the seminary. He advised me that a decision had been made some two years earlier by the seminary faculty, that I be excluded from public ministry. This decision, up until then, had never been communicated to me. It was revealed only after I had applied for re-admission to the post-graduate course.

The deceit and betrayal I felt was bewildering and heart-wrenching. I felt deceived, betrayed, angry and humiliated. Knowing that this decision had been withheld triggered an angry response within me. I wrote a letter of protest to the president of the church, complaining about the way the decision had been made without consultation. After a three-month delay, the president of the church issued me with the one-line reply, "We are sorry you see things the way you do." Karen and I felt totally dismissed, disrespected, abandoned, and helpless.

I felt my rejection by the church very keenly. It was a source of enormous pain. What hurt the most was their challenge to my integrity. I became consumed by the psychological trauma of trust that had been betrayed. What followed was four years of unemployment, a substantial loss of income, severe stress headaches, and a general deterioration in health, as I began the long road back to normalcy. During most of this period I grieved over my loss of opportunity for public ministry – something that at the time, I felt called upon by God to do. Instead, I had to deal with my anger, rejection, loss of face, and severe lowered self-esteem.

My inner voice took over from the 'men of the church' and became my critic;

"How could they do this to Karen and I?"

"Why won't they talk to us about it?"

"You are too set in your ways – they are threatened by you."

"You wouldn't have made a good pastor anyway."

"They didn't really want you Mike. You're not one of them."

After four years, my doctor – who knew my emotional pain – said, "Mike, you are the one displaying the symptoms." He was referring to the symptoms of stress and negativity felt in my body. My career psychologist taught me to slow down, get to know my inner voice, and start working on the four-step process to reframe the negative messages in my head, pounding away day and night. My psychologist helped me to accept that the men who ran the church – and who had not counselled me about their decision to exclude me from the ministry, nor had they subsequently acknowledged my pain of rejection – were doing the best they could, given their level of awareness at the time. He said, "You are talking to the wrong kind of people!"

At last here was a path forward.

I used the cognitive-behavioural strategies now encapsulated in *Emotional Leadership* and *The EASEQuadrant® Workshop*, to deal with my appraisals and negativity. Slowly, I put the pieces together and began the road back. My self-esteem returned. I completed an MBA degree, enrolled in a PhD program and served as a visiting lecturer in a Polytechnic in Singapore. I set up my own human support organisation with Karen in Singapore, created *The EASEQuadrant® Workshop* – a human development program on emotional leadership – and wrote a book with Karen; *Emotional Leadership. Using emotionally intelligent behaviour to enjoy a life of EASE.* The children's version, *Emotional Leadership For Kids*, will be released in June 2005.

I finally realised that what I had seen in the men who had disenfranchised me from the public ministry in the church, I had failed to see in myself. My perception (appraisal) of the 'men of the church' was a mirror of what was going on inside of me.

I blamed them for excluding me from public ministry. And I had projected my angry feelings onto someone else. They had the problem, not me! And I was going to let them know. Who did they think they were? They couldn't treat me like this – without respect, and affirming my rights. But this attitude only fuelled my anger.

I saw in the pastors and presidents of the church what I failed to see in myself. I had determined that the men of the church were 'the enemy'. But my enemy was within me. My perception justified my need for vindication. And my response was anger.

Finally I realised the lesson in this terrible experience – I was the one who made me angry, no one else!

In turning my loss of ministry in on myself I chose to deal with my pain as a reactive person. My response to a perceived attack on my integrity was anger. The chain of emotions I experienced; anger, disrespect, abandonment and guilt, led to depression and lowered self-esteem. My automatic response was the conditioned response of dealing with pain, as a reactive person.

My anger was a reflection of my own appraisal of events. I alone was responsible for my emotional distress, not the men of the church. In reacting to my experience of pain I had chosen anger over assertion – I had given away my power. I had opted for victim-hood, over a life of EASE.

My need for vindication (an attitude) triggered an appraisal that set off a reactive response (anger) in me. This is how a reactive person deals inappropriately with pain, until they let go of past conditioning.

I do not condone what was done to Karen and I by the men of the church. It forever changed my trust in organised religion – but not in my spirituality. However, had I been able to manage my emotion better at the time, and used the 4-Step Cognitive Framework, I would have immediately seen that I was the one displaying the symptoms – *I* was the one talking to the wrong kind of people. It would have saved me a lot of pain and time.

It took four years for me to learn that there is another, easier, way to deal with deep-rooted anger – change your attitude, belief, value, or expectation. A change of perception would have generated a different response to my experience – assertion.

In experiencing deep anger about my dismissal for ministry, I learned the truth of Aldous Huxley's words, "Experience is not what happens to you; it is what you do with what happens to you." I challenged my EAR-Identity and thereby aspects of my personality. I moderated my need for vindication (for truth) by rising from my point of view to my viewing point. I became more tolerant of ambiguity.

As events happen to me today, at the age of 55, I am a reactive person who uses the gap between event and response to moderate my behaviour. I choose to sit on my hands, take time-out, draw on my emotional intelligence, using the "breathing square" technique, and the 4-Step Cognitive Framework to generate positive emotion to balance the stress felt in my body. I process events into action in present moment awareness to enjoy the behaviour I want to be, and I enjoy a life of EASE."

4. CREATING TRANSITION – LIFE IS FOR MAKING MEMORIES

"The combination of the secular professional assistance I received, helped me to understand how I could deal with my pain and move on. It was the help of these professional people that gave me hope. Their advice helped trigger a compassionate response in me. Transformation first began by forgiving the men who had – or so it had seemed – dismissed me.

Emotional leadership reminds me of my essential purpose – to love and be loved. Life is for making memories. The events that cause you pain – those that you experience in unawareness – are the events you learn the most from. Make the choice – as I did – to be free from past conditioning, free to live a life of EASE.

Many of you will be motivated to change, by your experience of pain. Others will hold onto the agitation and irritation in your lives driven by the fear of not surviving.

> **Emotional Wisdom**
>
> Example 1: Mike learned that using anger in the short-term was effective in that it helped to ease his pain. In the long-term Mike's use of anger was injudicious, in that anger was channelled into maintaining his rage and directed outwards at others – with terrible results. By engaging with his anger and accepting his worst points, Mike was empowered to channel his anger into assertion. In doing so he now uses anger with wisdom and discernment to achieve his goals – without offending others, or turning his anger in on himself.

Life has a habit of holding us hostage to our lack of awareness. Only a fool is totally secure about himself. At the right moment the teacher will appear to help you release your pain.

As you begin your journey of awareness you may find your path blocked. You will find that the central impediment to change has been *you*. You will be overwhelmed by your character defects and low level of emotional ability. This is the beginning of meaningful change.

I chose assertion over anger. An inner change of attitude from anger and a need for vindication, to a life of EASE that transformed my life. Expert on Asian wisdom, Chin-Ning Chu (1992), says;

'Transformation' has no fixed formula. It results from your willingness to do battle within, and your unceasing courage to cultivate inner strength to overcome your liabilities. Through this self-cultivation, you will eventually produce the magical fruit that will transform your attitudes in every aspect of your life.[4]

My life experiences – together with my passion for helping people through times of change – have eventually led to Karen and I establishing a cognitive-behavioural counselling and behavioural coaching practice. We provide emotional intelligence testing and reporting, and employee assistance programs, to support people experiencing emotional distress and/or psychological problems. The mission of our organisation – Goslings International Pte Ltd – is to raise the well-being of people around the world."

My advice for moving forward:

"Life is for making memories. What you do should come from your desire to live fully – rather than from reasoning (explaining) and arguing (complaining) to justify yourself. Self-acceptance is releasing other people's opinions about you. Never let others' opinions affect your view of yourself. Always act with compassion toward others – be understanding, accepting and forgiving. Surround yourself with people who make you feel good – and leave the rest in the dust of your victories!"

KAREN'S JOURNEY FROM FEAR TO APPRECIATION

"I have always understood my feelings and articulated them well. As young as 14-years of age, I remember my mother telling me to "stop analysing everything". I was constantly thinking, interpreting, discussing or journaling the things that I felt.

I am a **sensitive** person. My parents never displayed conflict. And the message my siblings and I consistently heard was, "If you haven't got anything nice to say, then don't say anything at all." My nature and conditioning resulted in an innate and learned disability of not knowing how to behave in a conflict situation. The first person in my life to yell at me was Mike!

Early in our communication, if the tone of Mike's voice indicated that he was irritated or frustrated, I would interpret that as him being mad or angry with me. Feeling wounded and misunderstood, my response was to withdraw. I thought that withdrawing was the 'correct' thing to do. And I'd wait for an apology from Mike, who had 'lost his cool' and hurt my feelings. After all, I had done nothing wrong! I had certainly not said anything that wasn't nice.

I believed that Mike would know that I was a caring, calm and loving person, and that I would not deliberately irritate or frustrate him. If only he would simply tell me what the problem was – in a quiet and respectful tone – Not only would I listen gladly, but I would also be very willing to change my behaviour so he was not so upset.

I experience conflict as extreme anxiety in my body. Without any doubt, conflict, raised voices, and sarcastic tones, cause my body to become extremely aroused – in a negative way. Initially I thought that all people experienced this physical response. Even hearing people use raised or angry voices in another room can set off this physical response in me. Understanding this now, I realise that this is the reason I seek harmony in my environment wherever possible; at home, or work, or in my personal relationships. "Be pleasant, talk in a normal voice", I can hear myself requesting of others. I will usually avoid conflict – rather than deal with it – in an attempt to minimise the arousal I experience in a situation of conflict.

After the events of September 11, 2001 in the USA, my body manifestations escalated. On that day, I felt terror like I had never known it before. In the days that followed – especially as I counselled those affected personally by the tragedy – I became flooded with negative feelings. They were mostly irrational – but they were there nonetheless. During that time I felt; fearful, alarmed, trapped, unsafe, restricted, constrained, lost, inadequate, helpless, powerless, controlled, and anxious.

From that time on I became more irritable and short-tempered, frazzled and sometimes withdrawn. The smallest stress would set me off. My heart always seemed to be pounding and my chest racing. Any irritability displayed by Mike or the children would set off a reaction in me. I felt as though Mike should know what I was going through and try to be considerate of my feelings. I was often grumpy and would snap back at others.

My adrenalin was near saturation level. I recognised the feelings as anxiety, but I couldn't determine what I was so anxious about. Were terrorists coming to Singapore? Not likely. Yet I would wake in the morning with my heart pounding. It was just getting ridiculous!

I decided to try herbal medication to alleviate the physical symptoms. I found that calming tablets from the pharmacy helped to take the edge off the distressing sensations in my body. This not only helped me to remain focused during the day, but it also assisted me in getting a much better sleep at night. What I learned by this experiment with such calming medications was that my over-active mind was my own worst enemy. It kept me awake many nights with swirling thoughts.

Then in quick succession I read two amazing books; *The Highly Sensitive Person* by Elaine Aron (1997)[5] and *Peace From Nervous Suffering* by Dr Claire Weekes (1972)[6]. In both books I experienced astonishment, the "Oh my God, this is me" reaction, as I read about the physical manifestations associated with arousal as experienced by the sensitised person.

An explanation at last! This was real – it wasn't "just in my head". I truly felt the stress chemical adrenalin in my body. This now explained my tendency to withdraw, to become speechless, to instinctively want distance during times of emotional pain in a relationship. And it also explained why I needed time to "warm up" following an argument. As a **reactive** person, Mike always recovered much faster than me and often believed I was 'punishing' him by responding slowly with warmth and affection.

Weekes (1972, p. 7) writes;

Our feelings become calm because we change our mood. Changing mood (attitude) is the only conscious control – other than medication– we have over our involuntary nerves, and so over our symptoms of stress.

Since exploring the explanation of adrenalin and nervous suffering – and the techniques to manage first and second stages of fear once I recognise the state of arousal – I have understood even more about myself. The adage, "You are responsible for your own feelings" now registers as true. It is *my* body that feels these sensations, these pains. The thoughts that are associated with the pain are mine too – the irrational, anxious and blaming thoughts. Often these thoughts interpret the intentions or actions of others inaccurately. For example, when Mike would raise his voice to staff in a shop I would feel, "Mike is embarrassing me". In reality, I realise that he would not deliberately embarrass me, nor hurt me in any way. He loves me. I have mountains of evidence of that.

Yes, I may *feel* embarrassed – but Mike is not embarrassing me. Through blaming or "projecting out" my feelings it *seems* that Mike is embarrassing me. In fact, I am seeing in Mike what I have failed to see in myself – I am thinking "I feel embarrassed", and the arousal I feel in my body comes from my own thoughts.

I can now separate my feelings and judgemental, blaming thoughts, and work solely on reducing my arousal state by maintaining a positive mental attitude. In August 2002 I went to have some energy rebalancing done in order to clear the negative energies surrounding me. I felt validated to learn that the vast number of electro-magnetic devices we use today bombard our personal energy fields – causing feelings of stress and negativity. I also learned ways to strengthen and retain the positive experiences that I have.

> **Emotional Wisdom**
>
> Example 2: Karen learned that "blaming out" and expecting others to match up to her conditioned but unowned expectations, was effective in the short-term. It helped her deal with the pain she felt when in the presence of conflict. But in the long-term Karen needed another strategy to release the first and second fear she felt in her body. Managing her fear in the long-term meant not avoiding it or trying to switch it off by withdrawal, but training herself to be ready to go *through* fear.

Now, everyone is benefits – the children, Mike, the maid, our clients, and most of all me! I feel much more "in control". Through experiencing my pain

I know that I have finely tuned my body even better than before, and I am not beholden to it. I may still experience the arousal state, but I am able to manage it – I am in charge! For that I feel settled, which is the state in which I function best. So now I can create that settled state whenever the need arises.

I chose appreciation over fear. Enjoyment of family, friends, clients, and a life of EASE over fear, anxiety, and nervous illness."

MAKING NO-LOSE DECISIONS

"Be careful! You may make the wrong decision!"

Ever thought or heard this statement before? One of your biggest fears is that you have made, or will make, a wrong decision.

Susan Jeffers (1987), in her book, *Feel the fear and do it anyway*, says;

> The problem is that we have been taught, "Be careful! You might make the wrong decision!" A wrong decision! Just the sound of that can bring terror to our hearts. We are afraid that the wrong decision will deprive us of something – money, friends, lovers, status, or whatever the right decision is supposed to bring us.[7]

Making decisions can be a stressful time as people weigh up the reasons "for" and "against" the choice they are about to make. You may even put off making a decision as a way of handling the stress of having to make it. Or to avoid hurting someone in whom you've placed your trust, or to whom you've made a commitment – especially if your decision now is to break that commitment. Eventually, making a decision is something you will need to do on your own, after taking into consideration all the advice you can gather.

Susan Jeffers (1987, p. 112-117) tells us that, "… all you have to do to change your world is change the way you think about it." She presents decision making as a No-Win Model and a No-Lose Model (Figure 7.1).

Essentially, Jeffers sees the Choice Point as where your inner voice rules – making it difficult to make a decision. The No-Win Model is where you are constantly reassessing your decision. Each choice seems to be a no-win choice. The multitude of choices that pop into your head make it difficult to know which is the *right* choice.

Should I do this or should I do that? What if I go this way and that happens? What if it doesn't work out the way I plan? What if ..."
Jeffer's views the No-Lose Model as the way forward. "If you stand at the No-Lose Choice Point, your 'fearless' self takes over."

Figure 7.1

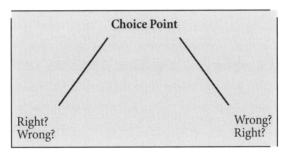

NO-WIN MODEL

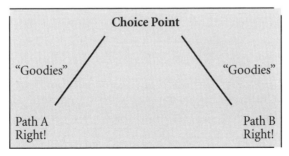

NO-LOSE MODEL

CASE STUDY 7.1 – MAKING NO-LOSE DECISIONS

Dave agonises over a decision to marry or not marry, and the commitment he has made to Cynthia.

Dave came to counselling looking for clarity about making a commitment to his partner in a future marriage relationship. He had been engaged to Cynthia for six or seven months and all arrangements were in place for the wedding. But Dave had struggled during this period with his anxiety as to whether Cynthia was the "right" partner for him. Dave was European and Cynthia was Asian – there were social and cultural issues involved.

Dave had a need to feel loved. He felt that this need was met when Cynthia said, "I love you" – which wasn't often. Cynthia felt it wasn't necessary to continually profess her love to Dave. As Dave agonised over his decision to marry he took the absence of these words from Cynthia as a sign that she didn't love him. He needed her to pay attention to him. In return, he wanted to make sure she was happy. He wanted to make her feel good and be her protector.

Dave felt that Cynthia did not meet his expectations. He felt she was clumsy and wasn't as well educated as him. He wondered if she would meet his long-term need for intelligent conversation. Dave was an organised person and planned everything years in advance. Cynthia didn't like to plan too far ahead. She preferred to take things as they came. This worried Dave. And yet, Cynthia's spontaneity was the very thing that attracted him to her in the first place.

Cynthia had visited with Dave's overseas relatives on one occasion. Back home, some of Dave's friends felt that he was rushing into the marriage. They had found Cynthia to be quiet and reserved – quite the opposite of her natural behaviour. They were concerned that she didn't "join in" with their visits to the local pub.

Dave felt that if he decided to marry Cynthia he would lose his friends back home. Some had told him that they could never accept Cynthia as one of them. Other significant losses on marrying Cynthia would be that he may have "missed out" on the woman of his dreams. He would be marrying someone who did not use language such as "I love you". And he would have to make sacrifices in terms of spending less time with his friends, and learning to adjust to the cultural differences between himself and Cynthia.

Dave kept asking himself, "How would he feel when she wanted to go clubbing on her own, when I don't enjoy clubbing? What if there is someone else out there more suited to me with whom I could share my life? What if the 'perfect' partner appeared just after my wedding? What if Cynthia doesn't really love me? What if my friends never accept her? How will we manage if she finds living in my home country too cold? Would I be happy to live permanently in Asia?"

Dave felt that if he decided not to marry Cynthia, he would also lose. He would never again experience her vitality and aliveness, and would miss the learning experience of a cross-cultural relationship. He recalled that he got on well with Cynthia's family and they had always welcomed him into their circle. He would experience significant pain over his loss of her warmth and presence. He would lose a relationship with someone he truly cared for.

When he thought of not marrying Cynthia, Dave kept asking himself, "What if she is the right person for me? What if we can learn to manage the different family backgrounds and cultures? How would I feel if I just accepted that she isn't going to say, "I love you" every day? What if my friends don't accept Cynthia, would we still have each other?

What should Dave do? On what basis should Dave make his decision?

Dave's no-lose decision

Using Jeffer's No-Lose Model of decision-making puts Dave in control. Dave's first fear arises when he thinks of his upcoming wedding. He feels acute arousal from the fear of just knowing that he must make a decision, and soon – as the wedding day draws ever closer. First fear changes to second fear when Dave does not know if he is making the 'right' decision. Soon the "what if's" fill his mind. Dave's fear turns into anxiety and the longer these negative, confused thoughts go around in his head, the more he starts to feel out of control and unable to make a decision. He sees himself in a no-win situation. If he marries Cynthia, its no-win and if he doesn't marry Cynthia, its no-win.

Furthermore, being a sensitive person, Dave experiences heightened arousal as he is confronted by all the various alternatives that flood his mind at decision time. For anyone suffering emotional distress at this heightened level of arousal, it is generally not a good time to be making decisions. Your body will be experiencing stress beyond optimal level – which makes thinking and reasoning more difficult.

As Dave grapples with his decision, he is confronted by his value of "following through on his commitments". He has come to know Cynthia's family well, and he feels responsible for causing them a loss-of-face. He is experiencing guilt about this, about "letting Cynthia down". And these thoughts are only adding to his level of stress.

The No-Lose Model provides Dave with two alternatives – both of which will give him a way forward, and both of which will involve pain. However, each path is an opportunity for change – despite the outcome! Whichever path Dave takes he will have learned something new about himself that he can carry into this or his next long-term relationship. He needs to make his decision based on an analysis of the costs and benefits of either no-lose path, given his current level of awareness.

Which path should Dave take? He needs to weigh up the costs versus benefits.

1. Dave sets an objective, his intent – "I want to be established in my home country by January 2003 to complete my post-graduate studies."
2. Having established an objective, a goal, Dave needs to become detached from the goal. Let it sit there and not let himself be driven by it. Being goal-focused is the "I'm in a no-win scenario."
3. Dave must set down all the facts (benefits and costs) for Alternative 1; "I will marry Cynthia and we will settle in my home country". Write out all the pros and cons for this decision.
4. Dave needs to set down all the facts (benefits and costs) for Alternative 2; "I will not marry Cynthia and therefore not settle with her in my home country."

5. When Dave makes his no-lose decision based on his level of awareness and the information available to him at the time, he cannot look back later and say, "Oh dear, I made a mistake." (see Making 'right choices' below).

Making decisions using Jeffer's No-Lose Model, is assisted by what you feel in your "gut" – in your abdomen. Trust your body in that it will tell you what it needs, and coupled with the above strategy you can have absolute confidence in your ability to make decisions.

MAKING "RIGHT" CHOICES

Making "right" decisions causes many people anxiety. How often have you weighed up all the "for and against" factors before making a decision, and yet still not be *completely* sure that you have made the right decision. You may ask yourself, "What if I've made a mistake? What if I should have chosen Path A instead of Path B"?

You will have heard the cliché, "If you're not making mistakes now and then, you are not doing anything." Recall our earlier discussion on "mistake" in chapter three;

Mistake is a label you apply in retrospect. When you realise you could have done something more reasonable – even though, the decision was right at the time you made it. Mistake is a label you apply to your behaviour at a later time, when your awareness has changed.

How often have you heard someone say, "I have a gut feeling about this. I just know intuitively that it's the right choice to make. It feels right." This is your intuition – your identity – speaking to you. Intuition is the mind having an immediate insight to something – but it's felt in your abdomen. You 'know' that you have made the right choice by the feeling inside of you.

On making a right choice, Deepak Chopra (1996, p.42) says,

When you make a choice – any choice at all – you can ask yourself two things: First of all, "What are the consequences of this choice that I'm making?" In your heart you will immediately know what these are. Secondly, "Will this choice that I'm making now bring happiness to me and to those around me?" If the answer is yes, then go ahead with that choice. If the answer is no, if that choice brings distress either to you or to those around you, then don't make that choice. It's as simple as that.

People feel emotion as sensations in different parts of their body. You may feel emotion in your heart, abdomen, head, arms or legs. Wherever you feel emotion strongest in your body is where you will know which choice is right for you. Listen to your body. It is key to your power of choice. Your body won't lie to you. It will speak to you and tell you what it needs to enjoy a life of EASE.

POWER OF SELF-MANAGEMENT

Power of self-management means;

- Managing emotion within you. Give yourself free reign to experience emotions within you at appropriate times – rather than repressing the feeling. This will enable you to generate and use emotion to be a better problem-solver and decision maker.
- Being objective in how you perceive, use, and understand emotion states – rising from your point of view to your viewing point.
- Acting with intention and wisdom in how you react to events – rather than responding without thinking, or being driven by your inner voice.
- Making no-lose decisions by engaging with your emotions. Trusting and valuing emotions as a tool in the process of change – preparing you for revitalisation and renewal.

Summary

Power of choice is about sowing emotional leadership – trusting your emotional abilities to make no-lose decisions that will serve you, your partner, family, workmates, and community. In sowing emotional leadership you are choosing to give to others in a way that honours their right to be loved, respected, empowered, and treated with dignity. Paradoxically, by sowing emotional leadership for a life of EASE, in return you will reap an abundance of love, gratitude, and respect, to meet your own needs.

Ultimately, power of choice is to engage with your emotions – trusting and valuing emotions as tools in the process of change, preparing and transforming you for revitalisation and renewal to **enjoy** a life of EASE.

EMOTIONAL LEADERSHIP CHECKLIST

Use this checklist and sow emotional leadership to make no-lose decisions and right choices for self-management.

- Do I know what the power of choice brings?
- Have I created my right path forward?
- Can I apply emotional intelligence to self-management?

EMOTIONAL LEADERSHIP POINT 1
Do I know what the power of choice brings?

☐ Learn to trust your emotions.

Motivating yourself to deal fully with the difficult emotions you experience is your point of transformation.

Power of choice is regaining your control to perceive, use, understand, and manage your emotions for effective decision-making and regulation of life tasks.

☐ **Sowing emotional leadership.**

In choosing to behave with emotional intelligence you are giving to others in a way that honours their right to be loved, respected, empowered, and treated with dignity.

Choosing to sow emotional leadership will reap an abundance of love, gratitude, and respect, to satisfy your need for these same things.

EMOTIONAL LEADERSHIP POINT 2
Have I created my right path forward?

☐ **Emotional leadership is the onward path.**

Emotional leadership is your path to reshaping and reprogramming your thinking to heal emotional wounds and choose behaviour you want to be.

Only you can challenge your EAR-Identity to create the kind of person you want to be.

☐ **Give in to self.**

First you must give in to self – give in to awareness, give in to your point of view, and give in to the old patterns that have brought you negativity and pain.

☐ **Rise to your viewing point**

Conditioning has you trapped in fixed patterns of thought, feelings, and actions. Break out. Choose who you want to be.

[ ] **A word of caution – you get to want what you want.**

You can become trapped, stifled by the anxiety of wanting – which drives you further from what you want. In fact, you get to want what you want – instead of achieving what you want.

It's far better to manage your arousal state and feel settled. In this settled state you will function at your best. You can create that settled state – the required mood – whenever the need arises.

EMOTIONAL LEADERSHIP POINT 3

Can I apply emotional intelligence to self-management?

[ ] **Learn to trust your emotions.**

Learn to trust your "gut feeling". This is your intuition – your EAR-Identity – speaking to you, telling you how to behave with emotional intelligence.

Intuition is the mind having immediate insight to something, but it's felt in your abdomen. You "know" that you have made a "right choice" from the feeling in your body. Your body doesn't lie to you, choose to listen to its message.

If your choice brings distress either to you or to those around you, then choose not to make it. Learn to trust in your emotions.

[ ] **Emotion management tasks.**

Motivating yourself to deal fully with the difficult emotions you experience is the point of transformation for you.

Power of Choice is you regaining your control to perceive, use, understand, and manage your emotions for effective decision-making, and regulation of emotional self-management tasks.

☐ **Power of choice.**

Act with intention and emotional wisdom in how you respond to events in your life – rather than reacting without thinking, or being driven by your inner voice.

Make no-lose decisions by engaging with your emotions. Trusting and valuing emotions as a tool in the process of change, preparing and transforming you for revitalisation and renewal to **enjoy** your life of EASE.

Notes

1   Chopra, D. (1996) *The seven spiritual laws of success*. Bantam Press, London. pp. 39-40.
2   Laurence, A.M 1990, *You've got what it takes. A Guide to self-discovery and effective living*, Lotus Publishing House, Sydney, p. 4.
3   Quoted in Goleman, D. (1995) *Emotional Intelligence. Why it can matter more than IQ*, Bantam Books, New York, p. xiii.
4   Chin-Ning Chu (1992) *Thick face black heart*. Allen & Unwin, Sydney. pp. 173-174.
5   Aron, Elaine N (1997) *The highly sensitive person*, Broadway Books, New York.
6   Weekes, Dr Claire (1972) *Peace from nervous suffering*, Angus & Robertson, UK.
7   Jeffers, S. (1987) *Feel the fear and do it anyway*, Random House, London. p. 111.

CHAPTER 8

$A \cdot E$
$E \cdot S$

LIFE OF EASE

SET YOUR INTENTIONS, DESIRES, AND GOALS INTO THE
SPIRITUAL REALM. REMAIN DETACHED FROM THE OUTCOME
AND LET WISDOM WORK ITS WORK.

INTRODUCTION

A time of crisis is also a time of opportunity.

The Chinese define risk as the combination of danger and opportunity. Greater risk means you have an increased opportunity to do well – but also an increased danger of doing badly.

As share values plummet some people view a downturn in the stock market as a crisis – a time of danger and financial loss. On the other hand, some see plummeting share prices as a once-in-a-lifetime opportunity – a chance to buy solid equities at a low price! A crisis in the stock market may also be an opportunity. While the crisis precipitated lower share prices for some investors, others may view this situation as an opportunity to buy.

Change can be a time of crisis *or* opportunity – depending on your perception of change. Crisis has within it the potential for change that is seldom present in the normal course of events. A crisis in the workplace – such as retrenchment; in the home – such as infidelity; and also within – such as lowered personal esteem and depression, are all opportunities for change!

You may be involved with managing change in teams, in the workplace, or within yourself. Most people are reluctant to embrace change. This book helps you manage crises and opportunities by teaching you how to manage your feelings, actions, and thoughts (FAT), in times of crisis *and* in everyday life. *Emotional Leadership* will empower you. It encourages you to make the most of opportunities that crises and everyday life events present to you.

In chapter four we learned that fear and threat are major arousers of anxiety. Fear of what change will bring, and the threat of losing what you already have – what you are comfortable with, and what is known to you – creates a crisis in many people.

But change is an opportunity to:

- Experience emotions you have never felt before.
- Confront your reality – perhaps for the first time.
- Make no-lose decisions that affirm your identity.

Everyone has some negativity within them. Stress rises as negativity increases – which can lead to a feeling of being out of control. *Emotional Leadership* helps you to:

- Stop the negative spiral before you let negativity take control.
- Move from your point of view to your viewing point, where you continue to see things rationally – even when everything else seems to be going wrong.

Chapter eight challenges you to recognise that you are today, what you have chosen to be. You will learn the secrets of what makes an intimate relationship special. Are you communicating effectively? Are you giving love according to how your partner receives love? Have you built your sandcastle of trust?

Both chapters seven and eight help you manage **change** through self-management and social management, so you can **enjoy** a life of EASE.

RELATIONSHIP CYCLE

One place where most people experience change is in their close personal and family relationships. As stated in chapter eight, relationships fail for three major reasons; (1) unresolved hurts, (2) ineffective communication, and (3) each person in the relationship not knowing how to give and receive love, in order to meet the needs of the other person.

The relationship cycle (Figure 5.1) describes the four major components of a relationship; effective communication, emotional intimacy, sensuality, and sexuality.

In chapter two we described how;

Women typically enter a relationship through communication and emotional stability, wanting a caring, loyal, and understanding partner. Women will only seek sexual fulfilment once emotional intimacy and trust has been established.

Men typically enter a relationship as provider and protector, wanting a supportive and understanding partner. Men seek sexual fulfilment in order to establish and secure emotional intimacy and trust.

Whilst this is not true for all men and women, it does highlight a major difference between the genders that is the cause for some relationship breakdowns. Men need to understand how women operate, and women need to understand how men operate. Additionally, men are typically not effective communicators in relationships – but they can learn to be.

Figure 5.1. Relationship Cycle*

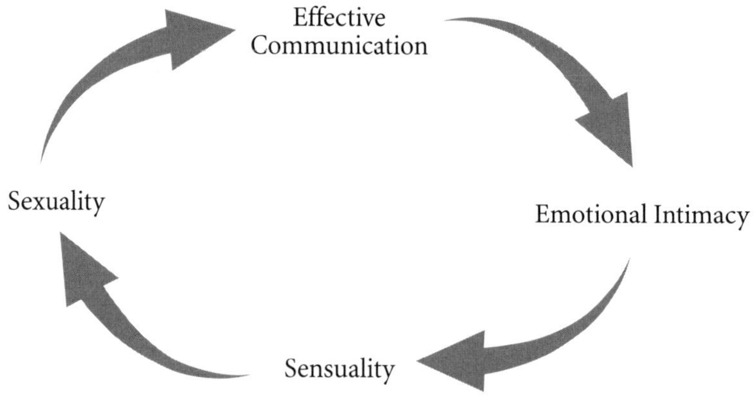

Effective Communication

Emotional Intimacy

Sensuality

Sexuality

*Adapted from "Continuum of Bonding Behaviours" - Dr Rosie King (1997), Good living, Great Sex, Ramdom House, Sydney, p.228.

There are four different levels of intimacy to be experienced within the relationship cycle.

1. **Effective communication** – is for building relationships in the workplace, at home, and in the community. Through levelling, listening, and validating, you honour the other person's right to be heard. Refer back to chapter six for a refresher on this topic.

2. **Emotional intimacy** – is a place where people feel safe when discussing issues that are important to a relationship. Emotional intimacy is definitely for close friends, family, and lovers. A degree of emotional intimacy is necessary in some workplace environments where people need to share information in an atmosphere of trust – medical practitioners, for example.

3. **Sensuality** – is experienced by people who delight in the senses, but it is a non-sexual component of a relationship. It is often shared by close friends in greeting or to comfort. For example, hugs, stroking, touching.

4. **Sexuality** – the final step in intimate relationships, covering a broad range of sexual behaviours.

The relationship cycle is particularly useful in illustrating what areas in a relationship need working on. For example, a sensitive person – male or female – who has been distancing himself or herself due to emotional arousal, will often have a need for quality conversation or time with their partner. It is common that until this need has been met, a sensitive person is unlikely to want to participate in sensuality or sexuality.

Sex therapist and sex educator, Dr Rosie King (1997), writes that couples who fall in love for the first time enjoy a period of limerence for between 12 to 18 months.

Limerence is a term coined by American psychologist Dorothy Tennov to describe the fabulous feelings most of us experience in the early stages of a romantic relationship.[1]

When limerence is at its peak, all four segments of the relationship cycle may be operating as the partners experience their love and bond together. As limerence fades and people get tired of being the "perfect partner", and little arguments and irritations creep into a relationship, different parts of the relationship cycle will fade. Throughout *Emotional Leadership* there are strategies and ideas, to help couples work on these aspects of their relationship, so that real love can take over and the relationship continues to flourish.

Emotional Leadership helps you to:

- Self-manage your emotions, releasing stored hurts.
- Conduct social management of the emotions of others, so you don't misinterpret cues and information.
- Communicate effectively with your partner, so he or she feels listened to and validated.
- Practise giving love to meet your partner's felt need for love. Which paradoxically, gives you an abundance of his or her love in return.

FIVE WAYS TO GIVE AND RECEIVE LOVE

Each of you has different needs that signal changes in emotions. You all have a basic need for love, affection, and esteem. Gary Chapman (2000) in *The five love languages,* describes wonderfully the different ways in which people have their need for love met. That is, the way you give and receive love. The "five ways to give and receive love"[2] are:

1. **Words of affirmation**

   You receive love through affirmation. For example, you like to be told that you look good, are competent at what you do, or have cooked a wonderful meal.

"Wow! You are such a good cook. Your chilli crab was simply delicious, the best I've had in a long, long time."

2. Quality time

People who receive love through quality time are those who enjoy close, deep, intimate conversation. Quality time can also just be enjoying something together, such as; riding bikes, playing tennis, or simply just sharing the Sunday paper.

Many women seek quality conversation and will respond with vigour to others who take the time to be active listeners.

3. Receiving gifts

Some people like to receive gifts as confirmation that they are loved. For example, a box of chocolates, a bunch of flowers, a holiday, or regular gifts of jewelry can meet a person's need for love.

A husband being present at the birth of a couple's child can be regarded as a gift of his time, and will always be remembered.

4. Acts of service

Acts of service are one sure way to express your love for someone. Cooking dinner, cleaning the house, running errands, and ensuring your partner's need for creature comforts, are all examples of acts of service that signal love.

5. Physical touch

Giving and receiving love by physical touch includes body massages, back rubs, holding hands, stroking, and sexual intercourse.

The ways of giving and receiving love above can also be a trap. **ATRAP** is an acronym to remember the five ways of giving and receiving love – Affirmations, Time, Receiving gifts, Acts, Physical. You may think that you are doing everything necessary to love your partner, and yet you've become "trapped" in a way of responding that does not meet his or her need at all!

Chapman says that individuals typically have one primary "love language". Many couples with whom we have shared these ways of giving and receiving love in our clinical practice have been amazed at how reflective of their needs the "love languages" are.

One male client recoiled in a counselling session when first being made aware of the ways to give and receive love, "Oh dear, I thought I was doing everything right! I've now discovered that I've been doing it wrong for the last 15 years!" He had fallen into the "trap" of thinking he did not need to change the way he was behaving toward his wife.

We use the acronym **APART** to remember the five ways to give and receive love – Affirmations, Physical, Acts, Receiving gifts, Time – because if you are not giving love to your partner according to his or her needs, you may end up apart. In order for your partner to feel loved, you need to love according to his or her needs, not your own.

The way that you give love is not necessarily the way your partner receives love. However, the way you give love to others is typically the way you like to receive love. For example, if you like to perform acts of service for people, it is highly likely that your primary way of receiving love is through acts of service. If you don't know which one of the five ways to give and receive love is your most preferred, ask yourself, "What have I most often requested of my partner?" That will most likely be your primary "love language" – the way you most like to receive love.

In your relationships you need to communicate your need for love to others so it can be met – be it affirmations, quality time, receiving gifts, acts of service, or physical touch. Most people in relationships don't know their partner's primary and secondary "love language", and this can be a major reason why relationships experience difficulties and often fail.

Emotional Leadership Practice

ELP 8.1   Giving and receiving love

Reflect on what may be your and your partner's primary and secondary ways of receiving love. Write them down below. Are you brave enough to share this with your partner? You'll be pleased that you did!

Your **primary** way of receiving love:	Your partner's **primary** way of receiving love:
Your **secondary** way of receiving love:	Your partner's **secondary** way of receiving love:

SANDCASTLE OF TRUST

Dr Rosie King (1997, p. 171), describes the sandcastle of trust.

> In clinical practice I use the sandcastle model of trust to explain to couples how trust can be built and destroyed in a relationship. Imagine that your trust in your partner is built like a sandcastle on the seashore, using beach sand and a spade. Trusting types possess first-class equipment to rapidly build sizeable sandcastles – a good-sized emotional spade and firm damp sand to work with. Each time your partner turns up at the agreed time, you pile sand on your castle. Each time your partner is there for you, each occasion your partner tells you the truth, each time your partner places commitment to the relationship over attraction to another – on goes another spadeful of sand.

Building your sandcastle of trust, is building special relationships based upon an identity that values trust as foundational to social behaviour. For many people, trust lies at the heart of relationships in the home and in the workplace. Dr King (1997, p. 170) says, "We all start out as trusting individuals – it is life that teaches us not to trust."

The father who goes out drinking with friends and comes home late night after night, despite assurances to his wife that, "I'll be home early tonight," will eventually lose the trust of his wife, as she stops asking where he has been – convinced that he will lie anyway.

The woman who never tells her husband how she spent her day, whom she has been with or where she has been, will lose the trust of her husband as he becomes suspicious that she is seeing someone else.

An employee who "moonlights" or slanders his employer, does not show integrity, loyalty, and commitment to his job, workplace, superiors and subordinates, will lose the trust of employer.

An employer who does not honour agreements with staff, does not pay staff legal entitlements, reneges on commitments made to employees, and does not behave toward staff in a way that respects and honours their rights, will lose their employee's trust.

As trust begins to fade, the sandcastle is demolished and needs to be rebuilt, spade-by-spade. Sometimes the pain from hurts – verbal, physical, sexual, and emotional abuse – is too severe, and the sea of time washes the sandcastle out to sea, never to be rebuilt. We all know the cost of broken relationships on the parties concerned, particularly children.

Trust is a choice. If your sandcastle of trust is beginning to slip away, try implementing the lessons you have learned from this book. You may be surprised at what happens in your life and relationships.

FORGIVENESS

Some of you reading *Emotional Leadership* will view the concept of "forgiveness" as essentially religious. Others will see the concept as simply a denial of a hurt that has been placed on you unjustly, and thus has no place in real healing. Whatever your position, forgiveness is included in this chapter as that final element that flows out of the compassionate response (chapter five). Forgiveness follows understanding and acceptance – the final letting go of a past or anticipated hurt, that holds you in your point of view. Forgiveness is to rise to your viewing point in new awareness – "I forgive you and set you free, as you were acting in limited awareness." This is release from pain.

Karen and I view forgiveness as an essential part of healing emotional pain, and alleviating emotional constipation. We have sought and obtained permission from Dr David Benner, Director of the Institute for Psychospiritual Health, to include as a reading, his work "Forgiveness and the healing of emotional wounds". This reading is adapted, with the author's permission, from *Free at Last: Breaking the Bondage of Guilt and Emotional Wounds* (Essence Publishing, 1998), and is included in *Emotional Leadership* as Appendix C.

Forgiveness carries with it responsibility. As you are the more aware person in your relationship, family, or workplace environment, you have a responsibility to conduct self-management and social management. Help lift others up to your viewing point, so that all may enjoy what you have achieved.

LIFE OF EASE

We have counselled our children:

"Think about **what sort of person you are going to be** when you grow up. Not **what you are going to be** when you grow up."

"Ask yourself, 'What am I passionate about?' For herein lies the answer to what is your unique talent. What will be your unique contribution, your vocation to the world and the people you come into contact with?"

Develop **emotional wisdom** – knowing how to behave when you don't know what to do. Combine your unique talent, emotional wisdom, and experience of spirituality, to go beyond your ego to your EAR-Identity. This is your reality. This is where you will find the person you are going to be when you grow up.

A life of EASE means allowing yourself to engage with your emotions – the best signal of what your body needs. Get in touch with your arousal triggers. If your belief, value, memory, perception, or expectation, is outdated and causing you pain, change it.

If you are a **reactive** person, learn to recognise anger and anticipate how others will interpret and react to your behaviour – choose to become more sensitive.

If you are a **sensitive** person, learn to trust your feelings within. Let go of your fear and the need to analyse and rationalise everything – choose to become more reactive.

Everything in life requires balance between two extreme states of emotion; rage (felt as unbridled anger) versus nervous illness (felt as fear and anxiety). The secret is to discover which EAR-Identity and emotional style – reactive or sensitive – masks the true you, and then change that EAR-Identity to live in emotional freedom.

Life is a series of events. Every event is an opportunity for change. And it is from the most painful events that you change the most. In 1985, I set up a take-away food shop on the Gold Coast in Queensland, Australia. Karen and I worked for 12 hours each day, dealing with members of the public who frequented our shop. One day an elderly chap, a fruit seller, came into the shop. We got talking about the difficulties of running a business, dealing with the public, suppliers, staff, and so on. He said to me, "You know Mike, we start out in business as nice guys trying to be tough, but we end up as tough guys trying to be nice."

The old man's intent was that our experiences harden us and make us stop giving. They stop us being the person we want to be. I have reflected on his comment many times over the years when once again someone has taken advantage of my kindness, my generosity. Sure, I'm tougher now then I was 20 years ago, but I have not given up on building the EAR-Identity I want to be. Now, from each event that happens to me, I ask myself, "What can I learn from that experience. What is that experience telling me about *me*, and how I want to behave?" It's tough work. And I constantly fall back into old patterns of behaving. But creating my EAR-Identity is my life's work – the only path forward that will create joy and happiness for me, and those with whom I have contact. I have not given up on giving.

Life is for living in the present moment. Free of pain felt from present moment hurts, free of pain from recalled memory of the past, and free of pain perceived from predictions in the future. Life is about living in present-moment awareness – moving from anger to assertion, from fear to appreciation; **living with ease** in emotional freedom.

Set your intentions, desires, and goals into the spiritual realm and practise detachment – a state of emotional freedom, for what will unfold before you. Remain detached from the outcome and let wisdom work its work.

Enjoy your life of EASE.

CASE STUDY 8.1 – CREATING CHANGE THROUGH AWARENESS

Ruth and Tom had become housemates (see The Housemate Syndrome, chapter six). Their marriage had deteriorated to a point where communication was ineffective and each had a bundle of unresolved hurts. They sought counselling to repair their marriage. They sat at either ends of the couch, Ruth visibly stressed and crying, Tom outwardly calm and rational. There was clearly tension between them. Their body language read, 'We don't communicate well'.

It seemed that as Ruth could not formulate words – due to her visible emotional distress – it fell to Tom to describe the sorry saga of unresolved and ongoing hurts, ineffective communication, and angry outbursts by Ruth, that had caused Tom to suggest that she needed counselling, to help her sort out her problems.

Over several counselling sessions Tom described the marriage as having started well. They were married older than most and had a good idea of each other's personality and behaviours. Tom felt that he had a good understanding of interpersonal skills and behaviour management and coped well with Ruth's angry outbursts – although he now felt that it was time for her to address them. Ruth revealed little of her perceptions of the difficulties in the marriage.

The counsellors introduced a sense of reality into the sessions by getting each person to examine their EAR-Identity, exploring who they wanted to be, and what kind of partner they wanted to be. Effective communication techniques as well as the various ways to give and receive love were discussed, and Ruth and Tom agreed to spend time together using these strategies as a way to rebuild their marriage.

Some months passed. Ruth and Tom returned for a second period of counselling saying that whilst they started out using the techniques they had learned earlier, they had now returned to the old patterns of behaving toward one another. A severe argument – with Ruth demanding Tom show some affection and respect toward her – had brought them back to counselling, as they agreed they could not continue their relationship in this way.

Ruth was now more vocal, she verbalised her considerable frustration with her unmet expectations by angrily demanding that Tom meet her needs. Tom, always outwardly calm and rational, was at a loss to understand Ruth's behaviour. He had withdrawn from all attempts to communicate with her using the techniques they had learned.

In an individual counselling session, Ruth revealed that an angry father – always demanding and disrespectful of her mother and her – had marred her young life. Challenged to own her angry feelings and unmet expectations, and not project them onto Tom, Ruth began to see how she had caused so much unhappiness for Tom and their children by her actions.

Ruth then disclosed that her drinking was an associated problem. This was a significant step. Until that stage in counselling, neither Ruth nor Tom had mentioned Ruth's problem with alcohol. Ruth experienced a major transition when she began to accept that her anger and loss of control through alcohol abuse had caused her to be a poor role model for her children, and had been a major factor in Tom withdrawing from her and not providing the warmth and physical hugs she so desperately craved.

Over the next brief period, Ruth undertook to stop drinking and make immediate changes to her language and demands on Tom. She was still not having her need for affirmations, physical affection, and quality time met by Tom, but she now recognised that in order to receive Tom's love she had to meet his needs. The counsellor explained that paradoxically, by meeting Tom's felt need for love, she would in time be loved again by him.

Outcome: Ruth took ownership of her inner voice and negative behaviour and committed to changing them to save her marriage.

 Emotional Leadership Practice – Small Group Exercise
ELP 8.2   Creating change through awareness

Reflect on case study 8.1 and write answers to the questions raised in the spaces provided below.

Questions

1. What emotions were Ruth and Tom experiencing, and what behaviours were they each demonstrating, when they first attended counselling? What type of emotional style did Ruth and Tom display – *sensitive* or *reactive*?

2. What emotions were Ruth and Tom experiencing, and what behaviours were they each demonstrating, at the end of the second period of counselling?

_____

_____

_____

_____

_____

3. Did either Ruth or Tom address their EAR-Identity? How? What were their negative thoughts before and after counselling?

_____

_____

_____

_____

_____

4. How can Ruth and Tom turn this into a "No-Lose" situation, where each feels validated and motivated to make necessary changes in themselves, to help repair their marriage?

_____

_____

_____

_____

_____

EMOTIONAL LEADERSHIP CHECKLIST

Use this emotional leadership checklist to recognise pitfalls and opportunities for effective social management and ways to build trust in relationships.

- Do I know what a life of EASE is?
- Have I committed to emotional leadership to build trust?
- Can I apply emotional intelligence in social management?

EMOTIONAL LEADERSHIP POINT 1
Do I know what a life of EASE is?

☐ Emotional freedom.

You will know that you have a life of EASE when you have created emotional freedom, your path to emotional wisdom – knowing how to behave when you don't know what to do.

You are emotionally wise when you know your mood and emotional style and its impacts on others. And you are able to respond with emotional intelligence to internal and external crises and opportunities in your life.

People who have emotional freedom experience better health and live a life of EASE.

☐ Social management in relationships.

You are emotionally free to live a life of EASE when you are engaged in the relationships in your life. Resolving past hurts, communicating effectively, and giving and receiving love according to your partner's needs.

Business and professional relationships fail through unresolved hurts and ineffective communication. Social relationships fail for these two reasons *and* one other – not giving and receiving love according to each other's needs.

☐ **Giving and receiving love.**

The way you give love is a sure sign of the way you like to receive love. Don't assume that your partner wants to receive love just like you do.

To live a life of EASE, learn to meet your partner's need for love. Paradoxically you will have your own need for love met.

EMOTIONAL LEADERSHIP POINT 2
Have I committed to emotional leadership to build trust?

☐ **Building your sandcastle of trust.**

Leadership is about building a long-term feeling of trust. Emotional leadership is learning and applying behaviours that gain long-term trust.

Trust is at the centre of any relationship. Build your sandcastle of trust slowly and surely. Don't give in to your inner voice by using behaviour that will destroy the sandcastle you have built.

☐ **Trust is foundational to social behaviour.**

Create an EAR-Identity that views trust as foundational to your social behaviour. Turn your life around by rejecting behaviour that teaches you not to trust.

EMOTIONAL LEADERSHIP POINT 3
Can I apply emotional intelligence in social management?

☐ **Behaviour you want to be.**

You are emotionally free and living a life of EASE when you are using emotionally intelligent behaviour – managing your emotions.

☐ **Social management.**

Incorporate your emotions when making decisions that impact on other people. Feel your feelings rather than blocking them. Use your awareness and acceptance of emotions to help you solve problems. Use the gap between event and response.

Apply your ability to perceive emotion. Use emotion in a judicious way to honour and respect the rights of others, and understand chains and blends of emotion to manage emotion effectively.

Use your interpersonal skills, personality, influencing style, emotional style, and emotional abilities to foster meaningful social relationships to **enjoy** a life of EASE.

Notes

1   King, Rosie 1997, *Good loving, Great sex*, Random House, Sydney. pp. 104-105.
2   Adapted from Chapman, Gary. 2000, *The five love languages. How to express heartfelt commitment to your mate*. Strand Publishing, Sydney.

APPENDIX A

THE EASEQuadrant®.
A FRAMEWORK FOR APPLYING EMOTIONAL INTELLIGENCE.

Mike Gosling MBA

Executive Behavioural Coach

Managing Director

Goslings International Pte Ltd

Creator of *The EASEQuadrant® Workshop* www.easequadrant.com

Co-Author of *Emotional Leadership. Using emotionally intelligent behaviour to enjoy a life of EASE*

www.goslings.net/coaching/coach.htm

EASEQuadrant® is a registered trade mark of Goslings International Pte Ltd.

THE EASEQuadrant®

The EASEQuadrant® is a theoretical framework for interpreting your emotional intelligence abilities scored using the MSCEIT™ – Mayer-Salovey-Caruso Emotional Intelligence Test (see Appendix B). *The EASEQuadrant®* is my vision of how emotional intelligence may be applied to everyday living; exercising leadership in your relationships in the home, community, and workplace.

The EASEQuadrant® (Figure 1) is a matrix for emotionally intelligent leadership. Set on two axes of experiential emotional leadership and strategic emotional leadership, *The EASEQuadrant®* comprises four quadrants. Each quadrant is a right of passage along your journey to learning and applying emotionally intelligent behaviour to build a long-term feeling of trust in your relationships.

Figure 1. The EASEQuadrant®

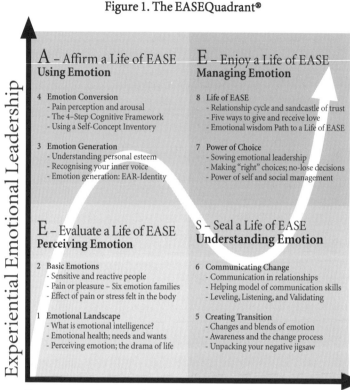

Experiential Emotional Leadership

A – Affirm a Life of EASE
Using Emotion

4 Emotion Conversion
 - Pain perception and arousal
 - The 4–Step Cognitive Framework
 - Using a Self-Concept Inventory

3 Emotion Generation
 - Understanding personal esteem
 - Recognising your inner voice
 - Emotion generation: EAR-Identity

E – Enjoy a Life of EASE
Managing Emotion

8 Life of EASE
 - Relationship cycle and sandcastle of trust
 - Five ways to give and receive love
 - Emotional wisdom Path to a Life of EASE

7 Power of Choice
 - Sowing emotional leadership
 - Making "right" choices; no-lose decisions
 - Power of self and social management

E – Evaluate a Life of EASE
Perceiving Emotion

2 Basic Emotions
 - Sensitive and reactive people
 - Pain or pleasure – Six emotion families
 - Effect of pain or stress felt in the body

1 Emotional Landscape
 - What is emotional intelligence?
 - Emotional health; needs and wants
 - Perceiving emotion; the drama of life

S – Seal a Life of EASE
Understanding Emotion

6 Communicating Change
 - Communication in relationships
 - Helping model of communication skills
 - Leveling, Listening, and Validating

5 Creating Transition
 - Changes and blends of emotion
 - Awareness and the change process
 - Unpacking your negative jigsaw

Strategic Emotional Leadership

I chose the Mayer-Salovey-Caruso ability model of emotional intelligence (MSCEIT™), along with cognitive-behavioural constructs, as the theoretical underpinning of *The EASEQuadrant®*, as I could see immediately that I could apply this model in my clinical counselling and behavioural coaching practice to assist people to better understand their emotions and behavioural change.

The MSCEIT™ is also central to my PhD research, which I commenced in 1999, examining the emotional intelligence of managers in Singapore. 81 managers completed the test. My research shows that whilst emotional intelligence in itself is valued as a capacity required of star performers, what *is* hard is getting successful leaders to apply their emotional intelligence skills, to achieve positive long-term change in behaviour – for themselves, their teams, and their relationships. In 2002 I created *The EASEQuadrant®* *Workshop* to teach successful leaders and others how to apply their emotional intelligence abilities in every day living.

THE EMOTIONALLY INTELLIGENT LEADER

Leadership is about building a feeling of long-term trust in relationships. Emotional leadership is learning and applying emotionally intelligent behaviour to build that long-term feeling of trust in your business, professional, and social relationships.

Learning about emotions involves emotional practise; applying your emotional intelligence – your capacity to identify, use, understand and manage emotion. Throughout this book we integrate and explain how applying your emotional intelligence can help you be an emotionally intelligent leader in your relationships – mastering your emotional abilities and behaving with emotional wisdom.

You begin your journey of learning to practise emotional leadership with an **evaluation** of your emotional landscape – your capacity for emotional intelligence and level of emotional awareness. Next you explore your EAR–Identity (the behaviour you want to be) and learn a key cognitive technique to **affirm** (reframe) your memory, thoughts, values, beliefs and expectations. To **seal** your new identity you learn to understand emotion chains and blends, and practice effective communication skills. Finally, making right choices about how you want to behave, and learning the secret of building long-term trust through improved self and social management, will guarantee you emotional wisdom to **enjoy** a life of EASE – to be an effective leader.

Delegates attending *The EASEQuadrant® Workshop* complete two online emotional intelligence tests – the MSCEIT™[1] and BarOn EQ-i®[2] – reporting on their emotional abilities and competencies respectively, and receive feedback on areas for emotional development.

Those who complete the MSCEIT™ emotional intelligence test may record their score below:

MSCEIT™ Total EIQ Score
Experiential EIQ Area Score:
Branch 1 Score – Perceiving Emotion
Branch 2 Score – Using Emotion
Strategic EIQ Area Score:
Branch 3 Score – Understanding Emotion
Branch 4 Score – Managing Emotion

Participants attending *The EASEQuadrant® Workshop* plot their MSCEIT™ experiential EIQ area score and strategic EIQ area score on *The EASEQuadrant®* (Figure 2), on the experiential emotional leadership and strategic emotional leadership axes, respectively. The point at which a participant's experiential EIQ area score and strategic EIQ area score cross is where they sit in their journey toward practising emotional leadership – applying emotional intelligence. The goal of each person is to achieve a meeting of their MSCEIT™ experiential EIQ area score and strategic EIQ area score in the top right hand corner of *The EASEQuadrant®*. At point **x** on *The EASEQuadrant®* a person demonstrates significant strength in both experiential and strategic emotional intelligence – emotional wisdom. If your scores cross at this point it is highly likely that you are a person who exhibits consistent emotionally intelligent behaviour valued of an effective leader – someone who builds a feeling of long-term trust in your business, professional, and social relationships. A score at point **x** on the grid is you exercising emotional leadership – behaving with emotional intelligence. Most of you will have scores crossing other than at point **x.** This is your opportunity to develop your emotional intelligence abilities. To develop emotional wisdom – knowing how to behave when you don't know what to do – through practising emotional leadership.

Figure 2. Plot your MSCEIT™ Branch EIQ scores on *The EASEQuadrant®*

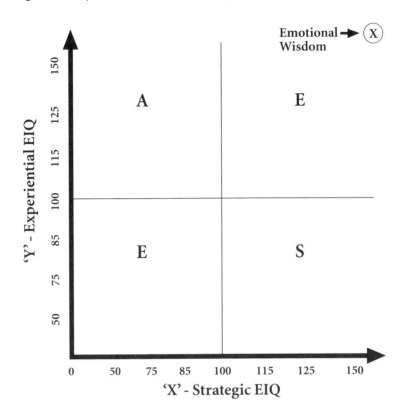

THE EASEQuadrant® WORKSHOP

For the experienced emotionally intelligent practitioner *The EASEQuadrant® Workshop* offers the chance to empower personal and relationship change, for the novice in emotional awareness it offers direction and a way to get started on your EAR-Identity, and for everyone there is the opportunity to discover the key to the most vital issue in your life – emotional wisdom; behaving with emotional intelligence.

For those interested in attending *The EASEQuadrant® Workshop*, we use film and media, real-life case studies on emotional issues, role-play, slide presentations, reflective individual exercises, and small group discussions to facilitate the learning process. Throughout this book and the workshop you will find many workshop examples and exercises that illustrate real world applications of emotional leadership. For example, understanding what comprises the compound emotion of disgust serves as a lead-in to discussing other compound emotions. In this book, as in the workshop, the exercises and case studies are styled as Emotional Leadership Practice (ELP).

I am accredited by Multi-Health Systems Inc. (MHS), Toronto, Canada to administer the MSCEIT and EQ-i emotional intelligence tests. If you interested in attending *The EASEQuadrant® Workshop* (two-days) and/or completing the two emotional intelligence tests online, contact me by email at MikeGosling@goslings.net; call +65 6256 7710; or visit my website at www.easequadrant.com. Alternatively, the MSCEIT™ and EQ-i® may be ordered from MHS at www.mhs.com. The MSCEIT™ may also be ordered from Dr David Caruso at www.emotionaliq.com.

APPLYING EMOTIONAL INTELLIGENCE

To assist readers to apply in your daily life what you have learned in *Emotional Leadership*, I set out general feedback on the MSCEIT emotional intelligence test. What follows is my summary of what each branch score of the MSCEIT describes about a person's emotional intelligence.

In a discussion on teaching emotional knowledge, the authors of the MSCEIT™ (Mayer, Salovey, & Caruso 2002, p. 21-22) state:

> Emotional intelligence is a part of personality. Research on the biological bases of personality suggests that most personality aspects are partly inherited and partly learned. No research has yet addressed the degree to which emotional intelligence is inherited. It is entirely possible that some of the capacity is biologically based and some is a consequence of learning.

A further distinction can be drawn between emotional intelligence and emotional knowledge. Emotional intelligence refers to the capacity to reason with emotions, whereas emotional knowledge refers to what one has learned about emotions. Assuming one has average emotional intelligence, it is possible to learn about emotions, and the more learning one has, the better one may perform in the area of emotional reasoning.

(MSCEIT™: Copyright © 2002, Multi-Health Systems Inc. All rights reserved. Reproduced with permission.)

The authors of the MSCEIT™ conclude that teaching emotional knowledge may be an effective way of compensating for lower levels of emotional intelligence and suggest that good evidence exists that emotional knowledge can be taught.

If you choose to complete the MSCEIT™ emotional intelligence test, either individually or as part of *The EASEQuadrant® Workshop,* the report you receive presents you with an opportunity to understand and consolidate new emotional knowledge about your emotional abilities. We have found in our clinical practice that individual task scores from the MSCEIT™ more often than not portray accurately a person's level of emotional ability. We have used task scores from the MSCEIT™ to assist us in counselling and coaching clients to learn and develop their emotional knowledge and thereby their emotional intelligence. Suggestions for development can be derived from a client's low task scores and information on skills or untapped abilities derived from well above average task scores.

For example:

Client A reported that she has been greatly helped by the MSCEIT™, discovering an emotional intelligence she didn't know she had. An increased understanding of her emotional abilities has helped her in her business and social relationships. She has gleaned valuable information from her task scores and now understands why she has been successful in her work as a manager and recognises areas she can improve on.

Client B now finally understands why people have told her that they don't want to continue a friendship with her. Her MSCEIT™ result showed a very low score on sensations – what we describe as an ability to be empathetic. She realised that her inability to empathise with others and by being quite blunt and self-focused in her talk with friends, has caused her the loss of relationships. By addressing with her what the MSCEIT™ says about her emotional abilities and the potential for change we have helped her address this issue, for which she was very grateful.

Client C was blown away by the discovery that many of his perceptions of his team member's feelings were so inaccurate. He understood immediately why he received so much flak from employees, because of his misinterpretation of their emotions – as signalled by their facial expressions. This was reinforced for him by a Branch 1 MSCEIT™ score of 86. He then made changes to his behaviour in this area, now that he is aware of how often he misreads people.

The MSCEIT™ helps people raise their well-being by assisting them in developing increased awareness of their emotional intelligence and highlighting areas for change.

When coaching clients in developing and nurturing emotional intelligence we will explore any dissatisfaction or discontent they may feel by working with them using the structure of PPE – Person, Problem, or Environment. If the issues relate to the **person** themselves we coach people on topics such as developing awareness, anger or anxiety management, lowered personal esteem, and understanding emotions and the impact of negativity (stress) on their bodies. The **problem** may present as dissatisfaction a person feels due to the job or task a person is required to perform, and coaching will need to focus on vocational issues. The problem may have arisen because of a person's **environment**, including situational factors like work and living location, an autocratic boss, or an unhappy home environment.

Understanding and consolidating new emotional knowledge about your emotional abilities (emotional intelligence) will assist greatly in you using emotion to enhance your reasoning about your PPE.

Placing your MSCEIT™ area scores on *The EASEQuadrant®* illustrates where you are in the eight stages of emotional leadership, your journey to emotional wisdom. Ideally, when you can place your "x" – where your experiential emotional intelligence score crosses your strategic emotional intelligence score – in the top right hand corner of *The EASEQuadrant®*, you are emotionally free to deal with events in your life, applying your emotional intelligence in present-moment awareness.

MSCEIT™ BRANCH 1 – PERCEIVING EMOTION

In this task you are asked to identify how a person feels based upon his or her facial expression, and the extent to which images and landscapes express emotion.

(MSCEIT™: Copyright © 2002, Multi-Health Systems Inc. All rights reserved. Reproduced with permission.)

People who score low on perceiving emotion are not very capable of reading people. Such people often also score low on the self-management tasks because their inability to read people often means they cannot manage emotional situations.

People who receive low scores in perceiving emotion are often taken aback as it could mean a change in self-image is required, something people are initially reluctant to do. Such people can be egocentric and fixed in their "point of view". They need to ask themselves if there was ever a situation in which someone acted in a way he or she had failed to predict. This may get them to acknowledge that they have a need to change and develop this ability.

People who have strength in perceiving emotion are delighted to discover their "hidden asset" that may lead them into a new and exhilarating career, such as; marketing, communications, counselling, and coaching – where their "hidden" emotional ability can be put to good use.

In chapters one and two of *Emotional Leadership* you completed exercises on perceiving emotion in film and in faces. We have shown you how emotions function to signal a need. The book highlighted Bar-On's emotional competencies – environment and personality traits that you exhibit. You have a written report on your self-test of these competencies and can explore further reading on how do develop them. You have read about how you see and interact with others using the Johari Window – are you an Open Person, Bull in a China Shop, Interviewer, or Turtle? We have described the biological connection in your brain between your neocortex and limbic system where perception occurs and have explained how stress occurs in the body. In chapter two we provided new emotional language, including increasing your understanding of different intensities of emotion.

In chapters one and two of *Emotional Leadership* we have assisted you to **evaluate** your life of EASE by correctly perceiving emotions (Branch 1 of the MSCEIT™ ability model of emotional intelligence).

MSCEIT™ BRANCH 2 – USING EMOTION TO FACILITATE THOUGHT

The two elements of this branch are the sensations (empathy) tasks and facilitation (moods) tasks. In the sensations (empathy) tasks of the test you will compare different emotions to different situations such as light, colour, and temperature.

(MSCEIT™: Copyright © 2002, Multi-Health Systems Inc. All rights reserved. Reproduced with permission.)

A high score here indicates you are able to generate a certain amount of emotion, and then compare it to the sensory modalities in the task. A low score indicates you have difficulty in generating emotions to compare and contrast with the sensory modalities. For example, you do not have a strong ability to generate empathy for someone who is feeling exhilarated at winning a senior position at work.

In the facilitation (moods) task you are assessed on your ability to generate a mood to assist and support thinking and reasoning. Strong performers can easily see the relevance of emotions to performance and motivation. Those with low average abilities in this task are less able to generate the right mood to enhance performance, productivity, and teamwork.

People who are open to experience, those who are good at accessing emotions (that is, those who are empathetic), and those with a vivid imagination, often score very high on facilitation (generating mood).

People who block emotions, those who are emotionally constipated and generally fight against negative feelings, choose consciously or unconsciously to not feel, because it hurts too much (it is too painful), and are not able to generate mood, are conscious of a feeling in their head and not in their body. Because the feeling is in their head they cannot generate emotion in their body. As a consequence, they tend not to feel much at all and score low on ability to generate empathy and mood to facilitate thinking and reasoning.

In chapters three and four of *Emotional Leadership* we have assisted you to develop your ability to use emotion to facilitate thought. We have described how emotion is generated and negative emotion reinforced and maintained by the inner voice. The concept of your EAR-Identity was introduced to provide you a model for understanding how you appraise events that happen in your life and the responses that you generate. We emphasised the importance of you gaining control over the "gap". We explained autonomic arousal felt in the body and how to move from anger to assertion and fear to appreciation using the 4-Step Cognitive Framework. We ended this section with a review of your self-concept inventory.

Chapters three and four of *Emotional Leadership* have assisted you to **affirm** your life of EASE by using emotion to enhance thinking and reasoning (Branch 2 of the MSCEIT™ ability model of emotional intelligence).

MSCEIT™ BRANCH 3 – UNDERSTANDING EMOTION

In this task you will be asked to analyse blends of emotions for their parts and assemble simple emotions into compound emotions. For example, what emotions combine to form a feeling of contempt?

Secondly, you are assessed on your knowledge of emotional "chains"; how emotions transition from one to another. For example, how anger can change into rage.

(MSCEIT™: Copyright © 2002, Multi-Health Systems Inc. All rights reserved. Reproduced with permission.)

A high score in this branch of the MSCEIT™ indicates high emotional insight, but does not necessarily indicate a strong ability to *feel* emotions (Branch 2). Someone with a low score in understanding emotional chains and blends will not pick up on cues from others and may find it difficult to read people (Branch 1). Alternatively, a woman who scores low on understanding emotions may perceive well that her partner is feeling depressed, yet be unable to understand *why* her partner is depressed. This person has little empathy (no awareness of the usual emotion likely to be experienced following a certain event) because she has difficulty understanding emotional chains and compound emotions. She believes that all people should respond to an event as she would.

In chapters five and six of *Emotional Leadership* we have taught you chains and blends of emotions and reminded you to keep looking at things from a perspective other than you own. You have learned how to convert weaknesses and negatives in your self-concept inventory into affirmations by revising the way you think about an experience. We have described the process of change and have encouraged you to build on your awareness by contrasting the Freudian non-biological model of personality, to our biological concept of EAR-Identity – unpacking your negative jigsaw, practising affirmations, and acting with compassion.

Chapters five and six of *Emotional Leadership* have assisted you to **seal** your life of EASE by understanding emotions (Branch 3 of the MSCEIT™ ability model of emotional intelligence).

MSCEIT™ BRANCH 4 – MANAGING EMOTIONS

The emotion management tasks of Branch 4 measure your ability to;

1. Regulate your own emotion in decision making (self-management), and
2. Incorporate your emotions and the emotions of others into decision making that impact on other people (social management). You were assessed on how effective different actions would be in achieving an outcome involving other people.

MANAGING EMOTION IN SELF (SELF-MANAGEMENT)

In this task you are asked to rate the effectiveness of alternative actions in achieving a certain result in situations where a person must regulate his or her own emotions.

(MSCEIT™: Copyright © 2002, Multi-Health Systems Inc. All rights reserved. Reproduced with permission.)

Low score   Those who score low in self-management tasks are prone to misread a situation and blame out, blame others, feel a victim, feel others hurt them, get angry or withdraw, and want others to do something to make them feel better. Using the 4-Step Cognitive Framework (chapter four) will assist such a person to improve his or her self-management abilities by incorporating his or her own emotions into cognitive reframing and decision making.

High score   Those who score highly in self-management tasks take responsibility for their feelings, know that despite emotional pain they can do something to make themselves feel better, and can think about an event from a number of different perspectives. Such a person is skilled at regulating his or her emotions to make well-balanced emotional decisions.

MANAGING EMOTION IN OTHERS (SOCIAL MANAGEMENT)

In this task you are asked to incorporate your own and others' emotions into decision making.

Low score   Those who score low in social management tasks may or may not be able to identify/empathise with another's emotions, but will react to another's emotion with self-judgement. Person A with low self-management abilities does not acknowledge or give permission for Person B to have the feeling. As a consequence, Person B does not feel emotionally safe with Person A, as Person B perceives Person A's reaction to be generally unpredictable. People with low self-management task scores find it difficult to solve problems effectively using the emotions of others.

High score Those who score highly in social management tasks are able to empathise with another's feelings and have the ability to convey that understanding. They have strong interpersonal skills. Such a person allows another to have a negative emotion without taking it personally. They will encourage another to express or experience an emotion safely, that is, they will not judge the other person. A person with a high task score for social management will make optimal decisions that incorporate all elements of a problem, including recognising and using the emotions of others.

In chapters seven and eight of *Emotional Leadership* we have encouraged you to sow emotional leadership; trust in your emotional abilities and competencies to make no-lose decisions that will serve you, your partner, family, workmates, and community. Define your path, give in to awareness, and make right choices. Work on the relationship cycle and ways to give and receive love in your social relationships. Build your sandcastle of trust using your emotional intelligence for effective long-term business, professional and social relationships.

Chapters seven and eight of *Emotional Leadership* have assisted you to **enjoy** your life of EASE by regulating and incorporating emotions into decision making that involves you and other people (Branch 4 of the MSCEIT ability model of emotional intelligence).

Notes

1   MSCEIT™ Copyright ©1999, 2002. Multi-Health Systems Inc. All rights reserved.
2   BarOn EQ-i® Copyright ©1997, 1999. Multi-Health Systems Inc. All rights reserved.

APPENDIX B

Dr John (Jack) Mayer

Professor of Psychology

University of New Hampshire, Department of Psychology, Durham (New Hampshire, USA)

Co-Formulator of the theory of emotional intelligence

Co-Author of the MSCEIT ability measure of emotional intelligence

www.unh.edu/psychology/faculty/fac_mayer.htm

Dr Peter Salovey

Dean of Yale College

Chris Argyris Professor of Psychology and Professor Epidemiology & Public Health

Yale University, Department of Psychology, New Haven (Connecticut, USA)

Co-Formulator of the theory of emotional intelligence

Co-Author of the MSCEIT ability measure of emotional intelligence

www.yale.edu/psychology/FacInfo/Salovey.html

Dr David Caruso, Psychologist

VP of Assessment at Harris-McCully Associates – a NYC-based human resources consulting firm.

Founder, Work-Life Strategies

Research Affiliate, Department of Psychology at Yale University

Co-Author of the MSCEIT ability measure of emotional intelligence

www.emotionaliq.com/About.htm

NOTE: This reading is adapted from Mayer, JD, Salovey, P & Caruso, DR 2002, *Mayer-Salovey-Caruso Emotional Intelligence Test (MSCEIT) User's Manual*, Multi-Health Systems Inc., Toronto, Canada and Dr David Caruso's website at <www.emotionaliq.com/MSCEIT.htm>. The permission of Dr Caruso has been obtained to reproduce this Appendix B on the Mayer-Salovey- Caruso Emotional Intelligence Test. Also note that copies of the MSCEIT™ emotional intelligence test may be ordered from the publisher on-line at www.mhs.com; by e-mail customerservice@mhs.com; by fax 416 492 3343 or (888) 540 4484; or by surface mail at MHS Inc., 3770 Victoria Park Ave., Toronto, Ontario, M2H 3M6, Canada. Alternatively, the MSCEIT™ may be ordered online from Dr David Caruso at www.emotionaliq.com, or email at david@emotionalIQ.org.

MSCEIT™ Copyright © 1999, 2002, Multi-Health Systems Inc. All Rights Reserved.

In 1990, Mayer and Salovey published two articles on emotional intelligence. The first article (Salovey & Mayer, 1990) reviewed literature throughout the disciplines of psychology and psychiatry, artificial intelligence, and other areas, concluding that there might exist a human ability fairly called emotional intelligence. The idea was that some people reasoned with emotions better than others, and also, that some people's reasoning was more enhanced by emotions than others. The companion article (Mayer, DiPaolo, & Salovey, 1990) presented a first ability model of emotional intelligence — a suggestion that emotional intelligence, measured as a true intelligence, might exist. Since that time, Mayer, Salovey, and their colleagues refined their model of emotional intelligence (see Mayer & Salovey, 1997), and expended considerable efforts toward developing a high-quality ability measure in the area. The newly developed Mayer-Salovey-Caruso Emotional Intelligence Test (MSCEIT™) is the result of this theoretical and empirical research.

MSCEIT™ IS BASED ON AN <u>ABILITY</u> MODEL OF EMOTIONAL INTELLIGENCE

A Brief Introduction to the Four-Branch Ability Model of Emotional Intelligence

In this model, emotional intelligence is viewed as consisting of four separate components or branches. Here is a summary of this Four-Branch Model of Emotional Intelligence:

1. **Perceiving and Identifying Emotions** – the ability to recognise how you and those around you are feeling.
2. **Facilitation of Thought** – the ability to generate emotion, and then reason with this emotion.
3. **Understanding Emotions** – the ability to understand complex emotions and emotional "chains", how emotions transition from one stage to another.
4. **Managing Emotions** – the ability which allows you to manage emotions in yourself and in others.

Further reading on the ability model:
Salovey, P & Mayer, J D 1990, 'Emotional intelligence', *Imagination, Cognition, and Personality*, 9, 185-211.

Mayer, J D & Salovey, P 1997, 'What is emotional intelligence?', in P. Salovey & D. Sluyter (eds), *Emotional development and emotional intelligence: Implications for educators*, Basic Books, New York, pp. 3-31.

Different approaches to emotional intelligence are discussed in:
Mayer, J D, Salovey, P & Caruso, D 2000, 'Models of emotional intelligence', in R.J. Sternberg (ed), *The handbook of intelligence*, Cambridge University Press, New York, pp. 396-420.

MEASURING EMOTIONAL INTELLIGENCE WITH THE MSCEIT™

Different definitional approaches to emotional intelligence have also led to different measurement approaches. Three different approaches are;

MSCEIT™[1] – "Emotional intelligence involves the ability to perceive accurately, appraise, and express emotion; the ability to access and/or generate feelings when they facilitate thought; the ability to understand emotion and emotional knowledge; and the ability to regulate emotions to promote emotional and intellectual growth."

Bar-On EQ-i®[2] – Emotional intelligence is "an array of noncognitive capabilities, competencies, and skills that influence one's ability to succeed in coping with environmental demands and pressures."

ECI[3] **– Emotional Competence Inventory** – "Emotional competence is 'a learned capability based on emotional intelligence that results in outstanding performance at work'."

Also see Mayer, J D, Caruso, D R, & Salovey, P 2000, 'Selecting a measure of emotional intelligence: The case for ability testing', in R. Bar-On & J. D. A. Parker (eds.), *Handbook of emotional intelligence,* Jossey-Bass, New York, pp. 320-342.

MSCEIT™

Description

The MSCEIT™ is an ability test of emotional intelligence designed for adult aged 17 years and above. Normative data is from a sample of 5,000 individuals.

The MSCEIT™ consists of 141 items that yield a total emotional intelligence score, two Area scores, and four Branch scores. The eight task-level scores are reported for research and qualitative use only.

The MSCEIT™ asks test takers to;

1. *Identify* the emotions expressed by a face or in designs.
2. *Generate* a mood and solve problems with that mood.
3. *Define* the causes of different emotions. Understand the progression of emotions.
4. *Determine* how to best include emotion in our thinking in situations that involve ourselves or other people.

Examples of MSCEIT™ items:

Branch 1. Identifying Emotions

Indicate the emotions expressed by this face.				
Happiness	1	2	3	4	5
Fear	1	2	3	4	5
Sadness	1	2	3	4	5

Branch 2. Using Emotions

What mood (s) might be helpful to feel when meeting in-laws for the very first time?

	Not Useful				Useful
Tension	1	2	3	4	5
Surprise	1	2	3	4	5
Joy	1	2	3	4	5

Branch 3. Understanding Emotions

Tom felt anxious, and became a bit stressed when he thought about all the work he needed to do. When his supervisor brought him an additional project, he felt _____. (Select the best choice.)

a. Overwhelmed

b. Depressed

c. Ashamed

d. Self conscious

e. Jittery

Branch 4. Managing Emotions

Debbie just came back from vacation. She was feeling peaceful and content. How well would each action preserve her mood?

Action 1:   *She started to make a list of things at home that she needed to do.*
            Very Ineffective.. 1..... 2..... 3..... 4..... 5.. Very Effective

Action 2:   *She began thinking about where and when she would go on her next vacation.*
            Very Ineffective.. 1..... 2..... 3..... 4..... 5.. Very Effective

Action 3:   *She decided it was best to ignore the feeling since it wouldn't last anyway.*
            Very Ineffective.. 1..... 2..... 3..... 4..... 5.. Very Effective

Notes

1   MSCEIT™ Copyright © 1999, 2002, Multi-Health Systems Inc. All Rights Reserved.
2   Bar-On EQ-i® Copyright © 1997, 1999, Multi-Health Systems Inc. All Rights Reserved.
3   Emotional Competency Inventory (ECI) Copyright © 1999 Hay/McBer. All Rights Reserved.

APPENDIX C
FORGIVENESS & THE HEALING OF EMOTIONAL WOUNDS

Dr. David G. Benner, Ph.D., C.Psych.

Distinguished Professor of Psychology and Spirituality
Psychological Studies Institute, Atlanta (Georgia, USA)

Chief Psychologist
Child and Adolescent Services, Hamilton (Ontario, Canada)

Director, Institute for Psychospiritual Health - www.psy.edu/iph

NOTE: This reading is adapted, with the author's permission, from "Free at Last: Breaking the Bondage of Guilt and Emotional Wounds" (Essence Publishing, 1998). Also note that copies of this book may be ordered from the publisher on-line at www.essence.on.ca; by e-mail at info@essence.on.ca; by fax (613 962 3055); or by surface mail at Essence Publishing, 44 Moira Steet West, Belleville, Ontario, Canada K8P 1S3.

First, two observations:

1. A small percentage of people who come for psychotherapy sometimes get worse. A small percentage who come for help in counselling or therapy and are depressed (that is, have emotional wounds) sometimes leave feeling better about themselves, but they're angry or obnoxious.

Therapists sometimes confuse expressing anger with releasing anger. What is needed for emotional healing is the release of anger. Expression of anger is a part of that, but the real challenge is expression moving us towards the end of release. Forgiveness is that mechanism of releasing anger.

2. We may have a feeling of being quite incapable of forgiving a person and being quite angry with ourselves for having so much trouble with it. We feel we should be able to forgive. We can read all the books on a subject and know what has to be done, but never have the experience of actually forgiving someone whom we feel caused us a past hurt.

FORGIVENESS – WHAT IT IS AND WHAT ITS ROLE IS IN HEALING

The concept of forgiveness is conspicuously absent from psychotherapeutic theory and practice. A literature search on articles over the past 25 years shows fewer than 50 articles on forgiveness. In contrast anger is discussed in thousands of articles in these same journals. But the concept of release of that anger through forgiveness is not an option that's even been seriously considered by most psychotherapists. Some who have considered it reject its place in psychotherapy, considering that forgiveness ignores the demands of justice since many people simply do not deserve to be forgiven. These people hold that forgiveness in therapy is utterly unprofessional and irresponsible because if somebody doesn't deserve to be forgiven we are doing them a disservice by forgiving them and letting them off the hook. I think this is tragic.

Others feel uncomfortable with a concept they view as essentially religious. Others feel that forgiveness has no place in psychotherapy as they think of forgiveness as based on denial and that it leads therefore only to symptom suppression, not real healing. This they suggest makes it inappropriate in psychotherapy.

But what possibility is there for the healing of emotional wounds if forgiveness does not have any place in the process? I think very little. Given the tremendous amount of time therapists spend with people who have been abused, damaged, neglected and mistreated I've come to feel that the single most important thing that psychotherapists need is an understanding of the important place of forgiveness in the healing of emotional wounds.

DEFINITION OF FORGIVENESS

1. Forgiveness is not forgetting. The popular adage of "forgive and forget" (see Smedes, who said the publisher chose the title of his book because that's what sells) is misleading as it implies that forgiveness is easy, which it isn't. It also suggests that we can tell its outcome once we've forgotten, that is, we know that forgiveness is complete once we no longer remember. To forget a hurt is to repress it. Forgiveness does not eliminate memory. Acts that have been forgiven are still available for recall. However, over time they should have less and less emotional pain attached to them. And more importantly they should have less and less anger associated with them.

2. Forgiveness is not to excuse. If we can excuse (condone) the behaviour of the person who hurt us, forgiveness is unnecessary. But on the other hand it is precisely because the behaviour of the person who hurt us is so inexcusable that we must forgive. Forgiveness is the only healing response to injustice. There are always reasons why the other person did as they did, but reasons are not excuses. To make excuses for the other person is to engage in rationalisation as a way of defending against the hurt. But in most instances of serious hurt, the behaviour that caused the hurt is genuinely inexcusable.

3. Forgiveness isn't the same as ignoring. Attempts to ignore the pain and hurt are also based on denial. Denial has no role in genuine forgiveness, which involves facing and dealing with the pain head on. Forgiveness involves accepting the experience as real, not attempting to minimise it.

To ignore or overlook it is an attempt to change reality by selective attention. But such magical thinking does not produce genuine healing.

4. To forgive is not necessarily to extend unconditional trust. Some people resist forgiveness because they assume that if they forgive the person who hurt them they'll have to trust them. Trust has to be earned. Forgiveness doesn't have to be earned. Trust does. We will remember and we must act in the light of the memory if we are to be responsible to ourselves and to the other person. Genuine forgiveness does not mean that we must assume that others will never again hurt us. Nor does it mean that we should not take steps to minimise this possibility.

There are always reasons why the other person did as they did, but reasons are not excuses. To make excuse for the other person is to engage in rationalisation, as a way of defending against the hurt, but in most instances of serious hurt, the behaviour that caused the hurt is genuinely inexcusable. An inability to extend unconditional trust is often the most appropriate thing. It does not mean however that we have not genuinely forgiven the other person. So forgiveness is not the same as unconditional trust.

If true forgiveness has nothing to do with fairness, forgetting, or even trustworthiness, what is it? Most simply, forgiveness is the conscious decision to let go. To let go of:

1. resentment,
2. the right to retaliate,
3. the right to hang on to the emotional consequences of the hurt.

When people are able to do this they move from victim-hood to healing. No longer in bondage to the past, they're now free to live their lives in the present. Free to live with vitality and to work towards the future with hope. This is emotional healing.

Forgiveness, according to Jewish philosopher Han Ahrent, is the only available remedy to the injustices of life. Apart from forgiveness people are destined to be victims of the unjust things that happen to them. This is precisely the way so many people who consult therapists feel. But their feelings obscure the truth. That is, they feel that they are victims of the bad things that have happened to them. True, bad things have happened to them, things that they did not deserve, things that they would have never chosen, but properly understood and experienced, forgiveness holds the key to change. Not to change the past, but to change their reactions to the past and their bondage to it. By means of forgiveness victims can become free of the tyrannising bondage of injustice and can experience healing of their emotional wounds. This should never be thought of as easy. For any significant emotional injury will make forgiveness the hardest thing that anybody can be asked to do. But it is possible and it has therefore an important role in psychotherapeutic work designed to help people who have experienced emotional wounds.

THE FORGIVENESS PROCESS

Three models of the forgiveness process have been developed within the last decade.

1. A Five Stage Model – Lynn & Lynn (Catholic Brothers)
   Building on the stages of death and dying, described by Elizabeth Kubler-Ross. Lynn & Lynn describe stages of denial, anger, bargaining, depression, and acceptance, as characterising the process of moving from hurt to forgiveness.

2. My own model of the forgiveness process describes three tasks of the forgiveness process:
   a. Re-experiencing the feelings – the emotional aspects of forgiveness
   b. Re-interpreting the experience – the cognitive (intellectual) aspects of forgiveness
   c. Releasing the anger – the volitional aspects.

3. Vitz and Mango's five-stage model of forgiveness: denial, anger and hatred, resistance, depression, and resolution.

The models developed by Lynn & Lynn and Vitz & Mango are quite similar to each other. The differences between my model and theirs are more pronounced. At core these differences are differences in focus. The other two models describe stages in the process of forgiveness whilst my model describes the tasks (what to do) of the forgiveness process, rather than provide a map to help determine how well one is moving through the forgiveness process. I do not assume that there is anything automatic about this forgiveness process and am more concerned in describing what must be done to move from hurt to forgiveness. Mine is about TASKS – what to do. I assume that without genuine painful hard work people never arrive at forgiveness of significant hurt. The passage of time may be sufficient for forgetting and a degree of emotional numbing, but it is not sufficient for genuine forgiveness.

Genuine forgiveness requires that a person engage in the emotional, intellectual, and volitional work described by the three tasks that I have identified in my model. The model provides some tools to help people get unstuck in the forgiveness process.

WHAT IS AN EMOTIONAL WOUND?

Before reviewing the work involved in moving from the bondage of an emotional injury to the freedom of forgiveness and emotional healing it may be helpful to first consider what we know about the dynamics of emotional wounds. What is an emotional wound? The best-developed model for the dynamics of emotional pain is that presented by Hargrave. He applies a contextual family therapy perspective to the understanding of emotional wounds, because he thinks they normally occur within the family. Hargrave points out that the essential dynamics of an emotional injury are a violation of trust. Emotional wounds, he points out, occur when trust is betrayed:

Parents physically or sexually abuse their children, spouses are sexually un-faithful to those to whom they promised fidelity, etc. In these ways people in relationship with each other violate the trust of those with whom they are in relationship and the result is an emotional wound.

While Hargrave is correct in identifying the core of an emotional wound as the violation of trust, it would perhaps be more precise to identify the cause as the perceived violation of trust. It is quite possible for a person to feel emotionally wounded in the absence of an objective violation of trust. Perception is (we must never forget) everything. Similarly many violations of trust go unnoticed and do not result in an emotional wound. Given these facts, we can say that emotional wounds have their origins in perceived violations of trust. Perceived violations that may have been either implicit or explicit.

But what exactly is an emotional wound? Hargrave suggests two optional feelings and behavioural consequences that form the essential dynamic of an emotional wound.

People who's sense of trust has been violated are likely to feel either;

1. **rage**, as they experience uncontrolled anger towards the person whom they perceive as violating their trust, or
2. **shame**, as they accuse themselves of being unlovable and not deserving a trustworthy relationship.

In addition, they are likely to either behave in other relationships in an overly controlling manner or in a chaotic manner. Overly controlling as they seek to minimise the risks of further hurt, or chaotic, as they seem to despair of any hope that anything they can ever do will minimise the chances of further hurt.

While Hargrave's understanding of the behavioural expressions of emotional pain is helpful, my clinical experience suggests a different emotional dynamic. Rather than two optional feelings and that is people experience either anger or shame, I suggest two alternating feelings, that people go through both of them. These are anger and sadness (or depression). Sadness sometimes manifesting itself in terms of clinical depression and despair, sometimes manifesting itself as a lower level sadness.

Although anger appears to be the first response to an emotional injury, it is actually a defence against an earlier and even more painful feeling. The first response to the experience of an emotional injury is usually a sense of loss. It is common for this loss to be covered by anger so quickly that most people are unaware that loss is a part of the response to hurt. However, it is a very important part of the whole process and we cannot gain freedom from the anger without facing the underlying sense of loss.

Emotional wounds always leave people with some diminished sense of self. It may be a loss of self-esteem, or possibly a loss of a sense of self-confidence, or competence. Often people report their emotional wound to be associated with a loss of innocence or possibly a loss of trust. Shadowing the basic assumptions by which life has been lived before the emotional wound also form an important part of the loss experience. Belief in one's invulnerability, the belief that events are predictable or controllable, the belief that life is fair, the belief that the world is benevolent or at least benign, or the belief that the self is worthy can all be shattered by traumatic experiences. The loss of these basic life operating assumptions is a major one. But whatever its form, feelings of loss form the deep and fundamental core of emotional wounds. While anger quickly comes as a defence against this feeling of loss, the first response to emotional hurt always seems to be that of violation, experienced as something "having been taken away from me".

The dominant feelings associated with the experience of loss are those of vulnerability and sadness. The secondary feelings are being helpless, demoralised, abandoned, guilty, and shameful. These feelings are so distressing that few people are able to tolerate them for long. Anger arises as a way to defend against them.

Together then, anger and sadness form the two complementary faces of the experience of an emotional wound. However, because it is difficult to sustain both feelings at the same time it is most common to respond to hurt by alternating between the two feelings. For a while the person may be self-occupied and aware to some extent of the damage they have sustained by the experience of hurt. In this stage they experience sadness and possibly depression. They feel acutely vulnerable to further hurt and feel the need to retreat to some safe corner of their world. But then the pain gets too intense and they end their introspection by shifting their attention to the one who has hurt them. In so doing they move from sadness to angry feelings. Anger is thus a secondary emotional consequence. It serves as a defence against the sadness.

People can get stuck in either of these stages of sadness or anger. Chronic depression is a result of getting stuck in the feelings of loss. Such people are more in touch with their loss than with their anger. They shut down their emotions so as to no longer feel the hurt and the pain. They also tend to withdraw from other people and consequently feel increasingly estranged from themselves and others. Their life becomes more and more filled with despair and self-pity until they become so comfortable with their depression that they sometimes prefer it to restored life. Ironically depression has become so much a part of them that while its a source of great pain it becomes a stable part of their identity.

On the other hand, chronic anger in any of its manifestations is also an easy place to get stuck in the healing process. Anger may be preferable to the painful feelings of loss because the individual experiences some relief from the vulnerability through their rage. Part of this comes from the sense of empowerment. People who have been emotionally wounded know what it feels like to be powerless and vulnerable. Their anger provides a welcome source of new strength. Letting go of this anger is therefore often difficult.

Before discussing the work of forgiveness in this healing process, we should note that a failure to address the underlying dynamics of loss is not the only reason why people get stuck in their anger and have trouble with forgiveness. In an excellent analysis of forgiveness from an object relation's point of view, John Gardiner notes that borderline personality disorder patients have an enormous difficulty with forgiveness because of their reliance on splitting and projection. He suggests that authentic forgiveness requires an integrated realistic perception of both the positive and negative aspects of self and others. Borderlines have difficulty with this. This is the reason that splitting (a tendency to see oneself as all good or all bad or to see others as all good or all bad) and projection (the tendency to project onto others the unacceptable bad within self), whether it occurs in borderline patients or others, makes forgiveness so difficult.

Gardiner's study of borderline pathology also leads him to suggest that a reliance on splitting results in impairment in empathy and that this also make forgiveness more difficult. This is a profoundly helpful observation. As we'll see in what follows, the development of empathy for the offender is an essential component in the work of forgiveness. Any serious impairment in the capacity for empathy therefore will be an impediment to forgiveness.

THE THREE TASKS OF THE FORGIVENESS PROCESS

One of the most commonly encountered problems in therapeutic work with Christians who have experienced emotional wounds is that knowing the extremely high value placed on forgiveness by Christianity, they are often too hasty to clear their conscience and attempt to forgive whomever hurt them. Christians don't have a monopoly on premature forgiveness, but they do show a massive tendency towards this. In fact, often very devout Christians will come for help quickly assuring the therapist that they have already forgiven who has hurt them. But they're telling the therapist that through clenched teeth. They're saying that they're not angry, that they've forgiven, but clenched hands and tight faces and teeth, show it's quite apparent that they haven't forgiven.

As a result of this they find themselves still stuck in anger or depression that they don't understand. The reason for this "stuckness" is that their acts of forgiveness were premature. Often somewhat ritualistically, before engaging in the hard work of the forgiveness process such efforts can actually impede genuine forgiveness because they suggest the work is already done. Genuine forgiveness, that is, the deep and meaningful release of resentment, victim-hood, and the right of retaliation, comes only as a result of hard work.

This hard work involves three spheres of personality and three different sets of therapeutic tasks. These tasks are interwoven and progress through them is never linear, so don't think you do one, then you finish it then you do another, and then you do the next. In process theories these tasks are interwoven. It's important therefore not to interpret this model in a mechanical manner. In describing the tasks of emotional healing, each of which addresses one primary sphere of personality, we're artificially separating things that in reality go together. Not only do the tasks overlap, but to some extent each involves the spheres of personality that are dominant in the others.

Whilst somewhat arbitrary therefore in describing separate emotional, intellectual, and volitional tasks that must be accomplished in the process of forgiveness, it does have the advantage of emphasising the fact that emotional healing must involve more than the emotions. Too often therapists specialise in one sphere of personality, their therapy just addresses feelings, or they're cognitive therapists and just address thinking. They fail to address all the components of an emotional injury. Some may be very adept in uncovering repressed or denied emotions but fail to do the necessary intellectual processing of the trauma. Others bring a cognitive orientation and quite adequately help the person do the necessary intellectual work, but may fail to pay sufficient attention to the emotional and volitional work. Yet others bring a behavioural orientation to forgiveness work and correctly emphasise the choices that the person must make without adequately engaging in the emotional and cognitive tasks.

While each individual will differ in what emphasis is required, all three components of work are essential. So let's go through the three tasks in order.

TASK 1: RE-EXPERIENCING THE PAIN – THE EMOTIONAL CHALLENGE

The fact that the healing of emotional wounds requires dealing with the emotions is quite obvious. But what exactly has to be done with those emotions? The principle lesson that has been learnt from the past 15 or so years of work in the emerging field of trauma psychology is that the individual must reconnect with the underlying pain in order to experience any genuine healing.

Efforts to resolve emotional wounds that resist or ignore reconnection with the underlying pain are based on denial or repression. Thus when people attempt to move towards forgiveness without passing through this stage of meaningfully re-experiencing the pain, have set themselves up to never experience genuine healing. Resistance to re-experiencing the pain has often felt like a step backwards. People often state that they felt those feelings deeply when the hurt occurred and feel therefore no need at present to go back to those feelings. But it is almost inevitable in emotional wounds of any significant magnitude that the pain gets short-circuited in the original experience. Attempts to escape the pain are so strong that the pain does not get processed. Instead the pain gets repressed, split-off, in some way not dealt with. This is the emotional work of feeling.

Processing the feelings is not the same as talking about them. The feelings must be re-experienced and expressed. Expression of the feelings associated with the emotional injury is a psychological damage repair mechanism. This is the reparative nature of mourning. Cathartic release of the underlying feelings associated with emotional wounds is necessary even if not sufficient for emotional healing. The essence of the emotional work of healing is allowing the person to experience all the feelings associated with the hurt. But as we noted earlier, at the basis of these feelings and at the core of emotional injury, is the experience of loss. Experiencing and expressing anger therefore is not sufficient. Anger needs to be explored but its roots in the experience of loss must also be identified. Mourning of these losses must be a central part of the emotional work that needs to be undertaken.

Mourning the losses associated with the emotional injury obviously requires identifying these losses. Patients often need help with this. A young woman seeking help around ambivalence about a relationship that was rapidly moving towards marriage reported in the first session childhood physical abuse at the hands of a cruel father. Fairly quickly she was able to get in touch with her anger at what had happened to her but she had much trouble moving beyond her anger. When asked what things she felt she might have lost as a result of living for so many years in a house with this tyrannical father she indicated that she couldn't think of anything. After a bit of prodding and further exploration and explanation of what the therapist was thinking about, she somewhat tentatively offered that well, "maybe what you mean is that I lost my sense of trust." That was a good beginning. Opening this gate then led to a number of other feelings of loss: a loss of childhood, a loss of innocence, a loss of a sense of safety, a loss of ideas about her family and about family in general – this may be a clue to the patient's ambivalence about marriage – and her loss of trust in God. "Where was God that this happened to me? Where was God when it was happening to me?" All of these losses were part of the sense of violation she experienced at the hands of her father. Opening herself to these experiences of her loss quickly moved her beyond her initial feelings of anger. She now felt a profound sense of sadness, feelings of grief for the little girl that had once been, but so quickly had to be changed into an adult. These feelings were profound. And mourning this loss, as well as expressing the associated anger, was the core of the emotional work that she had to undertake. Most therapists know how to help people with such work, and do it quite well. This is the bread and butter of what we do.

TASK 2: RE-INTERPRETING THE PAIN – THE INTELLECTUAL CHALLENGE

The second major task often introduces something new. That's reinterpreting the hurt, because emotional healing involves not just release of emotions but also reinterpreting the experience of the hurt. As recently identified by the proponents of narrative psychology, and as long recognised by advocates of cognitive approaches to therapy, its our construal of what happens to us, more than that which actually happens to us, that either keep us sick or make us well. It's the stories we make up to make sense of our experience that either keep us ill or make us healthy.

The stories that we make up to make sense of our experience become parts of ourselves. This is the reason why victim-hood is so powerful. Victim-hood is not merely an explanatory story to make sense of something that happened, it becomes a part of identity. What we know about victim-hood as an identity is that it's not a good place to be. The cognitive challenge associated with the second major task in emotional healing is helping people re-story (re-tell the story of) their traumatic experiences. Make no mistake about it, they have already formed stories about what happened and why it happened. Humans do that automatically. It doesn't seem to be something about which we have a choice. The choice lies in what stories we create, that is, how we understand our experience.

Re-interpreting one's experience begins by exploring the story that has already been formed to make sense of experience. Narrative repair is the process of re-integrating the experience, of reconstructing its meaning. It involves taking the broken fragments about the person's assumptions about themselves and life and reweaving these together into a fabric that restores meaning. It involves a careful re-interpretation of the events of the trauma separating out events from interpretation. The events are what happened. The interpretation is the story, the attributions, the patterns of blame and responsibility, and the meaning or significance of the events. The interpretation is the adjustment of one's story to make the trauma and its consequences part of the narrative. It's the rebuilding of a worldview. The search persists until the negative events can be integrated into a coherent stable and adaptive conceptual framework that provides a source of predictability and order to life. Therapists can help in this process by helping the person tell their story. This is why it is so important that people just tell it over and over. One of the most important things that we do in therapy is helping people learn their story and they learn it by telling their story. This narrative part of the work is very essential.

Therapists can help in this process just by helping people tell their story bit by bit and with increasing coherence and by gently challenging assumptions as to how the story was formed. Remember the story isn't automatic. I created the story. The story was not imposed on me by external events or by what people did to me. I made up the story. That's the difference between the story and the events. By this sort of involvement we help people reconstruct their story.

In helping people deal with emotional wounds and move towards forgiveness, therapeutic reconstruction of a story involves three separate but closely related accomplishments. All are related to the ability to see the offender with empathy and to see the self with realism.

1. Seeing the offender is like me. The first of these is helping the person see the offender as like him or herself, to see the offender like me. This involves seeing the one who hurt me as like me, weak, needy, coping with inadequacies, acting out of self-interest that have impaired my abilities to see the needs of others.

2. Seeing the offender as separate from what they did to me. The second aspect of reinterpreting the experience is seeing the offender as separate from what they did. This involves moving beyond seeing the offender as a caricature, the villain, the monster, the devil, but seeing them as a person. Not only seeing them as the cause of their hurt. An inability to see the person who hurt us as a person, makes forgiveness impossible.

3. Seeing myself as like the offender. Finally, forgiveness will only be possible when the one who has been hurt can see themselves as like the one who has hurt them in some basic ways.

When we can see ourselves as like those who have hurt us in basic ways then we can move towards forgiveness. When I can see that I also have hurt others not necessarily out of malice, often out of insensitivity, when I can see myself as one who has needed and hopefully received forgiveness, then forgiveness of others is possible. I am unsure how someone who themselves has never been forgiven could ever find in themselves the ability to forgive another. Recalling how others have forgiven me and released me of my resentment and retaliation opens the possibility for me to forgive. That's the second task.

TASK 3: RELEASING THE ANGER – THE VOLITIONAL CHALLENGE

When all is said and done, forgiveness is simply the conscious decision to release the anger, relinquish the right to retaliation, and be willing to move beyond victim-hood. What must be said and done before people are generally capable of doing this is the work of the preceding two tasks. When this has been done adequately this third task is often anti-climatic. When it has not been done adequately its often impossible. Most often it's some where between these two extremes. Difficult but possible.

Most people need help in being realistic about this third stage of releasing the anger. They need to understand that forgiveness is a process. They need to understand that it has to be done over and over again. I often compare it to an image of waves from the ocean under conditions of a receding tide. Even after forgiving the person who has hurt them they will likely be again washed over by fresh waves of anger and sadness. Once again, time after time the challenge is to release the anger and mourn the losses. As each wave washes up over them they begin to notice that the strength of successive waves is less and less. The tide is beginning to go out. When forgiveness rather than resentment is embraced the tide recedes. Its also helpful for people to realise that forgiveness is always offered in the midst of confusion. They will never have all the answers to why things happened as they did.

Finally, it's important to realise that forgiveness must be offered for what people do, not for who people are. Lewis Smedes, in "Forgive & Forget", says that we don't forgive people for who they are, we forgive them for what they did. I'm engaging in an unhelpful task for trying to forgive you for being an insensitive, uncaring, brutal slob, and monster. What I have to do is forgive you for what you did. I forgive that you did such and such to me. We need to understand that forgiveness needs to be about specific behaviours not about character traits.

Many people at this stage also need help in understanding the sources of their resistance to forgiveness. Some of those we talked about earlier. Sometimes this is a fear of returning to vulnerability. Other times it's a feeling that it's their right to hold a grudge. Other times it's a reluctance to relinquish the sense of power that their anger provides. Yet others may equate their non-forgiveness with the punishment of the one who hurt them. While others may feel they can only forgive if the other person requests it or deserves it. All of these are misunderstandings.

Each of these misperceptions regarding the nature of forgiveness must be addressed if they lie behind resistances to releasing one's anger. Vetz & Mangel suggest a number of signs of genuine forgiveness that can help both the therapist and patient assess progress through this volitional task. They point out that genuine forgiveness is associated with the ability to once again use one's anger constructively. I find this very helpful. They also point out that another evidence is an increase in genuine concern for and positive attitudes towards the person who has been forgiven. They point out how this contrasts to the signs of false forgiveness that is characterised by such things as denial and reaction formation. Such neurotic or pseudo forgiveness can easily be understood as being in the service of psychopathology that must be resolved before genuine forgiveness can be experienced.

Forgiveness and forgiveness alone has the power to break the controlling influence of the bad things that happen to people. When it does it forms an integral part of the healing of emotional wounds. When it is not a part of such healing people easily remain stuck in their anger. When it is a part of the healing process people can re-experience the pain of their hurt, re-interpret the experience and release the anger that results from it. This is the task that often requires the help of psychotherapists. Therapists who confront this task by being reminded of the crucial role of forgiveness will be better able to help those who seek their help.

APPENDIX D

COMMON MISCONCEPTIONS ABOUT ANTIDEPRESSANTS

Karen Gosling BA (Social Work), Master of Public Health

Counselling Director

Goslings International Pte Ltd

Co-Author of *Emotional Leadership. Using emotionally intelligent behaviour to enjoy a life of EASE.*

www.goslings.net/corporate/kgprofile.htm

Misconception: I don't need it. I can do it on my own.

Truth: You can't, you've tried. You've done your best already.

Misconception: It shows weakness of character.

Truth: Depression is an illness. The illness makes you weak.

Misconception: Medication is addictive.

Truth: Antidepressant medication is not addictive.

Here is a chart to explain the difference.

Addictive substance:

- Gives you a high when you take it, eg, Ecstasy.
- You need more and more of it to achieve the same effect.
- Withdrawal of the substance causes problems.
- You will spend the rest of your life looking for it.

Antidepressants:

- Does not give you a high, rather it calms you down.
- You don't need more and more of it.
- You get to your recommended dose and then you stay on it for as long as you need and then reduce.
- Withdrawal too quickly may cause problems. So follow the doctor's advice.

- You will then come off it and say, "I hope I never need those again."
- You will not spend your life wanting to go back on them. Rather, now you know the symptoms of depression/anxiety you will avoid getting so low in the future.

Misconception: Medication will dull my brain.

Truth: Anti-depressants usually enable you to think more clearly. The ability to smell, taste, and see more clearly, have also been reported.

Misconception: Once you start you cannot stop.

Truth: The idea of starting is so that you may eventually stop.

Misconception: If you stop the medication, the illness will relapse.

Truth: With some illnesses, yes. With depression, not often. The medication alters and corrects the imbalance of chemicals in the brain so that you no longer have the illness. Understanding your illness and the symptoms assists you to prevent the situation recurring in the future, using cognitive strategies.

LIFT OR STAIRCASE? One does not HAVE to take medication but medication fast forwards the recovery process. It is like going to a party on the fifteenth floor, and making a choice between taking the lift or the stairs. Both will get you to the same place, but the stairs will take longer, you will suffer exhaustion along the way, and will have missed out on most of the fun by the time you get there.

REFERENCES

Aron, E N 1997, *The Highly Sensitive Person*, Broadway Books, New York.

Averill, J R 1994, 'In the eyes of the beholder' in Ekman, P & Davidson RJ (eds) 1994, *The Nature of Emotion, Fundamental Questions*, Oxford University Press, New York.

Bar-On, R 1997, *The Emotional Quotient Inventory, Technical manual*, Multi-Health Systems, Toronto, Canada.

Bar-On, Reuven & Parker, James D A (eds) 2000, *The Handbook of Emotional Intelligence*, Jossey-Bass, San Francisco.

Brackett, M A & Mayer, J D 2003, 'Convergent, discriminant, and incremental validity of competing measures of emotional intelligence', *Personality and Social Psychology Bulletin*, 29, 1147-1158.

Caruso, Dr & Salovey, P 2004, *The Emotionally Intelligent Manager. How to develop and use the four key emotional skills of leadership*, Jossey-Bass, San Francisco.

Chapman, G 2000, *The five love languages. How to express heartfelt commitment to your mate*, Strand Publishing, Sydney.

Chopra, D 1993, *Ageless body, timeless mind. A practical alternative to growing old*, Harmony Books, New York.

Chopra, D 1996, *The seven spiritual laws of success*, Bantam Press, London.

Chu, Chin-Ning 1992, *Thick face black heart,* Allen & Unwin, Sydney.

Chu, Chin-Ning 1997, *The secrets of the rainmaker. Success without stress*, Stealth Productions, Australia.

Covey, S R 1989, *The 7 Habits of Highly Effective People*, Simon & Schuster, London.

Darwin, C 1872, 1998, *The expression of the emotions in man and animals. Definitive Edition.* Introduction, Afterword, and Commentaries by Paul Ekman. Oxford University Press, Oxford.

Ekman, P 1992, 'An argument for basic emotions', *Cognition and Emotion*, 6, 3/ 4, 169-200.

Ekman, P & Davidson RJ (eds) 1994, *The Nature of Emotion, Fundamental Questions*, Oxford University Press, New York.

Ekman, P 1994, 'All emotions are basic' in Ekman, P & Davidson RJ (eds) 1994, *The Nature of Emotion, Fundamental Questions*, Oxford University Press, New York.

Goleman, D 1995, *Emotional Intelligence,* Bantam, New York.

Goleman, D 1998, Working with *Emotional Intelligence,* Bantam, New York.

Harris, T A 1967, 1995, *I'm OK – You're OK*, Arrow Books, London.

Hay, L L 1984, *You can heal your life,* Specialist Publications, Concord, Australia.

Jeffers, S 1987, *Feel the fear and do it anyway*, Random House, London.

King, R 1997, *Good loving, Great sex*, Random House, Sydney.

Laurence, A M 1990, *You've got what it takes. A Guide to self-discovery and effective living*, Lotus Publishing House, Sydney.

Lewis, M & Haviland-Jones (eds) 2000, *Handbook of Emotions*, 2nd edn, Guilford Press, New York.

Mayer, J D 1999, September, 'Emotional Intelligence: Popular or scientific psychology?', *APA Monitor*, 30, 50. [*Shared Perspectives* column] American Psychological Association, Washington, DC.

Mayer, J D, DiPaolo, M T & Salovey, P 1990, 'Perceiving affective content in ambiguous visual stimuli: A component of emotional intelligence', *Journal of Personality Assessment*, 54, 772-781.

Mayer, J D & Geher, G 1996, 'Emotional Intelligence and the Identification of Emotion', *Intelligence*, 22, 89-113.

Mayer, J D & Salovey, P 1990, 'Emotional Intelligence', *Imagination, Cognition and Personality*, 9(3), 185-211.

Mayer, J D & Salovey, P 1993, 'The Intelligence of Emotional Intelligence', *Intelligence*, 17(4), 433-442.

Mayer, J D & Salovey, P 1995, 'Emotional Intelligence and the Construction and Regulation of Feelings', *Applied and Preventive Psychology*, 4, 197-208.

Mayer, J D & Salovey, P 1997, 'What Is Emotional Intelligence?', in P. Salovey and D. Sluyter (eds), *Emotional Development and Emotional Intelligence: Educational Implications,* Basic Books, New York.

Mayer, JD, Salovey, P & Caruso, DR 2002, *Mayer-Salovey-Caruso Emotional Intelligence Test (MSCEIT) User's Manual,* Multi-Health Systems Inc., Toronto, Canada.

McKay, M & Fanning, P 1992, 2000, *Self esteem,* 3rd edn, New Harbinger Publications, Oakland, CA.

McKay, M Rogers, P & McKay, J 1989, *When Anger Hurts: Quieting The Storm Within,* New Harbinger Publications, CA.

Montgomery, B & Evans, L 1984, 1995, *You and stress,* Penguin Books, Victoria, Australia.

Safran, J and Greenherg, L 1991, *Emotion, Psychotherapy, and Change,* Guliford Press, New York.

Thayer, R 1996, *The Origin of Everyday Moods,* Oxford University Press, New York.

Weekes, C 1972, *Peace from nervous suffering. A practical guide to understanding, confidence and recovery,* Angus & Robertson, London.

Weisinger, H 1995, *Anger at Work,* Morrow, New York.

Weisinger, H 1998, *Emotional Intelligence at Work,* Morrow, New York.

Winefield, H R & Peay M Y 1980, 1991, *Behavioural science in medicine,* 2nd edn, Helen R Winefield & Marilyn Y Peay, Adelaide, South Australia.

INDEX

A

ABC of communication skills, 227

Ability

model of emotional intelligence, 19, 302–307

to perceive emotion, 6, 17, 39, 48, 50

to use emotion, 102–108, 111–112, 155–160

to understand emotion, 171–178, 186

to manage emotion, 244–256, 268–282

to make decisions, 243, 251, 256, 261

Acceptance

as stage of grief, 190

being ready to practise, 126

feelings of, 170

forgiveness follows understanding and, 277

versus withdrawal, 179

Accepting: as part of the compassionate response, 197, 252

Accumulated stress

effects of, 74, 128

Addictive substance, 325

Adrenalin, 58, 72, 73, 75, 129, 130, 131, 151, 156, 176, 254

Affirmations, 157, 170, 193–197

Anger, 2, 3, 5, 30, 38, 69, 73, 106, 129, 136, 172, 186, 244

pain remembered in the past, 71

redirected inwards creates depression, 71

to assertion, 134

Anger and fear–based reactivity, 133

Antianxiety medication, 151

Antidepressants, 325

Anxiety – *see fear and anxiety*

pain perceived in the future, 71

Anxiety of wanting, 244

Anxiety state (nervous breakdown), 129

Appraisal, 97, 122

"trigger", perception, interpretation, 101

autonomic (involuntary) arousal, 128

Appreciation, 2, 256

fear to, 252

Assertion

anger to, 244

moving to, 135

rationale for, 139

six step strategy for, 136

Attachment to defence mechanisms, 183

Autonomic nervous system (ANS)

nerves, 128, 254

sympathetic (fight, flight), 129

parasympathetic (calming, restorative), 129

Awareness, 179

developing emotional, 38, 45, 279

hostage to our lack of, 251

Auto–response, 123

B

Bar–On, Reuven, 18

Bar–On EQ-i®, 21–23, 25, 27

Basic emotions, 58

Behaviour

aggressive, 10, 140–141, 172

assertive, 140–141

Define your path, 242

Definitions of health, 31

Depression, 186-187

Disgust, 2, 30, 38, 129, 174

Drama of life, 2, 15, 31, 100

E

EAR–Identity, 84, 100–102, 185, 243, 250, 277, 278

EASEQuadrant®, The, xxxvii, xxxiv, 11, 19, 249, 287–301

Effective communication, 65, 231, 271,

Emotion

  antecedents, 171

  appreciation, 256

  arousal, 171

  balancing, 75

  blends of, 176

  chains, 174

  compound: contentment, 176

  conversion, 121, 126

  families, 66

  generation, 83, 98

  in faces, 6

  in films, 4–6

  perceiving, 39, 50

  understanding, 171

  using, to facilitate thought, 118

Emotion–activating systems, 99

Emotional arousal

  antecedents, 171–174

  behavioural signs, 171–174

  creates awareness of your defence against change, 243

  consequences, 171–174

  describing, 171–174

  stages, 186-187

Emotional competencies:

  assertiveness, 22

  emotional self–awareness, 22

  empathy, 22

  flexibility, 23

  happiness, 23

  impulse control, 23

  independence, 22

  interpersonal relationship, 22

  optimism, 23

  problem solving, 23

  reality testing, 23

  self–actualisation, 22

  self–regard, 22

  social responsibility, 23

  stress tolerance, 23

Emotional constipation:

  "dis–*ease*", 70

  physiological impact of, 70

  negative emotion, 72

  pain from negativity, 127

Emotional health

  awareness and, 31

  intimacy and, 32

  signs of, 30

  spontaneity and, 32

Emotional intelligence

  arrival of, 17

  as important as IQ?, 23

  Bar–On EQ-i® – Competency model, 21, 22, 25, 27,

  behaving with, xxxiv

  MSCEIT™ – Ability model, 19–21, 25, 27, 302–307

  improve your, 37,

  is part of personality, 292

  ten rampant myths of, 8

Emotional intimacy, 269–270

Emotional leadership

  definition of, xxii, 289

  essential purpose of, 251

  experiential, xxvi, xxviii, xxx, 185, 288

  sowing, 240

  strategic, xxvi, xxviii, xxxii, 185, 288

NOTES